ACCA

P[illegible]

F8 (UK)

Audit and assurance (UK stream)

Welcome to IFP's study text for Paper F8 (UK) *Audit and assurance (UK stream)* which is:

- Written by tutors
- Comprehensive but concise
- In simple English
- Used around the world by Emile Woolf Colleges including China, Russia and the UK

International Financial Publishing in association with Emile Woolf International Training Professionals

First edition published by
International Financial Publishing Limited
Hitherbury House, 97 Portsmouth Road, Guildford, Surrey GU2 5DL
Email: info@ifpbooks.com
www.ifpbooks.com

British Library Cataloguing in Publications Data
A catalogue record for this book is available from the British Library.

ISBN 978-1-905623-37-2

Printed and bound in Great Britain.

Acknowledgements
The syllabus and study guide are reproduced by kind permission of the Association of Chartered Certified Accountants.

C

Contents

S

Syllabus and study guide

Aim

To develop knowledge and understanding of the process of carrying out the assurance engagement, and its application in the context of the professional regulatory framework.

Main capabilities

On successful completion of this paper, candidates should be able to:

A Explain the nature, purpose and scope of assurance engagements including the role of the external audit and its regulatory and ethical framework

B Explain the nature of internal audit and describing its role as part of overall performance management and its relationship with the external audit

C Demonstrate how the auditor obtains an understanding of the entity and its environment, assesses the risk of material misstatement (whether arising from fraud or other irregularities) and plans an audit of financial statements

D Describe and evaluate information systems and internal controls to identify and communicate control risks and their potential consequences, making appropriate recommendations

E Identify and describe the work and evidence required to meet the objectives of audit engagements and the application of the International Standards on Auditing (UK and Ireland)

F Evaluate findings and modify the audit plan as necessary

G Explain how the conclusions from audit work are reflected in different types of audit report, explaining the elements of each type of report.

Rationale

The syllabus for Paper F8, *Audit and Assurance,* is divided into seven areas. The syllabus starts with the nature, purpose and scope of assurance engagements, including the statutory audit, its regulatory environment, and introduces professional ethics relating to audit and assurance. It then leads into internal audit, including the scope of internal audit as well as the differences between internal audit and external audit. The syllabus then covers a range of areas relating to an audit of financial statements. These include planning and risk assessment, evaluating internal controls, audit evidence, and a review of the financial statements. The final section then deals with reporting, including statutory audit reports, management reports, and internal audit reports.

Syllabus

A Audit Framework and Regulation

1 The concept of audit and other assurance engagements
2 Statutory audits
3 The regulatory environment and corporate governance
4 APB ethical standards and ACCA's Code of Ethics and Conduct

B Internal audit

1 Internal audit and corporate governance
2 Differences between external and internal audit
3 The scope of the internal audit function
4 Outsourcing the internal audit department
5 Internal audit assignments

C Planning and risk assessment

1 Objective and general principles
2 Understanding the entity and knowledge of the business
3 Assessing the risks of material misstatement and fraud
4 Analytical procedures
5 Planning an audit
6 Audit documentation
7 The work of others

D Internal control

1 Internal control systems
2 The use of internal control systems by auditors
3 Transaction cycles
4 Tests of control
5 The evaluation of internal control components
6 Communication on internal control

E Audit evidence

1 The use of assertions by auditors
2 Audit procedures
3 The audit of specific items
4. Audit sampling and other means of testing

5 Computer-assisted audit techniques
6 Not-for-profit organisations

F Review

1 Subsequent events
2 Going concern
3 Management representations
4 Audit finalisation and the final review

G Reporting

1 Audit reports
2 Reports to management
3 Internal audit reports

Approach to examining the syllabus

The syllabus is assessed by a three-hour paper-based examination, consisting of five compulsory questions. The bulk of the questions will be discursive but some questions involving computational elements will be set from time to time.

The questions will cover all areas of the syllabus.

Question 1 will be a scenario-based question worth 30 marks. Question 2 will be a knowledge-based question worth 10 marks. Questions 3, 4 and 5 will be worth 20 marks each.

Study Guide

This syllabus and study provides more detailed guidance on the syllabus. You should use this as the basis of your studies.

A Audit framework and regulation

1 The concept of audit and other assurance engagements

(a) Identify and describe the objective and general principles of external audit engagements.

(b) Explain the nature and development of audit and other assurance engagements.

(c) Discuss the concepts of accountability, stewardship and agency.

(d) Discuss the concepts of materiality, true and fair presentation and reasonable assurance.

(e) Explain reporting as a means of communication to different stakeholders.

(f) Explain the level of assurance provided by audit and other review assignments.

2 Statutory audits

(a) Describe the regulatory environment within which statutory audits take place.

(b) Discuss the reasons and mechanisms for the regulation of auditors.

(c) Explain the statutory regulations governing the appointment, removal and resignation of auditors.

(d) Discuss the types of opinion provided in statutory audits.

(e) State the objectives and principle activities of statutory audit and assess its value (e.g. in assisting management to reduce risk and improve performance).

(f) Describe the limitations of statutory audits.

3 The regulatory environment and corporate governance

(a) Explain the development and status of International Standards on Auditing (UK and Ireland).

(b) Explain the relationship between International Standards on Auditing and the work of the Auditing Practices Board.

(c) Discuss the objective, relevance and importance of corporate governance.

(d) Discuss the need for auditors to communicate with those charged with governance.

(e) Discuss the provisions of international codes of corporate governance (such as the Combined Code on Corporate Governance) that are most relevant to auditors.

(f) Describe good corporate governance requirements relating to directors' responsibilities (e.g. for risk management and internal control) and the reporting responsibilities of auditors.

(g) Analyse the structure and roles of audit committees and discuss their drawbacks and limitations.

(h) Explain the importance of internal control and risk management.

(i) Compare the responsibilities of management and auditors for the design and operation of systems and controls.

4 APB ethical standards and ACCA's Code of Ethics and Conduct

(a) Define and apply the fundamental principles of professional ethics of integrity, objectivity, professional competence and due care, confidentiality and professional behaviour.

(b) Define and apply the conceptual framework.

(c) Discuss the sources of, and enforcement mechanisms associated with, ACCA's Code of Ethics and Conduct.

(d) Discuss the requirements of professional ethics and other requirements in relation to the acceptance of new audit engagements.

(e) Discuss the process by which an auditor obtains an audit engagement.

(f) Explain the importance of engagement letters and state their contents.

B Internal audit

1 Internal audit and corporate governance

(a) Discuss the factors to be taken into account when assessing the need for internal audit.

(b) Discuss the elements of best practice in the structure and operations of internal audit with reference to the Combined Code on Corporate Governance.

2 Differences between external and internal audit

(a) Compare and contrast the role of external and internal audit regarding audit planning and the collection of audit evidence.

(b) Compare and contrast the types of report provided by internal and external audit.

3 The scope of the internal audit function

(a) Discuss the scope of internal audit and the limitations of the internal audit function.

(b) Explain the types of audit report provided in internal audit assignments.

(c) Discuss the responsibilities of internal and external auditors for the prevention and detection of fraud and error.

4 Outsourcing the internal audit department

(a) Explain the advantages and disadvantages of outsourcing internal audit.

5 Internal audit assignments

(a) Discuss the nature and purpose of internal audit assignments including value for money, IT, best value and financial.

(b) Discuss the nature and purpose of operational internal audit assignments including procurement, marketing, treasury and human resources management.

C Planning and risk assessment

1 Objective and general principles

(a) Identify and describe the need to plan and perform audits with an attitude of professional scepticism.

(b) Identify and describe engagement risks affecting the audit of an entity.

(c) Explain the components of audit risk.

(d) Compare and contrast risk based, procedural and other approaches to audit work.

(e) Discuss the importance of risk analysis.

(f) Describe the use of information technology in risk analysis.

2 Understanding the entity and knowledge of the business

(a) Explain how auditors obtain an initial understanding of the entity and knowledge of its business environment.

3 Assessing the risks of material misstatement and fraud

(a) Define and explain the concepts of materiality and tolerable error.

(b) Compute indicative materiality levels from financial information.

(c) Discuss the effect of fraud and misstatements on the audit strategy and extent of audit work.

4 Analytical procedures

(a) Describe and explain the nature and purpose of analytical procedures in planning.

(b) Compute and interpret key ratios used in analytical procedures.

5 Planning an audit

(a) Identify and explain the need for planning an audit.

(b) Identify and describe the contents of the overall audit strategy and audit plan.

(c) Explain and describe the relationship between the overall audit strategy and the audit plan.

(d) Develop and document an audit plan.

(e) Explain the difference between interim and final audit.

6 Audit documentation

(a) Explain the need for and the importance of audit documentation.

(b) Describe and prepare working papers and supporting documentation.

(c) Explain the procedures to ensure safe custody and retention of working papers.

7 The work of others

(a) Discuss the extent to which auditors are able to rely on the work of experts.

(b) Discuss the extent to which external auditors are able to rely on the work of internal audit.

(c) Discuss the audit considerations relating to entities using service organisations.

(d) Discuss why auditors rely on the work of others.

(e) Explain the extent to which reference to the work of others can be made in audit reports.

D Internal control

The following transaction cycles and account balances are relevant to this capability:

- sales,
- purchases,
- stock,
- revenue and capital expenditure,
- payroll,
- bank and cash.

1 Internal control systems

(a) Explain why an auditor needs to obtain an understanding of internal control activities relevant to the audit.

(b) Describe and explain the key components of an internal control system.

(c) Identify and describe the important elements of internal control including the control environment and management control activities.

(d) Discuss the difference between tests of control and substantive procedures.

2 The use of internal control systems by auditors

(a) Explain the importance of internal control to auditors.

(b) Explain how auditors identify weaknesses in internal control systems and how those weaknesses limit the extent of auditors' reliance on those systems.

3 Transaction cycles

(a) Explain, analyse and provide examples of internal control procedures and control activities.

(b) Provide examples of computer system controls.

4 Tests of control

(a) Explain and tabulate tests of control suitable for inclusion in audit working papers.

(b) List examples of application controls and general IT controls.

5 The evaluation of internal control components

(a) Analyse the limitations of internal control components in the context of fraud and error.

(b) Explain the need to modify the audit strategy and audit plan following the results of tests of control.

(c) Identify and explain management's risk assessment process with reference to internal control components.

6 Communication on internal control

(a) Discuss and provide examples of how the reporting of internal control weaknesses and recommendations to overcome those weaknesses are provided to management.

E Audit evidence

1 The use of assertions by auditors

(a) Explain the assertions contained in the financial statements.[

(b) Explain the principles and objectives of transaction testing, account balance testing and disclosure testing.

(c) Explain the use of assertions in obtaining audit evidence.

2 Audit procedures

(a) Discuss the sources and relative merits of the different types of evidence available.

(b) Discuss and provide examples of how analytical procedures are used as substantive procedures.

(c) Discuss the problems associated with the audit and review of accounting estimates.

(d) Describe why smaller entities may have different control environments and describe the types of evidence likely to be available in smaller entities.

(e) Discuss the quality of evidence obtained.

3 The audit of specific items

For each of the account balances stated in this sub-capability:

- explain the purpose of substantive procedures in relation to financial statement assertions,
- explain the substantive procedures used in auditing each balance, and
- tabulate those substantive procedures in a work program.

(a) Debtors:

i) direct confirmation of debtors

ii) other evidence in relation to debtors and prepayments, and

iii) the related profit and loss account entries.

(b) Stock:

i) stock counting procedures in relation to year-end and continuous stock systems

ii) cut-off

iii) auditor's attendance at stock counting

iv) direct confirmation of stock held by third parties,

v) other evidence in relation to stock.

(c) Creditors and accruals:
  i) supplier statement reconciliations and direct confirmation of creditors,
  ii) obtain evidence in relation to creditors and accruals, and
  iii) the related profit and loss account entries.

(d) Bank and cash:
  i) bank confirmation reports used in obtaining evidence in relation to bank and cash
  ii) other evidence in relation to bank and cash, and
  iii) the related profit and loss account entries.

(e) Fixed assets and long-term liabilities:
  i) evidence in relation to fixed assets and
  ii) long term liabilities and
  iii) the related profit and loss account entries.

4 Audit sampling and other means of testing

(a) Define audit sampling and explain the need for sampling.

(b) Identify and discuss the differences between statistical and non-statistical sampling.

(c) Discuss and provide relevant examples of, the application of the basic principles of statistical sampling and other selective testing procedures.

(d) Discuss the results of statistical sampling, including consideration of whether additional testing is required.

5 Computer-assisted audit techniques

(a) Explain the use of computer-assisted audit techniques in the context of an audit.

(b) Discuss and provide relevant examples of the use of test data and audit software for the transaction cycles and balances mentioned in sub-capability 3.

(c) Discuss the use of computers in relation to the administration of the audit.

6 Not-for-profit organisations

(a) Apply audit techniques to small not-for-profit organisations.

(b) Explain how the audit of small not-for-profit organisations differs from the audit of for-profit organisations.

F Review

1 Subsequent events

(a) Explain the purpose of a subsequent events review.

(b) Discuss the procedures to be undertaken in performing a subsequent events review.

2 Going concern

(a) Define and discuss the significance of the concept of going concern.

(b) Explain the importance of and the need for going concern reviews.

(c) Explain the respective responsibilities of auditors and management regarding going concern.

(d) Discuss the procedures to be applied in performing going concern reviews.

(e) Discuss the disclosure requirements in relation to going concern issues.

(f) Discuss the reporting implications of the findings of going concern reviews.

3 Management representations

(a) Explain the purpose of and procedure for obtaining management representations.

(b) Discuss the quality and reliability of management representations as audit evidence.

(c) Discuss the circumstances where management representations are necessary and the matters on which representations are commonly obtained.

4 Audit finalisation and the final review

(a) Discuss the importance of the overall review of evidence obtained.

(b) Explain the significance of unadjusted differences.

G Reporting

1 Audit reports

(a) Describe and analyse the format and content of unmodified audit reports.

(b) Describe and analyse the format and content of modified audit reports.

2 Reports to management

(a) Identify and analyse internal control and system weaknesses and their potential effects and make appropriate recommendations to management.

3 Internal audit reports

(a) Describe and explain the format and content of internal audit review reports and other reports dealing with the enhancement of performance.

(b) Explain the process for producing an internal audit report.

CHAPTER 1

The meaning of audit and assurance

Contents

The meaning of audit

- Definition and objective of audit
- Concepts of accountability, stewardship and agency
- The audit report: independence, materiality and true and fair
- The statutory requirement for audit

1 The meaning of audit

1.1 Definition and objective of audit

A basic definition of an **audit** is '…an official examination of the accounts (or accounting systems) of an entity by an auditor'.

When an auditor examines the accounts of an entity, what is he looking for?

International Standard on Auditing (ISA) 200 *Objective and general principles governing an audit of financial statements* defines the **objective** of an audit as follows:

'…to enable the auditor to express an opinion whether the financial statements are prepared, in all material respects, in accordance with an applicable financial reporting framework.'

The applicable financial reporting framework is decided by:

- legislation within each individual country, and
- accounting standards (for example, International Accounting Standards/ International Financial Reporting Standards or UK Accounting/ Financial Reporting Standards).

The auditor seeks to express an opinion as the result of the audit work that he does. The type of work carried out by an auditor in order to reach his opinion is described in later chapters.

1.2 Concepts of accountability, stewardship and agency

An audit of a company's accounts is needed because in companies, the owners of the business are often not the same persons as the individuals who manage and control that business.

- The shareholders own the company.
- The company is managed and controlled by its directors.

The directors have a **stewardship** role. They look after the assets of the company and manage them on behalf of the shareholders. In small companies the shareholders may be the same people as the directors. However, in most large companies, the two groups are different.

The relationship between the shareholders of a company and the board of directors is also an application of the general legal principle of **agency**. The concept of agency applies whenever one person or group of individuals acts as an agent on behalf of someone else (the **principal**). The agent has a legal duty to act in the best interests of the principal, and should be accountable to the principal for everything that he does as agent.

As agents for the shareholders, the board of directors should be accountable to the shareholders. In order for the directors to show their **accountability** to the shareholders, it is a general principle of company law that the directors are required to prepare annual financial statements, which are presented to the shareholders for their approval.

1.3 The audit report: independence, materiality and true and fair

Audit has a very long history. The concept of an audit goes back to the times of the Egyptian and Roman empires. In medieval times, independent auditors were employed by the feudal barons to ensure that the returns from their stewards and their tenants were accurate.

Over time, the annual audit was developed as a way of adding **credibility** to the financial statements produced by management. The **statutory audit** is now a key feature of company law throughout the world.

An auditor reports **to the shareholders** on the financial statements produced by a company's management.

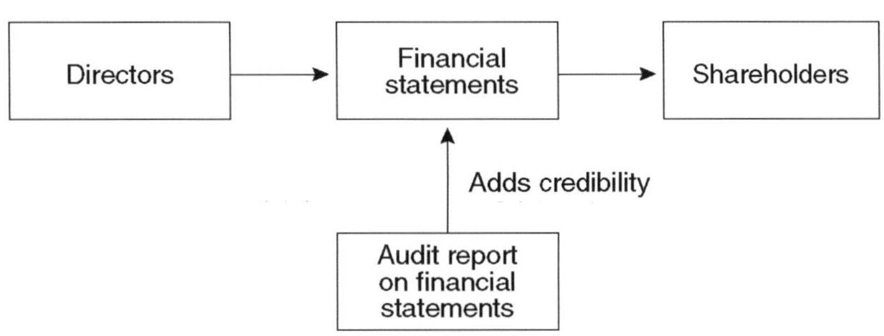

The key features of the audit report are as follows:

- The auditors producing the report are **independent** from the directors producing the financial statements
- The report gives an opinion on whether the financial statements "**give a true and fair view**" of the position and results of the entity.
- The report considers whether the financial statements give a true and fair view **in all material respects**. The concept of materiality is applied in reaching an audit opinion.

Independence of the auditor

The external auditor must be **independent** from the directors; otherwise his report will have little value. If he is not independent, his opinion is likely to be influenced by the directors.

In contrast to external auditors, internal auditors may not be fully independent from the directors, although they may be able to achieve a sufficient degree of independence. The work and status of internal auditors is covered in a later chapter.

The concept of independence of the auditor is considered in more detail in a later chapter.

True and fair view (fair presentation)

The auditor reports on whether (or not) the financial statements **give a true and fair view** of the position of the entity as at the end of the financial period and the performance of the entity during the period. **The auditor does not certify or guarantee that the financial statements are correct**.

Although the phrase 'true and fair view' has no legal definition, the term 'true' implies free from error, and 'fair' implies that there is no undue bias in the financial statements or the way in which they have been presented.

In preparing the financial statements, a large amount of judgement is exercised by the directors. Similarly, judgement is exercised by the auditor in reaching his opinion. The phrase 'true and fair view' indicates that a judgement is being given that the financial statements can be relied upon and have been properly prepared in accordance with an appropriate financial reporting framework.

Materiality concept

The auditor reports in accordance with the concept of **materiality**. He gives an opinion on whether the financial statements give a true and fair view, **in all material respects,** the financial position and performance of the entity.

Materiality is defined by International Standards on Auditing (UK and Ireland) as follows:

'Information is material if its omission or misstatement could influence the economic decision of users taken on the basis of the financial statements.'

For example, the shareholders of a company with assets of £1 million will not be interested if petty cash was miscounted with the result that the amount of petty cash is overstated by £10. This is immaterial. However, they will be interested if there are debtors in the balance sheet of £200,000 which are not in fact recoverable and which should therefore have been written off as a bad debt.

Applying the concept of materiality means that the auditor will not aim to examine every number in the financial statements. He will concentrate his efforts on the more significant items in the financial statements, either:

- because of their (high) value, or
- because there is a greater risk that they could be stated incorrectly.

1.4 The statutory requirement for audit

Most countries impose a statutory requirement for an annual (external) audit to be carried out on the financial statements of most companies. In the UK all public companies and all companies with an annual turnover above £5.6m are required to be audited each year.

However, in many countries, including the UK, smaller companies are exempt from this requirement for an audit. Other entities, such as sole traders, partnerships, clubs and societies are usually not subject to a statutory audit requirement. Small companies and these other entities may decide to have a voluntary audit, even though this is not required by law.

The meaning of assurance

- Definition of assurance
- Levels of assurance

2 The meaning of assurance

2.1 Definition of assurance

'Assurance' means confidence. In an assurance engagement, an 'assurance firm' is engaged by one party to give an opinion on a piece of information that has been prepared by another party. The opinion is an expression of **assurance** about the information that has been reviewed. It gives assurance to the party that hired the assurance firm that the information can be relied on.

Assurance can be provided by:

- **audit**: this may be external audit, internal audit or a combination of the two
- **review.**

A statutory audit is one form of assurance. Without assurance from the auditors, the shareholders may not accept that the information provided by the financial statements is sufficiently accurate and reliable. The statutory audit provides assurance as to the quality of the information.

The provision of this assurance should add credibility to the information in the financial statements, making the information more reliable and therefore more useful to the user.

However, there are differing levels or degrees of assurance. Some assurances are more reliable than others.

2.2 Levels of assurance

The degree of assurance that can be provided about the reliability of the financial statements of a company will depend on:

- the amount of work performed in carrying out the assurance process, and
- the results of that work.

Assurance provided by audit

An **audit** provides a **high, but not absolute,** level of assurance that the audited information is free from any material misstatement. This is often referred to as **reasonable assurance.**

The assurance of an audit may be provided by external auditors or internal auditors.

- An **external audit** is performed by an appropriately qualified auditor, appointed by the shareholders and independent of the company.
- **Internal audit** is a function or department set up within an entity to provide an appraisal or monitoring process, as a service to other functions or to senior management within the entity. Typically, internal auditors are employees of the entity. However, it is also common for entities to 'outsource' their internal audit function, and internal audit work is sometimes carried out by firms of external auditors.

Many of the practical auditing procedures that will be described in later chapters are the same for both internal and external audit work.

Assurance provided by review

A **review** is a 'voluntary' investigation. In contrast to "reasonable" level of assurance provided by an audit, a **review** into an aspect of the financial statements would provide only a **moderate** level of assurance that the information under review is free of material misstatement. The resulting opinion is usually (although not always) expressed in the form of **negative assurance**. Negative assurance is an opinion that nothing is obviously wrong: in other words, 'nothing has come to our attention to suggest that the information is misstated'.

A review does not provide the same amount of assurance as an audit. An external audit, for example, provides **positive assurance** that, in the opinion of the auditors, the financial statements **do** present fairly the financial position and performance of the company.

The higher level of assurance provided by an audit will enhance the credibility provided by the assurance process, but the audit work is likely to be:

- more time-consuming than a review, and so
- more costly than a review.

CHAPTER

2

Corporate governance and auditing

Contents

Corporate governance

- The meaning of corporate governance
- The responsibility of directors for the management of risks
- The main issues in corporate governance

1 Corporate governance

1.1 The meaning of corporate governance

As was seen in the previous chapter, a company is governed by its directors on behalf of the shareholders. Arguably, the directors also govern on behalf of other 'stakeholders' in the company, such as its employees. Corporate governance is **the system by which a company is directed and controlled.**

In many countries, rules or guidelines on 'best practice' in corporate governance have been developed. These are either applied on a voluntary basis or imposed by law.

An important aspect of corporate governance is the relationship between the owners of a company (its equity shareholders) and its governors (the board of directors). The strength of the relationship between owners and governors depends largely on the quality of the communication between them. The most important method of communication is the annual financial statements and accompanying reports (the 'report and accounts').

To promote good corporate governance, the financial statements should be reliable. This means that the directors should present reliable and relevant information in the financial statements, and those financial statements should be subject to independent audit to provide assurance to the shareholders.

1.2 The responsibility of directors for the management of risks

Another issue in corporate governance is the management of risks. Companies face many different risks, but most risks can be divided into two categories:

- **Business risks** or 'enterprise risks'. These are the risks associated with investing in products and services, and competing in markets.
- **Governance risks**. These are the risks that errors (deliberate or accidental) may occur due to weaknesses in existing 'internal' controls. For example, there may be excessive risks that financial transactions will be recorded incorrectly in the accounting system, or there may be an unacceptable risk that fraud could occur and remain undetected. There may be risks of failure to comply with regulations or laws. There may also be risks of operational errors in day-to-day operating activities, due to human error, machine breakdowns or poor supervision by management.

It is the **responsibility of executive management** to put in place a suitable system of **internal controls** to manage the **risks** of the company.

In the UK, internal controls are divided into three categories for the purpose of corporate governance:

- financial controls
- compliance controls (to ensure compliance with laws and regulations)
- operational controls.

Examples of financial controls are:

- controls that safeguard the assets of the company
- controls that ensure that adequate accounting records are maintained
- controls over the preparation and delivery of the annual financial statements.

Although it is the responsibility of management to design and implement internal controls, it is the responsibility of the company's governors (directors) to satisfy themselves that the system of internal control is adequate and that it functions properly.

1.3 The main issues in corporate governance

Corporate governance has attracted a large amount of attention in recent years, although measures to promote good corporate governance vary substantially between different countries.

The initial demand for better corporate governance occurred as a result of several 'corporate scandals', with major companies either collapsing or coming close to collapse. In the UK, several corporate failures in the 1980s (such as Maxwell Communications Corporation and Polly Peck International) were subsequently blamed on poor governance. In the US, corporate governance legislation was introduced in 2002 following the spectacular collapse of Enron and WorldCom, and other corporate scandals. There have also been major cases in Continental Europe, such as Ahold (the Netherlands) and Parmalat (Italy).

There are several key issues in corporate governance, although their perceived importance varies between different countries:

(1) There should be an effective board of directors. The directors should be independent-minded and should collectively have a wide range of skills, knowledge and experience. The board of directors should not be under the control or influence of an 'all-powerful' chairman and/or chief executive officer, who is able to dictate the board's decisions.

(2) The board of directors should have clearly-defined responsibilities that it must not delegate, and it should carry out these responsibilities properly.

(3) The directors should govern the company in the best interests of its shareholders (and possibly also other stakeholders); they should not run the company in their own self-interest.

(4) The financial statements of the company should be reliable. (In many cases of corporate collapse, the financial statements were proved to have been misleading and unreliable.)

(5) Risks should be controlled, and the directors should provide assurance to the shareholders about the systems of controls and risk management.

(6) The remuneration of directors should be fair. Directors should not fix their own remuneration, and their remuneration package should provide them with incentives to achieve the objectives of the company that are in the best interests of the shareholders. Directors should not be rewarded for failure.

(7) There should be active, open and constructive dialogue between the company's directors and its shareholders, in particular its major shareholders.

As far as audit and assurance are concerned, the main relevant aspects of corporate governance are items (4) and (5) above.

The role of the auditor in corporate governance

- The external auditor
- The internal auditor

2 The role of the auditor in corporate governance

2.1 The external auditor

The external auditor is part of the corporate governance system.

- He provides an independent check on the integrity of the financial information prepared by the directors for the use of shareholders and other stakeholders
- In public companies, he has a responsibility for forming an opinion on the extent to which the directors have complied with the specific corporate governance regulations imposed on them.

In order to fulfil these roles, the external auditor will **examine** the company's systems and controls. However, he is **not responsible** for those systems or controls. Responsibility remains with the directors and executive management.

The external auditor is also required by ISA 260 *Communication of audit matters to those charged with governance* to communicate with management periodically on matters of governance interest. These might include:

- weaknesses in internal control found by the auditor, or
- any limitation in the scope of his work.

In addition, all good corporate governance systems have procedures and arrangements designed to maintain the independence of the external auditor. For example:

- the external auditor may be required to report to an audit committee, as well as to work with the chief executive officer and finance director
- the nature and extent of non-audit services provided by the audit firm may be kept under review, to make sure that the auditor:
  - has not become excessively dependent on the company and its executive management for fee income, and
  - is not in danger of becoming too familiar with the company's management and systems of operation
- suitable procedures may be established for the discussion of contentious issues where the auditors and the finance director/chief executive officer have strong differences of opinion.

2.2 The internal auditor

Senior management is responsible for putting in place a system of internal controls that will prevent or detect errors and fraud. An internal audit function may be used by management as a means of **monitoring** these systems of internal control.

An internal audit function can therefore be used to obtain **assurance** that the system of internal controls is adequate and that it is functioning properly.

Companies are not required by law to have an internal audit function. However, in the UK, listed companies are required to set up an audit committee which is required each year to:

- monitor and review the effectiveness of internal audit activities, or
- where there is no internal audit function, to consider the need for an internal audit function and make a recommendation to the board. (The reasons for not having an internal audit function should also be explained in the annual report and accounts.)

Other companies and entities may also choose to have an internal audit function, because of the assurance it should provide about the adequacy of internal controls.

The role of the internal audit function is described in more detail in a later chapter.

Systems of corporate governance

- A voluntary or statutory approach
- General principles of corporate governance
- The Combined Code on Corporate Governance
- The use of audit committees

3 Systems of corporate governance

3.1 A voluntary or statutory approach

Many countries now have minimum corporate governance requirements. Typically, they are imposed only on listed companies, although smaller companies are also encouraged to comply. (Listed companies are companies whose shares are officially 'listed' by the financial markets regulator and traded on a major stock market.) In addition, some public sector organisations are also showing an increased emphasis on corporate governance matters.

In many countries, corporate governance guidelines are based on a **voluntary code of practice** rather than statutory regulation.

This is largely the case in the UK, where the Combined Code on Corporate Governance is applied to listed companies. Although this Code does not have any statutory force, the Listing Rules of the Financial Services Authority require listed companies to comply with every aspect of the Code or to explain their reasons for any non-compliance. This is known as 'comply or explain'. There are also some statutory requirements relating to corporate governance in the UK, such as the statutory requirement for an annual audit and a requirement for an annual 'directors' remuneration report' on which the shareholders must be invited to vote.

A **statutory approach** to the regulation of corporate governance has been taken in the United States, in the form of the **Sarbanes-Oxley Act (2002)**. This was introduced primarily as a result of the corporate failures in 2001 and 2002, including Enron and WorldCom. (One of the requirements of the Sarbanes-Oxley Act is for the chief executive and chief financial officer of each stock market corporation to submit an annual report to the Securities and Exchange Commission about the adequacy of their internal control system. This report must be supported by a formal statement from the external auditors.)

The detailed provisions of corporate governance regulations vary from country to country. The examiner has made it clear that you are not required to have a detailed knowledge of the regulations in any country other than the UK.

3.2 General principles of corporate governance

The five principles set out below were developed by the Organisation for Economic Co-operation and Development (OECD). They are intended to provide a general model of a good corporate governance system.

The OECD Principles state that a corporate governance framework should achieve the following objectives:

(1) Protect shareholders' rights, such as voting rights and the right to transfer ownership in shares.

(2) Ensure the equitable treatment of all shareholders, including minority and foreign shareholders. All shareholders should have the opportunity to obtain effective redress for any violation of their rights.

(3) Recognise the rights of stakeholders as established by law and encourage active co-operation between corporations and stakeholders in creating wealth, jobs, and the sustainability of financially secure enterprises.

(4) Ensure that timely and accurate disclosure is made on all material matters regarding the corporation, including the financial situation, performance, ownership, and governance of the company.

(5) Ensure the strategic guidance of the company, the effective monitoring of management by the board, and the board's accountability to the company and the shareholders. This includes ensuring:

   - the integrity of the corporation's accounting and financial reporting systems, including the independent audit
   - that appropriate systems of control are in place, in particular, systems for monitoring risk, financial control, and compliance with the law.

Items (4) and (5) above have the greatest relevance to audit and assurance.

3.3 The Combined Code on Corporate Governance

Introduction

All listed companies in the UK must comply with the Combined Code or else explain their non-compliance. The following are the main principles of the Combined Code:

Principles of the Code

Area	Main principles
The Board	■ Every company should be headed by an effective board, which is collectively responsible for the success of the company. ■ There should be a clear division of responsibilities between the running of the board and the executive responsibility for the running of the company's business. No one individual should have unfettered powers of decision.

	■ The board should include a balance of executive and non-executive directors (especially independent non-executive directors) such that no individual or small group of individuals can dominate the board's decision-making. ■ There should be a formal, rigorous and transparent procedure for the appointment of new directors to the board. ■ The board should be supplied in a timely manner with information in a form and of a quantity appropriate to enable it to discharge its duties. All directors should receive induction on joining the board and should regularly update and refresh their skills and knowledge. ■ The board should undertake a formal and rigorous annual evaluation of its own performance and that of its committees and individual directors. ■ All directors should be submitted for re-election at regular intervals, subject to continued satisfactory performance. The board should ensure planned and progressive refreshing of the board.
Remuneration	■ Levels of remuneration should be sufficient to attract, retain and motivate directors of the quality required to run the company successfully, but a company should avoid paying more than is necessary for this purpose. A significant proportion of executive directors' remuneration should be structured so as to link rewards to corporate and individual performance. ■ There should be a formal and transparent procedure for developing policy on executive remuneration and for fixing the remuneration package of individual directors. No director should be involved in deciding his or her remuneration.
Accountability and audit	■ The board should present a balanced and understandable assessment of the company's position and prospects. ■ The board should maintain a sound system of internal control to safeguard shareholders' investment and the company's assets. ■ The board should establish formal and transparent arrangements for considering how they should apply the financial reporting and internal control principles and for maintaining an appropriate relationship with the company's auditors.
Relations with shareholders	■ There should be a dialogue with shareholders based on the mutual understanding of objectives. The board as a whole has responsibility for ensuring that a satisfactory dialogue takes place. ■ The board should use the AGM to communicate with investors and to encourage their participation.

Example

Mrs Smith is both Chief Executive Officer (CEO) and Chairman of your client. The board of directors consist of five executive and two non-executive directors. Board salaries are set by Mrs Smith based on her assessment of all the board members, including herself, and not their actual performance.

Required

Explain why your client does not meet international codes of corporate governance, why this may cause a problem for the company, and recommend changes.

Answer

Chief Executive Officer (CEO) and Chairman

Why codes not met: Mrs Smith is both CEO and Chairman of the company. Good principles of corporate governance state that the person responsible for running the company (the CEO) and the person responsible for controlling the board (the chairman) should be different people.

Why a problem: This is to ensure that no one individual has unrestricted powers of decision.

Recommendation: That Mrs Smith is either the CEO or the Chairman and that a second individual is appointed to the other post to ensure that Mrs Smith does not have too much power.

Composition of board

Why codes not met: The current board ratio of executive to non-executive directors is 5:2.

Why a problem: This means that the executive directors can dominate the board proceedings. Corporate governance codes suggest that there should be a balance of executive and non-executive directors so this cannot happen.

Recommendation: That the number of executive and non-executive directors is equal to help ensure no one group dominates the board. This will mean appointing more non-executive directors.

Board remuneration

Why codes not met: Board remuneration is set by Mrs Smith.

Why a problem: This process breaches principles of good governance because the remuneration structure is not transparent and Mrs Smith sets her own pay. Mrs Smith could easily be setting remuneration levels based on her own judgements without any objective criteria. Remuneration should also be linked to performance, to encourage a high standard of work.

Recommendation: That a remuneration committee is established comprising three non-executive directors. This committee would set remuneration levels for the board, taking into account current salary levels and the performance of board members.

Directors' and auditors' responsibilities

In all aspects of corporate reporting there is a basic distinction between the role of the directors and that of the auditors:

- the directors are responsible for the preparation of information which complies with the relevant regulations
- auditors are responsible for reviewing that information and, in some cases reporting on the extent to which the directors have complied with their responsibilities. It is good practice in accordance with ISA 210 *Terms of audit engagements* to clarify the relative responsibilities of the directors and auditors in corporate governance matters.

With regards to the Combined Code, the respective responsibilities of directors and auditors can be outlined as set out below.

Note that where the auditor's role is to *read* a document, the objective is to seek to resolve any possible misstatements or any inconsistencies with the information contained in the audited financial statements. This is simply an application of the general principles of ISA 720 *Other information in documents containing audited financial statements* which is covered in a later chapter.

Area	Directors' responsibility in relation to the annual report	Auditors' responsibility
General compliance with the Combined Code	Disclose in a narrative statement as to how they have complied with the principles of the Code.	**Read** the narrative statement.
Detailed provisions of the Code	Present a statement as to whether they have complied with the provisions of the Code throughout the year.	**Review** nine defined items and report if there is non-compliance (see below). **Read** other material.
Directors' remuneration	Include a detailed statement of directors' remuneration.	**Audit** the statement as if it were part of the financial statements and include in the scope of the normal audit opinion.
Going concern status	Include a statement that the business is a going concern with any necessary supporting assumptions or qualifications.	**Review** and report if there is non-compliance.

The nine defined items in the Code which are to be reviewed by the auditor all relate to the main principles set out under "Accountability and audit". They are as set out below. Guidance on the auditors' work on these is contained in ASB Bulletin 2004/3 *The Combined Code: requirements of auditors under the listing rules of the London Stock Exchange.*

Main principle under accountability and audit	Related provisions reported on
The board should present a balanced and understandable assessment of the company's position and prospects.	■ The directors should explain in the annual report their responsibility for preparing the accounts and there should be a statement by the auditors about their reporting responsibilities (the latter will involve extending the usual statement made in the audit report setting out the auditors' responsibilities).
The board should maintain a sound system of internal control to safeguard shareholders' investment and the company's assets.	■ The board are required to review this system at least annually and to report to shareholders that they have done so. The review should cover all material controls, including financial, operational and compliance controls and risk management systems.
The board should establish formal and transparent arrangements for considering how they should apply the financial reporting and internal control principles and for maintaining an appropriate relationship with the company's auditors.	■ The board should establish an audit committee of at least three (two for smaller companies) independent non-executive directors. One of these must have "recent and relevant" financial experience. ■ The main role and responsibilities of the audit committee should be set out in written terms of reference and should include certain responsibilities (see next section). ■ The terms of reference of the audit committee should be made available and the work of the committee should be described in the annual report. ■ The audit committee should review arrangements for allowing company staff to raise concerns about possible improprieties and for those concerns to be independently investigated. ■ The audit committee should monitor and review the effectiveness of the internal audit activities. Where there is no internal audit function, the committee should consider annually whether there is a need for one and should make recommendations to the board. The annual report should explain the reasons for the absence of an internal audit function. ■ The audit committee should have primary responsibility for making a recommendation on the appointment, re-appointment and removal of the external auditors. If the board does not accept the recommendation a statement from the audit committee setting out the recommendation and explaining why the board has taken a different position should be included in the annual report. ■ The annual report should explain how, if the external auditor provides non-audit services, auditor objectivity and independence is safeguarded.

3.4 The use of audit committees

An audit committee is a **sub-committee of the board of directors**. The role of the audit committee is to carry out some delegated functions in connection with the external audit and internal audit, and to report and make recommendations to the main board of directors.

In the Combined Code, these arrangements are fulfilled by establishing an audit committee consisting entirely of at least three independent non-executive directors (or at least two in the case of smaller companies). The audit committee provides a counter-balance to the working relationship between the external auditors and the executive management of the company.

By having a requirement for the external auditor to have certain dealings with the audit committee, it should be possible to:

- reduce the dependence of the auditors on the executive management (in particular the chief executive officer and finance director)
- monitor the independence of the auditors
- provide assurance to the board that the auditors are performing their tasks to a suitable standard.

Functions of an audit committee

The functions of an audit committee may include the following tasks and responsibilities:

- To monitor the integrity of the financial statements, and to review any significant financial reporting judgements that have been used in the preparation of the statements.
- To review the adequacy of the company's internal financial controls, and possibly also its other internal controls (compliance controls and operational controls).
- To monitor the effectiveness of the internal audit function in the company.
- To make recommendations to the board about the appointment, re-appointment or removal of the external auditors, for submission to a vote by the shareholders.
- To approve the remuneration and terms of engagement of the external auditors.
- To monitor the independence and objectivity of the external auditors and the effectiveness of the audit process.
- To review and implement a policy on the employment of the external auditors to provide non-audit services to the company, so that the policy maintains the objectivity and independence of the auditors in their audit work.

The audit committee does not remove the need for the executive management to work directly with the external auditors. However, it provides an important extra channel of communication with the external auditors, to ensure that they fulfil their responsibilities properly.

Benefits and disadvantages of an audit committee

The existence of an audit committee should:

- increase user confidence in the credibility of financial information published by the company
- assist directors in meeting their responsibilities
- strengthen the independence of the external auditors by providing a point of liaison for them
- lead to better communication between the external auditors and the board of directors.

However, there are disadvantages, such as:

- the additional cost (and time) involved in having an audit committee
- the creation of a 'two-tier' board of directors: those directors closely involved in the preparation of the financial statements and the annual audit, and those who are not involved
- fear amongst executive directors that the aim of the audit committee is to 'catch them out'
- placing an excessive burden on those non-executive directors who are members of the audit committee.

CHAPTER

3

The statutory audit

Contents

The regulatory framework

- The requirement for an external audit
- Eligibility to act as an external auditor
- Appointment of auditors
- Resignation of auditors
- Removal of auditors
- Rights and duties of auditors

1 The regulatory framework

The detailed statutory regulation of auditing and the audit profession varies from country to country. The regulations in force in the UK are described in this chapter.

1.1 The requirement for an external audit

In most countries there is a legal requirement for listed companies and other large companies to have an external audit of their published financial statements. This requirement is imposed by law in order to protect the shareholders.

However, in smaller 'family' companies, where the shareholders are also the directors, the requirement for assurance in the form of an external audit is much less important.

As a consequence, many countries have a **small company audit exemption**. This exempts small companies from the need for an annual statutory audit. In the UK, companies are exempted from the requirement to have an external audit if their annual turnover does not exceed £5.6 million and their balance sheet assets do not exceed £2.8 million.

1.2 Eligibility to act as an external auditor

Self-regulation by the audit profession

Eligibility to act as an external auditor is usually determined by membership of an appropriate 'regulatory body', such as the ACCA.

The role of such regulatory bodies includes the following:

- Offering professional qualifications for auditors, to provide evidence that auditors possess a minimum level of technical competence.
- Establishing procedures to ensure that the professional competence of auditors is maintained. This includes matters such as:
  - ensuring that audits are performed only by 'fit and proper' persons, who act with professional integrity

  - requiring that the members carry out their audit work in accordance with appropriate technical standards (for example, in accordance with International Auditing Standards, known as ISAs)
  - ensuring that auditors remain technically competent and up to date with modern auditing practice (for example, by following a programme of continuing professional development)
  - providing procedures for monitoring and enforcing compliance by its members with the rules of the regulatory body. This includes rules and procedures for the investigation of complaints against members and the implementation of disciplinary procedures where appropriate.
- Maintaining a list of 'registered auditors', which is made available to the public.

Such a system is referred to as a system of **self-regulation**. In such a system, the regulation of auditors is carried out by their own professional bodies.

Regulation by government

The alternative is regulation by government. In the UK there is limited regulation by government, with self-regulation being much more important.

The Companies Act 2006 (which extended and consolidated the previous Companies Act, the Companies Act 1985) states that certain individuals are **ineligible** to act as an external auditor in the context of a given company, even if they are a member of an appropriate regulatory body. These exclusions are designed to help to establish the independence of the auditor.

The following individuals are prohibited by law from acting as the auditor of a company:

- an officer or employee of the company
- a partner or employee of an officer or servant of the company
- a partnership in which any of the above individuals is a partner.

1.3 Appointment of auditors

The external auditors are appointed by the shareholders at the **annual general meeting** (AGM) of the company, and hold office until the next AGM. At the next AGM the auditors are re-appointed by the shareholders, or different auditors are appointed.

However, directors may be allowed to appoint auditors in the following circumstances, as a matter of practical convenience:

- to fill a 'casual vacancy'; for example where the current auditor is no longer able to act
- to appoint the first auditor of a newly-formed company.

An auditor appointed by the directors will hold office only until the next AGM, when they will have to submit themselves for re-appointment by the shareholders.

If neither the shareholders of the company nor its directors have appointed auditors, company law allows for the Secretary of State at the DTI to make the appointment.

In principle, the **remuneration of the auditor** is set by whoever appoints the auditor. However in practice, where the shareholders make the appointment, it is usual to delegate to the board of directors the power to set the auditor's remuneration. The directors are likely to be more familiar than the shareholders with the nature and scope of the work involved in the audit process, and so the appropriate level of fees for that work. (The board of directors may delegate the task of recommending or approving the audit fee to the audit committee.)

1.4 Resignation of auditors

The auditor may choose to resign during his period of office. However, company law provides certain safeguards to ensure that the shareholders are made aware of any relevant circumstances relating to the auditor's resignation.

The procedures for the resignation of the current auditors include the following:

- The resignation should be made to the company **in writing**.
- The auditor should prepare a **statement of the circumstances**. This sets out the circumstances leading to the resignation, if the auditor believes that these are relevant to the shareholders or creditors of the company. For non-listed companies, if no such circumstances exist, the auditor should make a statement to this effect. (Listed companies are required to **always** make such a statement). This statement should be sent **by the company**:
  - to the Registrar of Companies
  - to all persons entitled to receive a copy of the company's financial statements (principally the shareholders).
- The auditors may require the directors to call a meeting of the shareholders in order to discuss the circumstances of the auditor's resignation.
- **Auditors** of listed companies **must notify the Registrar of Companies** when they cease to hold office. Auditors of other companies need only notify the authorities if they cease to hold office **before the end of their current term of office**. (This creates a double notification regime in case the directors fail to make such notification.)

1.5 Removal of auditors

In certain circumstances, the directors may be empowered to appoint auditors. However, it would not be appropriate for the directors to have the power to remove the auditors from office.

For example, it would be inappropriate for the directors to have the power to remove the auditors because there may be a disagreement between the directors and the auditors about an item in the financial statements or about the conduct of the audit. The directors could silence the auditors by dismissing them. Clearly, it would be more appropriate for the directors to recommend the appointment of new auditors to the shareholders, and for the shareholders to make a decision. Alternatively, auditors resigning from office will be required to give their reasons to the shareholders and in certain circumstances (see above), may also be required to notify the Registrar of Companies.

Therefore, as a general principle, only the ordinary shareholders should be able to dismiss the auditor. The detailed procedures involved are laid down in the Companies Act but the following general points apply:

- A simple majority (i.e. over 50%) of votes cast at a meeting of shareholders is sufficient to remove the auditor.
- The auditor is be allowed to attend such a meeting and make statements to the shareholders.
- Alternatively, the auditor can require written statements to be circulated to the shareholders in advance of the meeting.

These procedures should ensure that the shareholders are given all the relevant information to allow them to make a well-informed decision about the removal of the auditors.

1.6 Rights and duties of auditors

In addition to the rights and duties included above, the Companies Act contains provisions that both:

- impose certain duties on the external auditor, and
- grant him certain rights (or powers) to enable him to carry out his duties.

Duties of the external auditor

The primary duty of the external auditor is to:

- examine the financial statements, and
- issue an auditor's report on the financial statements, which is then presented to the shareholders together with the financial statements.

This auditor's report will set out the auditor's opinion as to whether (or not):

- the financial statements give a true and fair view of the financial position and performance of the company
- the financial statements have been prepared in accordance with the Companies Act 2006, and
- the information given in the directors' report is consistent with the financial statements.

The detailed provisions relating to the audit opinion are explained in a later chapter.

In addition, the Companies Act requires the auditor to consider a number of other matters as part of the statutory audit process. These include:

- whether adequate accounting records have been maintained

- whether the auditor has received all the information he required to carry out the audit
- whether the financial statements are in agreement with the underlying accounting records
- whether the information disclosed about directors' remuneration is accurate.

The outcome of the statutory audit is an **opinion** on the truth and fairness of the financial statements. The word 'opinion' implies that the auditor has applied his professional judgement in reaching his conclusion.

This point is arguably one of the limitations of the statutory audit. The audit report expresses an opinion, not a statement of fact. It is therefore open to disagreement.

In carrying out his audit work, the auditor is unlikely to check every transaction undertaken by the company during the period. There is therefore a risk that the judgement he forms may be inappropriate, because in performing the audit he has missed an item of significance.

Rights of the external auditor

The main statutory rights of the auditor include the following:

- The right of access to all accounting records at all times.
- The right to all information and explanations (from management) necessary for the proper conduct of the audit.
- The right to attend all meetings of shareholders.
- The right to speak at shareholders' meetings (restricted to speaking on matters affecting the audit or the auditor).

International Standards on Auditing (ISAs)

- The role of auditing standards
- The process of issuing auditing standards
- The authority attached to ISAs
- Scope and authority of APB pronouncements

2 International Standards on Auditing (ISAs)

2.1 The role of auditing standards

The role of the audit is to provide a high level of assurance to the users of the financial statements. This assurance will be of greater value to users if they know that the audit has been carried out in accordance with established standards of practice.

In addition, if users compare the financial statements of a number of companies, it is important that the user has confidence that consistent **auditing standards** have been applied to the audits of all of the companies.

International Standards on Auditing (known as ISAs) apply primarily to the external audit process. However their provisions can also often be seen as good practice for relevant areas of the work of the **internal** auditor.

2.2 The process of issuing auditing standards

Responsibility for ISAs

Both national and international bodies produce auditing standards. In the UK the Auditing Practices Board (APB) is responsible for preparing auditing standards for use in the UK and the Republic of Ireland.

It does this by looking at each International Standard on Auditing (ISA) issued by the International Auditing and Assurance Standards Board (IAASB), a committee of the International Federation of Accountants (IFAC). The APB supplements each ISA with any additional material that it believes is appropriate in the UK/Irish context, and then publishes it as an ISA (UK and Ireland).

In this book ISAs (UK and Ireland) are simply referred to as ISAs.

Producing a new ISA

The process of producing an ISA is as follows:

- A subject is selected by the IAASB for detailed study, with a view to eventually issuing an ISA.
- After a period of study and research, if there is agreement to proceed, an **exposure draft** is produced. The exposure draft is approved by the IAASB and then distributed widely amongst the profession and others for comment.
- Comments and proposed amendments are considered by the IAASB. The draft standard is then modified and approved by the IAASB.
- The new ISA is then published by the IAASB.
- The APB examine the new ISA and propose any supplementary material that they wish to add to the original IAASB wording.
- After consultation, the supplemented ISA is issued as a new ISA (UK and Ireland).

2.3 The authority attached to ISAs

ISAs have the following authority:

- The auditor should conduct an audit of financial statements in accordance with ISAs. (However, the requirements of ISAs need be applied only to material matters).
- ISAs are also to be applied (with suitable modification) to the audit of other information (in addition to the information in the financial statements) and to related services such as internal audit and review work.
- ISAs contain basic principles and procedures. These are highlighted in the published ISA document in bold type. The basic principles and procedures must be followed. ISAs also contain related guidance material.
- In exceptional circumstances auditors may need to depart from the provisions of an ISA in order to achieve their audit objectives. In these circumstances, the auditor must be prepared to justify the departure from the requirements of the ISA.

2.4 Scope and authority of APB pronouncements

This section is concerned with a document issued by the APB entitled *The scope and authority of APB pronouncements*. In addition to ISAs, the APB also issues a number of other documents as set out below:

- **Quality control standards** (not examinable in this paper).
- **The Auditors' Code**. This is set out in the document as an appendix. Its principles, which are set out below, have guided the development of the APB's Ethical Standards (see below) and the ISAs.
- **Engagement standards.** These include the ISAs (UK and Ireland) and the APB's Ethical Standards (ESs). The ISAs require compliance with both the ESs and with ethical pronouncements issued by the auditor's professional body. The ESs and

the ACCA Code are covered in a later chapter. Engagement standards apply to all audits carried out under the Companies Act 2006 and certain other audits.

- **Other guidance** such as Practice Notes (PNs) and Bulletins. These are persuasive rather than prescriptive. PNs assist auditors in carrying out audits in particular circumstances and industries. Bulletins provide timely guidance on new or emerging issues. A limited number of Practice Notes and Bulletins are examinable. They will be described in later chapters where appropriate.

The Auditors' Code

The Code sets out nine qualities which the APB believes should characterise the external auditor. As you will see in a later chapter, there is overlap between this code and the fundamental principles of the ACCA's own ethical code.

- **Accountability:** Auditors act in the interests of primary stakeholders (for companies, the shareholders), whilst having regards to the wider public interest.
- **Integrity:** Auditors act with integrity, fulfilling their responsibilities with honesty, fairness, candour, courage and confidentiality. Confidential information acquired in the course of audit is disclosed only when required by the public interest, or by operation of law.
- **Objectivity and independence:** Auditors are objective and provide impartial opinions unaffected by bias, prejudice, compromise and conflicts of interest. Auditors are also independent, this requires them to be free from situations and relationships which would make it probable that a reasonable and informed third party would conclude that the auditors' objectivity either is impaired or could be impaired.
- **Competence:** Auditors act with professional skill, derived from their qualification, training and practical experience. This demands an understanding of financial reporting and business issues, together with expertise in accumulating and assessing the evidence necessary to form an opinion.
- **Rigour:** Auditors approach their work with thoroughness and with an attitude of professional scepticism. They assess critically the information and explanations obtained in the course of their work and such additional evidence as they consider necessary for the purpose of their audit.
- **Judgement:** Auditors apply professional judgement taking account of materiality in the context of the matter on which they are reporting.
- **Clear, complete and effective communication:** Auditors' reports contain clear expressions of opinion and set out information necessary for a proper understanding of the opinion. Auditors communicate audit matters of governance interest arising from the audit of financial statements with those charged with governance of an entity.
- **Association:** Auditors allow their reports to be included in documents containing other information only if they consider that the additional information is not in conflict with the matters covered by their report and they have no cause to believe it to be misleading.
- **Providing value:** Auditors add to the reliability and quality of financial reporting; they provide to directors and officers constructive observations arising from the audit process; and thereby contribute to the effective operation of business capital markets and the public sector.

Advantages and limitations of statutory audits

- Advantages of statutory audits
- Limitations of statutory audits

3 Advantages and limitations of statutory audits

There are several advantages in having an external audit, but there are also some limitations.

3.1 Advantages of statutory audits

An external audit provides the following benefits:

- It increases the credibility of published financial statements.
- It confirms to management that they have performed their statutory duties correctly.
- It provides assurance to management that they have complied with non-statutory requirements, such as corporate governance requirements (where these are subject to audit or review).
- It provides feedback on the effectiveness of internal controls. Where internal controls are weak or inadequate, the auditor will give recommendations for improvement. This will assist management in reducing risk and improving the performance of the company.

Even where a statutory audit is not required, for example due to small company statutory exemption limits, an audit will increase the credibility of published financial statements. This may be important for potential lenders to the company. Potential lenders, such as banks, may insist on the company having an audit as a pre-condition for lending money.

3.2 Limitations of statutory audits

The main limitations of an audit are as follows:

- Its cost. The cost of an audit can be high. However, if the audit firm is already hired to carry out non-audit work such as accounts preparation or advisory work, the additional cost of an audit may be fairly small.
- The disruption caused to a company's staff during the audit. The company's staff may be required to assist the auditors by answering questions, providing documents and other information, and so on.

CHAPTER 4

Professional ethics and codes of conduct

Contents

Fundamental principles

- The application of professional ethics
- The fundamental principles
- Due skill and care
- The ACCA's disciplinary regime

1 Fundamental principles

1.1 The application of professional ethics

The law regulates some aspects of auditing, but not much. Company law regulates the requirement for external auditing, but internal auditing is not normally subject to statutory regulation.

However, all accountants who are members of a professional body such as the ACCA, are required to comply with the regulations of that professional body. Such professional regulations therefore apply to both external auditors and assurance providers and internal auditors.

This chapter describes the code of ethics of the ACCA, which should be followed by all members (including student members) whether they are operating as external auditors or assurance providers or internal auditors. The code also applies to the staff of an ACCA practice, regardless of whether they are members of ACCA, or any other professional body. The ACCA's ethical guide is known as the **Code of Ethics and Conduct**.

Although these rules apply to all members, the examination is primarily concerned with how the rules apply to an external auditor or assurance provider. In providing a code of ethics, the ACCA is complying with one of its regulatory functions, which is to ensure that statutory audits are performed only by 'fit and proper' persons who act with professional integrity.

The effect of these ethical rules on internal auditors is considered in a later chapter.

As discussed in a previous chapter, members of the ACCA in the UK who carry out audits are also required to comply with the APB's **Ethical Standards** (ESs). These ESs are as follows:

- ES1 *Integrity, objectivity and independence*
- ES2 *Financial, business, employment and personal relationships*
- ES3 *Long association with the audit engagement*
- ES4 *Fees, remuneration and evaluation polices, litigation, gifts and hospitality*
- ES5 *Non-audit services*
- ES *Provisions available for small entities*

Because both the ACCA Code and the ESs were developed with regard to the IFAC Code of Ethics (not examinable until Paper P7) they are broadly in line with each other. The following sections therefore refer to the ACCA Code, but any cases where the ESs are more restrictive are highlighted.

1.2 The fundamental principles

There are five **fundamental principles** in the ACCA Code of Ethics and Conduct. These principles are consistent with those in the APB's Auditors' Code discussed in a previous chapter and are set out below:

- **Integrity**. Members should be straightforward and honest in all professional and business relationships. Integrity implies not just honesty but also fair dealing and truthfulness.
- **Objectivity**. Members should not allow bias, conflicts of interest or undue influence of others to override their professional or business judgements.
- **Professional competence and due care**. Members have a duty to maintain their professional knowledge and skill at such a level that a client or employer receives a competent service, based on current developments in practice, legislation and techniques. Members should act diligently and in accordance with applicable technical and professional standards.
- **Confidentiality**. Members should respect the confidentiality of information acquired as a result of professional and business relationships and should not disclose such information to third parties without authority or unless there is a legal or professional right or duty to disclose. Confidential information acquired as a result of professional and business relationships should not be used for the personal advantage of members or third parties.
- **Professional behaviour**. Members should comply with relevant laws and regulations and should avoid any action which discredits the profession. They should behave with courtesy and consideration towards all with whom they come into contact in a professional capacity.

1.3 Due skill and care

It is a fundamental principle that ACCA members should carry out their work with **professional competence and due care**. This requirement reinforces a basic principle of the law of contract as it operates in many countries – that a contract for the provision of services should be performed with a reasonable degree of skill and care.

The concept of 'due care' or 'reasonable care' is important. The implication is that audit work performed by an auditor for a client must be adapted to the specific circumstances and characteristics of the client. There is no such thing as a 'standard' audit.

If the auditor fails to exercise a proper degree of care, a number of consequences may follow:

- There may be legal claims against the auditor in the law of contract or the law of tort. ('Tort' means wrongdoing.)

- There may be disciplinary proceedings against the auditor by the ACCA.
- The auditor or audit firm may earn a reputation in the business community for poor standards of work, and may therefore lose clients.

1.4 The ACCA's disciplinary regime

As discussed above, ACCA members are required to follow proper standards of professional conduct. The ACCA takes disciplinary action against members, firms and students where there is evidence of a sufficiently serious failure to observe those standards.

The ACCA's disciplinary committee hearings are generally conducted in public. Even if a complaint is withdrawn, the ACCA may decide to proceed with its investigation.

However, making a complaint is not a substitute for seeking damages or other compensation through the courts, as the maximum sum payable via the ACCA is £5,000.

The conceptual framework

- Introduction to the conceptual framework
- Threats
- Safeguards

2 The conceptual framework

2.1 Introduction to the conceptual framework

The application of the fundamental principles set out above is considered by the ACCA Code within a **conceptual framework**. This framework acknowledges that these principles may be threatened by a broad range of circumstances. This approach identifies five potential categories of **threats** to the fundamental principles. A sixth threat, the management threat, is added by ES1:

- **Self-interest** threat (for example, if the auditor earns a large proportion of his revenue from a particular client, he may be unwilling to upset that client by issuing an unfavourable audit report).
- **Self-review** threat (for example, if the auditor performs accountancy work for a client in addition to the audit, he may find himself in a situation where he is reviewing his own work and may therefore not be as critical of it as he might be if he was reviewing someone else's work).
- **Advocacy** threat (for example, supporting the client in a legal case may lead to a perceived loss of independence).
- **Familiarity** threat (for example, acting for a client for a long period of time may mean that the auditor becomes less critical of that client's reporting practices).
- **Intimidation** threat (for example, a strong finance director may intimidate junior members of the audit team and persuade them not to report errors found during their testing)
- **Management** threat (for example, doing work that involves making judgements and decisions that are the responsibility of management, such as the design and implementation of new IT systems).

Members are required to identify, evaluate and respond to such threats. If identified threats are anything but clearly insignificant, members must implement **safeguards** to eliminate the threats or reduce them to an acceptable level so that compliance with the fundamental principles is not compromised.

So, for example, an appropriate safeguard to mitigate the specific familiarity threat described above might be to change the partner in charge of the audit (and possibly the whole audit team) every few years. The ultimate safeguard, which might be appropriate, for example, in the advocacy threat above, would be either not to act for the client in that capacity or to resign from the audit.

Although the Code goes on to cover specific areas (such as gifts and hospitality, long association with an audit client and the provision of other services), this framework approach recognises that it is impossible to define every situation that creates threats and specify the appropriate mitigating action. The different types of threats and possible safeguards are considered in more detail below.

e

Example

Your assurance firm is auditor of Happy Goods. The audit manager has just become engaged to the managing director's daughter, who he met through a mutual friend. The managing director owns 51% of the shares in Happy Goods.

Required

List the threats to independence which might arise as a result of the above, explaining clearly why these are threats.

a

Answer

An **intimidation threat** might arise because the MD could exert influence over the audit manager via any influence he might have over his daughter. Alternatively, as the relationship between the audit manager and his future father-in-law develops direct intimation might be possible.

A **familiarity threat** might arise, again, as the relationship between the audit manager and the MD develops. The audit manager may become less critical of the reporting or operational practices at this client.

A **self-interest threat** might arise because the MD owns a majority shareholding in Happy Goods and his daughter (who may well inherit the shares at some point in the future) therefore has a vested interest in the performance of the organisation – as will her husband (i.e. this threat is probably greater once the marriage has taken place.)

2.2 Threats

In the exam you could be required to recognise threats in a given situation and to explain why those threats arise. The framework gives a list of circumstances which could give rise to each of the five threats. These are set out below but these lists are not exhaustive. The later sections of this chapter then look in more detail at some of the more common situations which might be tested in the exam, the threats which arise and the specific safeguards which should be applied.

Self-interest threats may occur as a result of the financial or other interests of members or their **immediate** or **close family members**. An immediate family member is defined by the Code as a spouse (or equivalent) or dependant. A close family member is a parent, non-dependent child, brother or sister, who is not an immediate family member.

Such financial interests might cause members to be reluctant to take actions that would be against the interests of the client. For example, if a member holds shares in a client company he may be unwilling to give an unfavourable audit report. This would threaten the fundamental principle of objectivity.

Circumstances which may give rise to self-interest threats for members include:

- financial interests, loans or guarantees
- incentive-based fee arrangements
- concern over employment security
- commercial pressure from outside the employing organisation
- inappropriate personal use of corporate assets
- close personal or business relationships
- holding a financial interest in a client or jointly holding a financial interest with a client
- undue dependence on fees from a client.

Self-review threats occur when a previous judgement needs to be re-evaluated by members responsible for that judgement. For example, where a member has been involved in maintaining the accounting records of a client he may be unwilling to find fault with the financial statements derived from those records. Again, this would threaten the fundamental principle of objectivity.

Circumstances which may give rise to self-interest threats for members include:

- business decisions or data being reviewed by the same person who made those decisions or prepared that data
- being in a position to exert direct and significant influence over an entity's financial reports
- the discovery of a significant error during a re-evaluation of the work undertaken by the member
- reporting on the operation of financial systems after being involved in their design or implementation
- a member of the assurance team being, or having recently been, employed by the client in a position to exert direct and significant influence over the subject matter of the engagement
- performing a service for a client that directly affects the subject matter of an assurance engagement.

Advocacy threats occur when members promote a position or opinion to the point that subsequent objectivity may be compromised. Although it is natural for members to support their client's or employer's position this could mean that they adopt a position so closely aligned with that of their client or there employer that there is an actual or perceived threat to the fundamental principle of objectivity.

Circumstances which may give rise to advocacy threats for members include:

- commenting publicly on future events
- situations where information is incomplete or where the argument being supported is against the law

- promoting shares in a listed company which is also an audit client
- acting as an advocate for an assurance client in litigation or dispute with third parties.

Familiarity threats occur when, because of a close relationship, members become too sympathetic to the interests of others. Circumstances which may give rise to familiarity threats for members include:

- where a member in a position to influence financial or non-financial reporting or business decisions has an immediate family member who could benefit from those decisions
- long association with business contacts influencing business decisions
- acceptance of gifts or preferential treatment, unless the value is clearly insignificant
- over-familiarity with the management of the organisation such that professional judgement could be compromised
- a former partner of the firm being a director or officer of the client or an employee being in a position to exert direct and significant influence over the subject matter of the engagement.

Intimidation threats occur when a member's conduct is influenced by fear or threats (for example, when he encounters an aggressive and dominating individual at a client or at his employer). Circumstances which may give rise to intimidation threats for members include:

- threat of dismissal or replacement of the member, or a close family member, over a disagreement about the application of an accounting principle or the way in which information is to be reported
- a dominant personality attempting to influence the member's decisions
- being threatened with litigation
- being pressured to inappropriately reduce the amount of work performed in order to reduce fees.

ES1 states that **management threats** occur when the audit firm undertakes work for the audit client that involves making judgements and taking decisions that are the responsibility of management (for example, where the firm has been involved in the design, selection and implementation of financial information technology systems). In such a situation the audit firm may become closely aligned with the views and interests of management and the auditors' objectivity may become impaired, or may be perceived to be impaired. Generally management threats arise on the provision of non-audit services.

2.3 Safeguards

- Safeguards which may remove or reduce threats to members fall into three categories:
- safeguards created by the profession, legislation or regulation

- safeguards in the work environment
- safeguards created by the individual.

Each of these categories is considered below. Later sections of this chapter consider the specific threats which might apply to specific situations.

Safeguards created by the profession, legislation or regulation include:

- educational, training and experience requirements for entry into the profession
- continuing professional development requirements
- corporate governance regulations
- professionals standards (such as ISAs)
- professional or regulatory monitoring and disciplinary procedures (such as the ACCA's own disciplinary procedures)
- external review by a legally empowered third party (such as a regulator appointed by the Government) of the reports or information produced by a member.

Safeguards in the work environment include the following:

- The employer's own systems of monitoring and ethics and conduct programmes (such as an internal training or a mentoring programme).
- Recruitment procedures, ensuring that only high-calibre, competent staff are recruited.
- Appropriate disciplinary processes.
- Strong internal controls.
- Leadership that stresses the importance of ethical behaviour and which expects employees to behave ethically.
- Policies and procedures to implement and monitor the quality of employee performance.
- Policies and procedures to implement and monitor the quality of engagements.
- Documented policies regarding the identification of threats to compliance with the fundamental principles, the evaluation of those threats and the implementation of appropriate safeguards. For example, as suggested in ES1, firms should require all staff to notify it of any:
  - family or other personal relationships involving audit clients
  - financial interests in audit clients
  - business relationships with audit clients
  - decision to take up a post at an audit client

  as these are all factors which could effect the independence of an individual.
- Communication of such policies and procedures and training on them.
- The use of different partners and engagement teams for the provision of non-assurance services to assurance clients.

- Policies and procedures to stop individuals who are not members of an engagement team from inappropriately influencing the outcome of the engagement.
- Policies and procedures to give employees the power to report ethical issues to senior staff at the employing firm, without fear of retribution from those about whom they are making the report.
- Discussing ethical issues with the client.
- Disclosing to the client the nature of the services provided and the fees charged (this could be done via the audit committee).
- Consultation with another appropriate professional accountant.

Safeguards created by the individual include:

- complying with continuing professional development requirements
- keeping records of contentious issues and approach to decision-making
- having a broader perspective on how other organisations operate by forming business relationships with other professionals
- using an independent mentor
- keeping in contact with legal advisors and professional bodies.

Example

Following on from the previous example, suggest specific, appropriate safeguards which could be put in place to mitigate the identified threats.

Answer

The most appropriate safeguards would be to:

- remove the manager from the audit of Happy Goods Ltd, and
- ensure that he has no significant influence over the audit team (for example, by ensuring that the members of the audit team are not close friends of his).

Failing that, the following safeguards could be implemented:

- Confirm that the MD's daughter is not dependent on him in any way (financially or otherwise).
- Review the manager's work on the audit.
- Ensure that the manager is aware of the requirement for independence.
- Discuss the potential ethical issue with the client and request that the manager has no involvement with the MD during the course of the audit (he is more likely to deal with the FD). (Though this will not help if the relationship between the manager and the MD is already developing (as they may meet outside the audit environment) or if the MD has significant influence over his fellow-directors. However, it may be that no such close relationship is forming, especially if the daughter is not close to her father and is not financially dependent on him.)

Independence, objectivity and integrity

- Actual and perceived independence
- Fees and pricing
- Family and personal relationships
- Close business relationships
- Financial interests
- Loans and guarantees
- Employment or former employment with assurance clients
- Long association of senior personnel with assurance clients
- Provision of non-assurance services
- Gifts and hospitality
- Actual and threatened litigation
- ES Provisions available for small entities

3 Independence, objectivity and integrity

3.1 Actual and perceived independence

For an audit or other assurance report to be of value, the assurance provider:

- **must be independent** (actual independence), and also
- **must be seen to be independent** (perceived independence).

The opinion of an assurance provider must be an independent opinion given by a professional person with appropriate skills in assurance work, and the opinion must not be influenced by anyone else. In particular, the assurance work must not be influenced by the opinions and views of the management of the client company. This is why the fundamental principle of **objectivity** is so important.

Independence of the assurance provider (and in particular, of a statutory auditor) is a matter of public confidence in the assurance or audit process. As discussed above, in the context of the conceptual framework, members need to be fully aware of situations that may damage their independence and objectivity. Such situations are referred to as **threats** to independence. Any threats to independence may be reduced by **safeguards** put in place by an assurance firm.

Although the ACCA Code provides a conceptual framework, which recognises that it is impossible to define every situation that creates threats and specify the appropriate safeguards, specific guidance is provided in a number of key areas where independence may be under threat, or may be seen to be under threat. The main areas are:

- fees and pricing
- family and personal relationships

- close business relationships
- financial interests
- loans and guarantees
- employment or former employment with assurance clients
- long association of senior personnel with assurance clients
- provision of non-audit services
- gifts and hospitality
- actual and threatened litigation.

3.2 Fees and pricing

Relative size of fees

Where the *total* fees generated by an assurance client represent a large proportion of an assurance firm's total fees, the dependence on that client and concern about the possibility of losing that client may create a **self-interest threat**.

Specific **safeguards** might include:

- discussing the extent and nature of fees with the audit committee or other appropriate persons at the client
- taking steps to reduce dependency on that client (for example, by refusing lucrative non-audit services or taking those on and resigning as auditor)
- having external quality control reviews
- consulting a third party, such as the ACCA or another professional accountant.

The Code states that the public may perceive that independence is impaired where the fees for audit and other recurring work paid by one client, or a group of connected clients, exceeds 15% of the income of the audit practice (10% for listed and other public interest clients). A review of independence is recommended when fees reach 10% (5% for listed clients).

It may be particularly difficult for new audit practices to satisfy this requirement; therefore, particular care on independence is required in these circumstances.

Overdue fees

If fees from an assurance client remain unpaid for a long time, a **self-interest threat** may arise. This will certainly be the case if a significant part of the overdue amount is not paid before the next year's report is issued.

The Code therefore recommends that payment of such fees should be required **before** the report is issued. Other **safeguards** might include:

- discussing the level of outstanding fees with the audit committee or other appropriate persons at the client
- involving an additional professional accountant who did not take part in the assurance engagement to provide advice or to review the work performed.

ES4 states that if fees remain overdue, the audit engagement partner, together with the ethics partner, should consider whether the firm can continue as auditors or whether it should resign.

Pricing

When an assurance firm obtains an assurance engagement at a significantly lower level than that charged by the previous firm, or quoted by other firms (known as "low-balling") a **self-interest threat** arises. This threat will not be reduced to an acceptable level unless:

- the firm is able to demonstrate that appropriate time and qualified staff are available, and
- all applicable assurance standards and quality control procedures are being complied with.

Contingent fees

Contingent fees are fees **calculated on a pre-determined basis**, relating to the outcome or result of a transaction or the work performed. For example, if an assurance report was provided in support of a loan application, a contingent fee might be one which is only payable by the client if the application was successful. Clearly this type of fee creates both **self-interest and advocacy threats**.

These threats are considered insurmountable and therefore the Code does not allow contingent fee arrangements.

3.3 Family and personal relationships

Family and personal relationships between a member of the assurance team and a director, officer or certain employees at the client may create **self-interest, familiarity or intimidation threats**, depending on the specific circumstances. The significance of these threats will depend on:

- the member's responsibilities on the assurance engagement
- the closeness of the relationship, and
- the role of the family member at the assurance client.

Clearly, a greater threat will exist where, say, the wife of one of the partners at the assurance firm is the finance director at the client than if, say, an audit junior's sister is the receivables ledger clerk.

Where an **immediate family member** (ie spouse or dependent) of a member of the assurance team is:

- a director, officer, or employee of the assurance client, and
- is in a position to exercise direct and significant influence over the subject matter of the assurance engagement

Then the only appropriate **safeguard** is to remove the individual from the assurance team. So, in the example above, that particular partner should have no involvement with the assurance engagement at his wife's company. Even then, this may not be a sufficient safeguard if all the partners enjoy a close relationship and the only safe approach may be not to take on that company as a client at all.

For a **close family member** (parent, non-dependent child, brother or sister) in the same position **safeguards** might include:

- removing the individual from the assurance team
- where possible, structuring the responsibilities of the assurance team in such a way that the member of the assurance team does not deal with matters which are the responsibility of the family member (so, in the example above, the audit junior would not be assigned to the receivables section of the audit)
- putting in place policies and procedures to allow assurance staff to communicate to senior staff at the assurance firm any independence issues which concern them.

Threats are not restricted to the family relationships defined above. It is the assurance firm's responsibility to consider any other personal relationships which might have a bearing on independence and consider what safeguards need to be put in place.

3.4 Close business relationships

A commercial or common financial interest between an assurance firm or a member of the assurance team and a client or its management may create **self-interest and intimidation threats**. The Code gives the following examples of such relationships:

- A material financial interest in a joint venture with the assurance client or its senior management.
- Arrangements to combine services or products, marketed with reference to both parties.
- The firm acting as a distributor or marketer of the client's products or services or vice versa.

If the relationship relates to the **assurance firm**, unless the financial interest is immaterial and the relationship clearly insignificant to the firm, the Code states that there are **no safeguards** which could reduce the threat to an acceptable level. Therefore the only possible courses of action are to:

- terminate the business relationship
- reduce the level of the relationship so that the financial interest becomes immaterial and the relationship insignificant, or
- refuse the assurance engagement.

If the relationship relates to a **member of the assurance team**, as opposed to the firm, unless the financial interest is immaterial and the relationship clearly insignificant to the individual, the only appropriate **safeguard** would be to remove the individual from the assurance team.

The **purchase of goods and services** from an assurance client by the firm or a member of the assurance team would not generally create a threat to independence provided:

- the transaction is in the normal course of business, and
- on an arm's length basis.

However, the nature or number of such transactions could create a **self-interest threat** and safeguards would need to be applied such as:

- eliminating or reducing the transactions
- removing the individual from the assurance team
- discussing the issue with the audit committee or appropriate senior management at the client.

3.5 Financial interests

A **financial interest** in an assurance client exists where shares or debt instruments are held either directly or indirectly. A **direct financial interest** is one held by an individual or the assurance firm or by a trust controlled by them. An **indirect financial interest** is one held by an individual or the assurance firm via a trust **not** controlled by them. Such a holding may create a **self-interest threat**.

Neither an assurance team member (nor his immediate family) or an assurance firm must hold a direct financial interest or a material indirect financial interest. Therefore the only safeguards would be to:

- dispose of any direct financial interest
- dispose of any indirect financial interest or reduce the holding to such a level that it is no longer material
- remove the individual from the assurance team
- resign from the audit.

If holdings are acquired by an individual as a gift or inherited:

- they should be disposed of as soon as practicable, or
- the individual should be removed from the assurance team.

3.6 Loans and guarantees

If the assurance client is a **bank or similar institution**, no threat to independence is created where the loan is made on normal terms to the assurance firm or a member of the assurance team.

If the assurance client is a **not a bank or similar institution** the **self-interest threat** would be so great that **no safeguard** could reduce the threat to an acceptable level, unless the loan is immaterial to both the firm/member and the client.

3.7 Employment or former employment with assurance clients

Employment with assurance clients

Individuals who have previously been on the assurance team could leave the assurance firm to work for the assurance client. Depending on:

- the seniority of the individual when he was on the assurance team
- the position he has taken up at the client
- the amount of future involvement he will have with the assurance team (as a member of the client's staff)
- the length of time that has passed since he was on the assurance team

significant **self-interest, familiarity or intimidation threats** could arise. This will be the case particularly if strong personal or financial links remain between the individual and the remaining members of the assurance team or the assurance firm.

The Code **specifies** that:

- the individual concerned must not be entitled to any benefits or payments from the firm, unless these are fixed, pre-determined arrangements
- any amounts owed to the individual (for example, in the case of an ex-partner) must not be so significant that they could threaten independence
- the individual must no longer take part (or appear to take part) in the firm's business
- in respect of **audit clients** a key audit partner should not accept a key management position with their audit client until at least **two years** after the conclusion of the audit.

ES2 puts a different slant on this last point by specifying that where a **former partner who has acted as the engagement partner** in the last two years joins the audit client as a director or in a key management position, the firm should resign and should not accept re-appointment for two years (unless the former partner leaves the client earlier than this). This reflects a situation where a partner leaving the firm negotiates with his (soon to be) ex-partners that the firm will resign from the audit on his decision to take up the post.

Other **safeguards** might include:

- modifying the assurance plan (perhaps to increase the amount of work on the area the ex-team member will be involved with)
- assigning an assurance team of sufficient expertise compared to the individual who has left (i.e. a team which will not be intimidated by the ex-team member)
- arranging for an additional professional accountant to review the work done
- carrying out a quality control review of the engagement.

Similar threats could also arise where a member of the assurance team knows he is to join the client in the future or has entered negotiations to do so. If the individual were to remain on the assurance team, objectivity could be impaired as the individual might be keen not to upset his potential future employer (**self-interest threat**). **Safeguards** would include:

- the firm having policies and procedures in place to require individuals to notify the firm when they are entering into serious negotiations with an assurance client
- removing the individual from the assurance team

Recent service with an assurance client

If a former director, officer or employee of an assurance client becomes a member of the assurance team there may be **self-interest, self-review or familiarity threats**. This will particularly be the case if, as a member of the assurance team, the individual has to report on work he carried out. He may also be reluctant to criticise the work of former colleagues.

The Code **specifies** that individuals who worked for an assurance client as a director, officer or employee in a position to exert a direct and significant influence over the subject matter of the engagement during the period covered by the assurance report, or the **preceding two years** should not be assigned to the assurance team.

If they were employed prior to this period the level of threat will depend upon:

- the amount of time elapsed
- the individual's position with the client
- the role of the individual on the assurance team.

Safeguards might include:

- arranging for an additional professional accountant to review the work done by the individual
- discussing the matter with the audit committee or appropriate senior management at the client.

3.8 Long association of senior personnel with assurance clients

Using the same senior personnel on an assurance engagement over a long period of time may create a **familiarity threat**. The level of threat will depend upon:

- the length of time that the individual has been on the assurance team
- the role of the individual on the assurance team
- the structure of the firm
- the nature of the assurance engagement.

Safeguards might include:

- rotating senior staff of the assurance team
- arranging for an additional professional accountant to review the work done by the senior staff
- carrying out independent quality control reviews.

However, because the threat would be so great for an audit client, the Code **specifies** the following for the **audit of listed or other public interest clients**:

- The engagement partner should be rotated after a pre-defined period. This should normally be no more than **five years** and he should not return to the engagement until after a further five years.
- Other key audit partners should be rotated after a pre-defined period. This should normally be no more than **seven years** and they should not return to the engagement until after a further two years (or five years if returning as the engagement partner).
- The individual responsible for the engagement quality control review should be rotated after a pre-defined period. This should normally be no more than **seven years** and he should not return to the engagement until after a further two years.

When an audit client **becomes a listed entity**, the length of time an individual has served that client in that capacity should be considered when deciding when the individual should be rotated. However, the Code **specifies** that the above categories of persons should only continue in those positions for another **two years**.

If the firm has such a limited number of staff that such rotation is not practicable, other safeguards should be applied such as arranging for an additional professional accountant to review the work done.

3.9 Provision of non-assurance services

The independence of an assurance firm may be threatened when the firm carries out a large amount of non-assurance work for an entity that is also its assurance client. This is particularly true where an audit firm carries out non-audit services for its audit client.

- The non-audit work may provide a large amount of income that makes the audit firm economically dependent on the company (**self-interest threat)**.
- In addition, employees of the audit firm who carry out the audit may be required to audit the work that has been done for the company by colleagues in the audit firm. It might be difficult for them to find faults with the work that has been done by other employees of the firm (**self-review threat)**.
- ES5 identifies another key threat – that there is a danger that the auditor could make, or be perceived to be making, management decisions (**management threat).**

Both the Code and ES5 consider various categories of non-assurance work. The ones of most relevance to your exam are considered below.

General non-assurance services

Although non-assurance (as opposed to non-audit) services are generally considered acceptable, subject to appropriate safeguards, the following activities are **prohibited** by the Code:

- Authorising, executing or completing a transaction.
- Deciding which recommendation of the firm should be implemented.
- Reporting, in a management role, to senior management of the client.

Any of the above would involve the firm acting in a management capacity and therefore constitute a threat to the firm's objectivity.

Appropriate **safeguards** for other activities would include the following:

- The firm having policies and procedures such that an individual is prevented from making any management decision on behalf of the client.
- Discussing independence issues with the audit committee or senior management at the client.
- The firm having policies covering oversight responsibility for the provision of other work to assurance clients.
- Involving an additional professional accountant in a review of independence or an aspect of the engagement.
- The client acknowledging responsibility for the results of the work performed by the firm.
- Disclosing to the audit committee or similar body the nature and extent of fees charged.
- Personnel carrying out the non-assurance services not taking part in the assurance engagement.

Preparing accounting records and financial statements

Preparing accounting records and financial statements and then auditing them creates a significant **self-review threat**. This may also apply where an assurance engagement involves reviewing subject matter (such as forecasts) prepared by the firm itself. ES5 also recognises the danger of a **management threat** if the auditor were to make decisions which should be those of management.

In providing such assistance, firms **must not make management decisions** such as:

- deciding on or changing journal entries without the client's approval
- authorising or approving transactions
- preparing source documents or originating data (including decisions on valuation assumptions).

The provision of advice on accounting principles and presentation in the financial statements given during the course of an audit will not generally threaten the firm's independence. Such advice is considered to be part of the normal audit process.

The Code **specifies** that for **listed or other public interest clients** the audit firm **may not provide** accounting or book-keeping services, including payroll services and the preparation of financial statements, except:

- in an emergency, or
- to a division or subsidiary of the client where the work is of a routine or mechanical nature

provided that:

- the fees are insignificant
- the division or subsidiary is immaterial to the client, and
- the services do not involve the exercise of judgement.

Where such services are provided, **all** of the following **safeguards** should be applied:

- the client must accept responsibility for the results of the work
- the firm must not assume any management role
- the team providing the services must be different to the audit team.

For **non-listed clients**, accounting or book-keeping services, including payroll services, of a routine or mechanical nature may be provided with appropriate **safeguards** such as:

- the service not being performed by a member of the audit team
- the firm having policies and procedures such that an individual is prevented from making any management decision on behalf of the client
- requiring the source data for accounting entries to be originated by the client
- requiring the underlying assumptions to be originated and approved by the client
- obtaining the client's approval for any changes to the financial statements.

Valuation services

A **self-review threat** might arise where an audit firm performs a valuation of an item which is to be included in the financial statements to be audited. Again, there is also a potential **management** threat per ES5. Therefore **audit firms** should **not provide valuation services** where:

- the matter is material to the financial statements, and
- involves a significant degree of subjectivity.

In other cases, appropriate **safeguards** might include:

- the client acknowledging responsibility for the results of the work
- an additional professional accountant reviewing the work done
- the client confirming their understanding of and approving the underlying assumptions and methodologies used
- the individuals carrying out the work not being involved in the audit.

Taxation services

Such services include compliance work, tax planning, the provision of advice and assistance in the resolution of tax disputes. Such assignments are not considered by the Code to threaten independence.

Internal audit services

The Code states that a **self-review threat** might arise where an audit firm provides internal audit services to an audit client. The following **safeguards** must be applied:

- the client being responsible for the internal audit activities (using a designated, preferably senior management, employee) and acknowledging its responsibility for the system of internal controls

- the client and audit committee approving the scope, risk and frequency of the work
- the client being responsible for evaluating recommendations and deciding which are to be implemented
- the client evaluating the adequacy of the procedures performed
- the findings and recommendations being reported to the audit committee or similar body.

In addition, the firm should consider whether such services should only be provided by individuals not involved in the audit.

ES5 is slightly more restrictive stating that an engagement to provide internal audit services for an **audit client** should **not be undertaken where**:

- the firm would place significant reliance on the work of internal audit as part of their external audit work, or
- in carrying out the internal audit services, the audit firm would undertake part of the role of management (i.e. there is an insurmountable **management threat**).

IT systems services

Where such services provided by the audit firm involve the design and implementation of Financial Information Technology Systems (FITS) a **self-review threat** might arise. Without the following **safeguards** the Code considers that this threat will probably be too significant for the work to be accepted:

- The client acknowledging its responsibility for the system of internal controls.
- The client designating a competent employee, preferably senior management, to be responsible for management decisions in respect of the design and implementation of the system. (ES5 refers to such an employee as **"informed management".**)
- The client making all such management decisions.
- The client evaluating the adequacy and results of the design and implementation of the system.
- The client being responsible for the operation of the system and the data generated by it.

Again, ES5 is slightly more restrictive stating that the audit firm **should not undertake** an engagement to design, provide or implement IT systems for an **audit client** where:

- the systems concerned would be important to any significant part of the accounting system or to the production of the financial statements and the audit firm would place significant reliance on them as part of their external audit, or
- in carrying out the IT services the audit firm would undertake part of the role of management (i.e. there is an insurmountable **management threat**).

Temporary staff assignments

If the audit firm lends staff to an audit client there is a potential **self-review threat** where the individual will be in a position to influence the preparation of the accounts or financial statements. Such assistance may be given provided that the individual **will not be involved in**:

- making management decisions
- approving or signing agreements etc
- exercising discretionary authority to commit the client to certain actions.

Safeguards should include:

- the individuals loaned having no subsequent audit responsibility for any area they were involved in during their assignment
- the client acknowledging its responsibility for directing and supervising loaned staff.

Litigation support services

Such services may include:

- acting as an expert witness
- calculating estimated damages
- assistance with document management and retrieval

and could create a **self-interest threat,** depending on the materiality of the amounts involved and the subjectivity of the matter concerned.

Safeguards might include:

- the service not being performed by a member of the assurance team
- the firm having policies and procedures such that an individual is prevented from making any management decision on behalf of the client
- the involvement of independent experts.

ES5 states that litigation support services **should not be provided** to an **audit client** where:

- the engagement would involve the estimation by the firm of the likely outcome of a pending legal matter that could be material to the financial statements, and
- there is a significant degree of subjectivity involved.

Legal services

The threat will depend on the nature of the service, whether the provider is also a member of the assurance team and the materiality of the matter. Safeguards are likely to include those listed under general non-assurance services above.

However, the Code states that acting for an **audit client** in the resolution of a dispute or litigation where the amounts involved are material to the financial statements creates such significant **advocacy and self-review threats** that the work **should not be taken on.**

Recruitment of senior management

The recruitment of senior management for an assurance client may create current or future **self-interest, familiarity, intimidation and management threats**. The level of the threat will depend on the role of the person to be recruited and the type of assistance sought.

The firm may review CVs and draw up a short-list of candidates for interview but the decision as to who is hired must be made by the client.

Corporate finance and similar activities

Certain types of corporate finance services may create such significant **advocacy and self-review threats** that the work should not be taken on. Assurance firms **should not**:

- promote, deal in or underwrite an assurance client's shares
- commit an assurance client to the terms of a transaction or complete a transaction on an assurance client's behalf.

In other cases, **safeguards** such as not making management decisions and using individuals who are not members of the assurance team should be considered.

ES5 also states that such work should not be taken on where:

- the audit partner doubts the appropriateness of an accounting treatment related to the advice provided, or
- it would involve the firm undertaking a management role (insurmountable **management threat**).

3.10 Gifts and hospitality

Accepting gifts or hospitality from an assurance client may create **self-interest and familiarity threats**.

The Code **specifies** that gifts or hospitality should only be accepted where the value is **clearly insignificant**.

3.11 Actual and threatened litigation

Actual or threatened litigation could create **self-interest or intimation threats**. The significance of the threat will depend on the materiality of the litigation, the nature of the engagement and whether the litigation relates to a previous assurance engagement.

Safeguards should include:

- disclosing the extent and nature of the litigation to the audit committee or senior management
- if the litigation involves a member of the assurance team, removing that individual from the assurance team
- an additional professional accountant reviewing the work done.

Example

Your firm is the auditor of Happy Days, an entity which provides hospitality packages at racecourses around a single country. The managing director of Happy Days has suggested the following to your managing partner:

- All members of the audit team are to be offered two free tickets to a major event at the racecourse of their choice.
- Last year's audit senior should be seconded to the organisation for a six-month period. The current year's audit is not yet underway.
- That the firm also provide internal audit services.

Required

Discuss which, if any, of the above proposals would be acceptable to your firm (and if not state why not), and set out the **main** safeguards, if any, which would be required.

Answer

Free tickets – not acceptable. The ACCA Code states that gifts or hospitality should only be accepted where the value is clearly insignificant (self-interest threat). This would be likely to be a considerable "perk" for audit team members and, in any case, would not give an appearance of independence.

Secondment – acceptable with the following safeguards.

- The senior should not be involved in future audits (as there would be self-review and familiarity threats).
- The composition of the current year's audit team should be reviewed to ensure that the secondee would not be likely to have significant influence over the members of that team (through personal relationships) (familiarity and intimation threats).
- The secondee should not be in a position to influence management decisions and management must take responsibility for all such decisions.

Internal audit services – acceptable with the following safeguards (self-review threat).

- That the management of Happy Days (via a designated senior employee) take responsibility for the scope and frequency of the work.
- That it is management's decision as to which recommendations are acted upon.

3.12 ES Provisions available for small entities

The APB has issued this additional ES, mindful of the fact that certain audit firms will find it difficult to comply with the five ESs, particularly when auditing a small entity.

This ES (the ESPASE) provides alternative provisions for auditors of small companies in respect of threats arising from economic dependence and where tax or accounting services are provided and allows exemption from certain of the requirements in ESs 1 to 5. Where an audit firm takes advantage of the ESPASE it **must disclose that fact in the audit report**.

Small entities are defined in the same way as companies eligible for audit exemption (see previous chapter) plus other entities such as small charities or clubs.

Alternative provisions and exemptions under the ESPASE

Economic dependence: Where total fees for both audit and non-audit services receivable from a non-listed client are expected to fall between 10% and 15% of the annual fee income of the audit firm, firms are not expected to comply with the requirement to arrange an external independent quality control review of the audit engagement before the audit report is finalised.

Self-review threat – non-audit services: When undertaking non-audit services the firm is not required to apply safeguards to address a self-review threat, provided that:

- the audit client has "informed management", and
- the firm extends the cyclical inspection of completed engagements that is performed for quality control purposes.

Management threat – non-audit services: When undertaking non-audit services the firm may act in a management capacity where there is no "informed management", provided that:

- it discusses objectivity and independence issues relating to the provision of non-audit services with those charged with governance, and
- it discloses the fact that it has applied the ESPASE.

Advocacy threat – tax services: The firm may act as an advocate for the audit client provided, again, that it discloses the fact that it has applied the ESPASE.

Partners joining an audit client: The firm need not comply with the requirement of ES2 whereby the firm is required to resign and not to accept re-appointment for two years after the partner joins the client, provided that:

- the firm takes appropriate steps to determine that there has been no significant threat to the audit team's integrity, objectivity and independence, and
- it discloses the fact that it has applied the ESPASE.

Confidentiality and conflicts of interest

- Duty of confidentiality
- Recognised exceptions to the duty of confidentiality
- Conflicts of interest

4 Confidentiality and conflicts of interest

4.1 Duty of confidentiality

One of the five fundamental principles of the ACCA Code is that of **confidentiality**. As discussed above, this principle states that information obtained in the course of professional work should not be disclosed to others, except where:

- **consent has been obtained** from the person or entity to which the information relates, or
- there is a **legal or professional right or duty to disclose** (as described below).

In addition, information gained when acting in a professional capacity should not be disclosed in order to:

- gain a personal advantage, or
- gain an advantage for another party.

One of the reasons for this requirement for auditors is that auditors need to obtain full and open disclosure of information from a client in order to carry out their duties. If the client cannot be assured of the confidentiality of this information, he may be unwilling to provide the auditors with all the information that they need.

4.2 Recognised exceptions to the duty of confidentiality

There are some recognised exceptions to the duty of confidentiality. Where one of these exceptions applies, the member may be required to disclose the information to a third party, or may voluntarily choose to disclose confidential information.

Obligatory disclosure

An auditor/ACCA member is **obliged** to:

- disclose relevant information to an appropriate authority if he knows, or has reason to suspect, that a client has committed **treason, terrorism, drug trafficking, or money laundering**
- disclose information **if forced to do so by the process of law** (for example, a court case might require the production of audit documents for inspection by the court).

In these circumstances, the requirements of the law override the duty of confidentiality.

Voluntary disclosure

Voluntary disclosure of confidential information is permitted in the following circumstances:

- to protect the member's interests (for example, in making a defence against an official accusation of professional negligence)
- in the public interest (for example, making disclosures to the tax authorities of non-compliance by a client company with tax regulations)
- when authorised by local statute
- to non-governmental bodies which have the power to force such disclosure.

4.3 Conflicts of interest

Conflicts between members and clients

ACCA members or firms should not accept or continue an engagement where there is a conflict of interest between the member or firm and its client. The test is whether a "reasonable and informed third party" would consider the conflict of interest as likely to affect the judgement of the member or the firm.

Examples of this might be:

- when members compete directly with a client
- the receipt of commission from a third party for the introduction of a client (for example, an audit firm may be paid a commission by another entity, such as a firm of brokers, for introducing the entity to its client companies).

Safeguards against a conflict of interest might include:

- disclosure of the conflict/commission to the client, and
- obtaining the informed consent of the client.

Conflicts between competing clients

A firm might act for two clients that are in direct competition with each other.

The firm has a professional duty of confidentiality, and so will not disclose confidential information about one client company to its competitor. Again, the test is whether a "reasonable and informed third party" would consider the conflict of interest as likely to affect the judgement of the firm.

The approach that the audit firm should take will be a matter of judgement and should reflect the circumstances of the case. Where the acceptance or continuance of an engagement would **materially prejudice the interests of any client**, the appointment should not be accepted or continued.

In other cases, possible **safeguards** might include the following:

- Giving careful consideration to whether it is appropriate to accept an assurance engagement from a new client that is in direct competition with an existing client, it may be appropriate to decline the offer from the potential new client.

- Careful management of the clients, for example by ensuring that different members of staff are used on the two engagements.
- Full and frank disclosure to the clients of the potential conflict, together with suitable steps by the firm to manage the potential conflict of interest.
- Procedures to prevent access to information (such as physical separation of the teams and confidential and secure data filing). Such an approach is known as creating "Chinese walls".
- Establishing clear guidelines on security and confidentiality and the use of confidentiality agreements.
- Regular review of safeguards in place.
- Advising one or both clients to seek additional independent advice.

Obtaining and accepting a new audit engagement

- Introduction
- Obtaining audit work
- Accepting an audit appointment: ethical matters
- Engagement letters (ISA 210)

5 Obtaining and accepting a new audit engagement

5.1 Introduction

Several commercial and ethical matters should be considered by an **external** auditor when considering the acceptance of a new audit engagement.

Audit practices are a business, and their objective is to make a profit. However, this does not mean that the practice should automatically accept every audit engagement that is offered to it, in order to maximise profit. Circumstances may arise where it is appropriate to decline the offer of an audit appointment, for either commercial or ethical reasons.

5.2 Obtaining audit work

Advertising and publicity

The ACCA Code allows members to seek publicity for their services and to advertise their services. However, whatever medium is used, it **must not reflect badly on the member, the ACCA or the accountancy profession**. Members must also take care that the way in which they market their services does not create a **self-interest threat** to the fundamental principle of **professional behaviour**.

The Code also states that advertisements and promotional material must not:

- discredit the services offered by others (for example by claiming superiority)
- be misleading
- fall short of any local regulations or legislation (such as, in the UK, the Advertising Standards Authority's Code which requires all adverts to be legal, decent, clear, honest and truthful).

Fees

Where reference is made in promotional material to fees:

- this must not be misleading with regard to the precise range of services and the time commitment covered
- comparison may be made to the fees of others, provided that this is not misleading and that it follows local regulations or legislation
- discounts on existing fees may be offered, or a free consultation at which the level of fees will be discussed.

Introductions

Fees and commissions may be paid to third parties for the introduction of potential new clients, **but safeguards must be in place** to reduce the threats to the fundamental principles. Such safeguards would include disclosure to the client.

Tendering

When making a decision to appoint a new firm of auditors, it is standard practice amongst larger companies to invite tenders for the audit work from a number of audit firms.

A tendering process typically requires the interested audit firms to provide a detailed written proposal including an approximate fee estimate, based on the estimated time to be spent on the audit and the grade of staff to be used. A presentation to the potential client may also be required.

Sometimes, an audit firm may use a technique known as '**low-balling**' when it tenders for audit work. As discussed above, low-balling means deliberately quoting a low (and perhaps unprofitable) fee in order to obtain the audit work. A low-balling strategy may be linked to an intention to:

- increase the fee to a more realistic level over a period of years, or
- make up the shortfall in the fee for the basic audit work with more profitable fees for non-audit services.

Low-balling itself is not considered unethical but, as discussed in a previous section, it creates a potential **self-interest threat** to independence. Therefore the firm must be able to demonstrate that appropriate time and qualified staff are available to ensure that a quality audit is performed in accordance with ISAs.

5.3 Accepting an audit appointment: ethical matters

The ACCA Code includes procedures that auditors must follow to assure that their appointment is valid.

Procedures before accepting an appointment

Before accepting an appointment, the audit firm should take the following steps:

- It should assess whether acceptance would create any **threats** to compliance with the fundamental principles. For example, a personal relationship between a partner at the firm and a senior member of the client's staff could create a threat to objectivity. Lack of technical expertise could create a threat to professional competence and due care.
- It should ensure that **resources** are available to complete the audit assignment; in particular, it must ensure that there will be sufficient staff (of the right level of expertise) available at the right time. Again, not to have sufficient resources available would create a threat to professional competence and due care.

- It should take up references on the proposed client company and its directors, if they are not already known to the auditors. This is usually referred to as **client screening**.
- It should **communicate with the current auditors**, if there are any, to establish if there are any matters that it should be aware of when deciding whether or not to accept the appointment. Although this is partly a matter of courtesy between professionals, this will involve discussion of the appointment, the client and the audit work. Such discussion will allow the firm to decide if the client is someone for whom it would wish to act.

The following points should be noted in connection with communicating with the current auditors:

- Client permission is required for any such communication. If the client refuses to give its permission, the appointment as auditor should not be accepted.
- If the client does not give the current auditor permission to reply to any relevant questions, the appointment as auditor should not be accepted.
- If the current auditor does not provide any information relevant to the appointment, the new auditor should accept or reject the engagement based on other available knowledge.
- If the current auditor does provide such information, the new auditor should assess all the available information and take a decision about whether or not to accept the audit work.

Note that even where the current auditor provides information that is judged to be relevant to the acceptance of the engagement, the proposed new auditor may still accept the assignment. However, he should exercise appropriate professional and commercial judgement in doing so.

Procedures after accepting an appointment

After accepting the appointment as auditor, the audit firm should take the following measures:

- It should ensure that the current auditor (if any) has resigned from the audit in a proper manner, or has been removed from office in accordance with any appropriate legislation.
- It should ensure that its appointment is valid in law and is properly documented.
- It should prepare and submit an engagement letter to the board of the new client (see below).

5.4 Engagement letters (ISA 210)

Having accepted an appointment as auditor of a client company, the audit firm should submit an engagement letter to the board of directors of the client company. The engagement letter can be seen as the basis for **the contract between the company and the auditor**. Its main objectives are to confirm:

- the auditor's acceptance of the appointment
- the scope of the audit work
- the basis of the audit opinion
- any other (non-audit) services to be provided, although this may be set out in a separate engagement letter
- the extent of the auditor's responsibilities in respect of the client's financial statements.

The content of the engagement letter

ISA 210 *Terms of audit engagements* states that the form and content of an audit engagement letter will vary depending on the circumstances of each client. However, a letter will generally include reference to the following:

- The objective of the audit.
- Management's responsibility for the financial statements.
- The scope of the audit, including reference to appropriate legislation and professional standards.
- The form of the audit report to be issued to the shareholders and the form of any other formal communication from the auditor to management.
- A clear statement of the fact that there is a risk that some material mis-statements could remain undetected after an audit, because of
  - the test nature of auditing
  - the inherent limitations of an audit, and
  - the inherent limitations of internal controls.
- The auditors' (statutory) right of unrestricted access to the accounting records of the client and to explanations from the client's employees.

In addition to the above, the auditor may feel that it is appropriate to include additional points in the engagement letter, such as:

- the basis on which fees are charged
- planning information, such as an outline timetable for the audit work
- a request for the management of the client company to formally acknowledge their acceptance of the contents of the engagement letter
- arrangements for the involvement of client staff in the audit process, including any internal auditors.

Example

Explain, for each of the additional points above, why their inclusion in the engagement letter might be appropriate.

Answer

Basis on which fees are charged – to ensure that there is no misunderstanding (for example that more senior staff cost more and that "time is money"). This may help to encourage the client to provide as much assistance as possible and not to insist that all work is carried out by more senior members of the team.

Outline timetable – to ensure that the client will be prepared for the arrival of the audit team (for example, draft financial statements and supporting schedules of all ready and key staff available (and not on holiday). If necessary, the audit timetable could be changed at this stage.

Formal acknowledgement of the contents of the letter– to ensure that the directors cannot later claim that they did not understand the scope of the audit and their responsibility for the financial statements.

Arrangements for the involvement of client staff – to ensure that the client is able to plan for the involvement of the necessary staff and that they are available at the required time.

Annual review of the engagement letter

The engagement letter issued on the initial appointment as auditors may state that its provisions will apply to all future annual audits, until it is revised. However, ISA 210 requires that the letter should be **reviewed annually** by the auditors in order to ensure that its provisions remain relevant.

In addition, the ISA suggests that the following factors may indicate that the issue of a revised engagement letter is appropriate:

- Revised or additional terms of engagement.
- Indications that management may not understand the nature of the audit.
- A change in senior management.
- A major change in the nature or size of the client's business.
- Any relevant changes in legal or professional requirements.

CHAPTER 5

Internal audit

Contents

Concept and role of internal audit

- Purpose, functions and limitations of internal audit
- Internal audit and risk assessment
- Management of risk
- Comparison of external and internal audit

1 Concept and role of internal audit

1.1 Purpose, function and limitations of internal audit

The exact scope and objectives of an internal audit department vary widely and depend on the size and structure of the entity and the requirements of its management. However, ISA 610 *Considering the work of internal auditing*, which is covered in a later chapter, states that internal auditing activities will usually include one or more or the following:

- **Monitoring of internal control**. The establishment of an adequate internal control system is a responsibility of management and is an important aspect of good corporate governance. Because the internal control system needs to be monitored on a continuous basis, large companies are likely to establish an internal audit function to assist management in this role. Internal audit is therefore usually given specific responsibility by management for reviewing internal controls, monitoring their operation and recommending improvements via a report to the directors.
- **Examination of financial and operating information**. This may include review of the means used to identify, measure, classify and report such information or specific inquiry into individual items including detailed testing of transactions, balances and procedures. As you will see from later chapters, work in this area is very similar to that carried out by the external auditor.
- **Review of the economy, efficiency and effectiveness of operations**. This could include a review of non-financial controls.
- **Review of compliance** with laws, regulations and other external requirements and with internal requirements such as management policies and directives.
- **Special investigations** into particular areas such as suspected fraud.

The majority of these activities will be classed as **operational internal audit assignments.** These are audits of specific processes and operations performed by the entity and are covered in Section 2 below. However, internal audit could also be asked to perform **other assignments** such as value for money and best value audits. These are covered in Section 3 below.

Whatever tasks are assigned to internal audit, the same **degree of independence** can never be achieved as that required of the external auditor. In order to achieve as much independence as possible it is therefore important that the internal auditor report to the highest level of management.

It is also a matter for the entity setting up the internal audit function what **qualifications or experience** it requires of the members of its internal audit team. In contrast, the external auditor has to comply with regulations set by government and his professional body covering technical and professional standards and qualifications. (Although an internal auditor who is a member of a professional body (such as the ACCA) will need to comply with the requirements of that body.)

The **limitations of the internal audit function** are considered further in a later chapter in the context of ISA 610.

1.2 Internal audit and risk assessment

Establishing an internal audit function is an important aspect of good corporate governance. This is because one of the key functions of internal audit is to:

- review the effectiveness of the organisation's internal control systems, and
- report to the directors or senior management their findings and recommendations.

Internal control systems are put in place by the directors (executive management) in order to help them manage the company's 'governance' risks. Risk can be thought of as anything which may prevent an organisation from achieving its objectives. It may be convenient in this context to think of risks as the risks of errors or fraud, or the risk that information will be unreliable.

Risk is extremely relevant to the role of the internal auditor. His work may often involve carrying out a risk assessment exercise, designed to identify the main areas of risk to which the organisation is exposed. The internal auditor will report these risks to management, and will perhaps make suggestions about how the risks can be managed.

It is useful to analyse the risks that are considered by internal auditors into three main categories. These are:

- **Operational risk**. These are the risks that the operating activities of an entity may be disrupted, either deliberately or unintentionally and in error. Employees may make mistakes, and do something wrong or forget to do something. Machines may break down. There may be poor security arrangements, poor supervision, weak management or an ineffective organisation structure. Operational risk refers to anything that might go wrong with operational activities.
- **Financial risk**. These are the risks of what might happen if there are changes in the financial environment, such as interest rates, taxation law or exchange rates. Financial risk also includes credit risk, which is the risk of non-payment or late payment by customers.

- **Compliance risk**. These are risks that the entity may fail to comply with relevant rules and regulations, resulting in penalties being imposed by regulatory authorities or fines being paid to injured parties. Examples of compliance risk vary according to the nature of a company's activities: they may include the risks of non-compliance with health and safety law, anti-pollution law, employment law, and so on.

1.3 Management of risk

In many cases, it is not possible for management to eliminate risk entirely. Instead, measures are taken to 'manage' risk, and:

- limit the probability that an adverse event will occur, or reduce the frequency of adverse events, and
- limit the impact of an adverse event when or if it does occur.

Approaches to risk management that an internal auditor may recommend to management include the following:

- **Acceptance**. Risk acceptance means accepting the risk and doing nothing to reduce the possibility that an adverse event will happen and doing nothing to limit the consequences if an adverse event does occur. This approach is normally only acceptable if the risk is insignificant.
- **Reduction**. Risk reduction involves taking measures to reduce the probability that an adverse event will happen, or reducing the consequences of an adverse event. Measures to reduce risk may involve instituting appropriate **controls** to minimise the risks to which the entity is exposed. Most **internal controls** are designed as **risk reduction measures**.
- **Avoidance**. Risk avoidance means avoiding transactions or situations that would create an exposure to a risk. For companies, it is normally impossible to avoid risks entirely without withdrawing from a business operation entirely.
- **Transfer**. Risk transfer means transferring the risk to a third party, often in return for a payment. The most commonly-used example of risk transfer is probably the use of insurance. With insurance, risks are transferred to an insurance company in exchange for the payment of a premium.

1.4 Comparison of external and internal audit

Internal and external auditors often carry out their work using similar procedures. This is something to bear in mind when answering 'practical' questions on auditing in an examination.

However, there are a number of fundamental differences between the two audit roles. These are summarised in the following table:

	External audit	Internal audit
Role and work	To express an opinion on the truth and fairness of the annual financial statements. The external auditor will therefore carry out whatever work he deems necessary to reach that opinoin.	To examine systems and controls and assess risks in order to make recommendations to management for improvement. The internal auditor's work programme will therefore to a large extent be dictated by management.
Qualification to act	Set out by statute. This ensures that the external autitor is independent of the entity and suitably qualified.	No statutory requirements – management select a suitably competent person to act as internal auditor. It is therefore possible that the internal auditor may not be as competent as the external auditor, depending on management's recruitment criteria.
Appointed by	The shareholders. This ensures independence.	Management. In order to give as much independence as possible the internal auditor should therefore report to the highest level of management.
Duties set out by	Statute. (See above under role and work.)	Management (See above under role and work.)
Report to	The shareholders. (See above, under appointed by.)	Management. (See above under appointed by.)

You should also bear in mind that the external auditor has no specific responsibility for fraud and error, other than to report whether or not the financial statements give a true and fair view; the external auditor will be concerned that there has been no **material** undetected fraud or error during the period. This is covered in a later chapter.

The internal auditor may be given specific responsibility for investigating suspected fraud or error by management, and he is likely to have much lower materiality thresholds.

Operational internal audit assignments

- Definition of an operational internal audit assignment
- General approach
- Specific processes
- Procurement operations
- Marketing operations
- Treasury operations
- Human resources management

2 Operational internal audit assignments

2.1 Definition of an operational internal audit assignment

Operational internal audit assignments involve the internal auditor being asked by management to look at a particular aspect of the entity's operations, such as marketing activities or the human resources department.

Operational internal audit assignments are therefore defined as audits of specific processes and operations performed by an organisation. They are also known as **management audits**, or **efficiency audits**.

The purpose of an operational internal audit assignment is to assess management's performance in the specific area of operations that is subject to the audit, and to ensure that company policy and control procedures are adhered to.

The audit will identify areas for improvement in efficiency and performance, and improvements in management.

2.2 General approach

The general approach to an operational internal audit assignment will be determined by the purpose of the audit. For each area of operations that is subject to an operational internal audit assignment, the internal auditor should assess:

- the **adequacy** of the policies, procedures and controls adopted, and
- the **effectiveness** of the policies, procedures and controls.

Adequacy of policies and procedures

The internal auditor should assess whether the policies and procedures are adequate for their purpose. The key question that needs to be answered is:

Will the policies achieve the relevant objectives?

The policies, procedures and controls should therefore be reviewed by the internal auditor in the context of the objectives which they are designed to achieve.

Effectiveness of policies and procedures

If policies and procedures seem to be adequate, the internal auditor should then ask whether they are being applied properly. The key question that needs to be answered is:

Are the processes operating effectively?

This will involve the internal auditor testing the processes, using techniques similar to those used in tests of control (covered in a later chapter).

2.3 Specific processes

For your examination, knowledge is required of four specific processes:

- **Procurement**: operations concerned with purchasing.
- **Marketing**: operations associated with obtaining information about customer needs and trying to increase sales demand.
- **Treasury**: Treasury operations are concerned with management of the entity's short-term and long-term financing. A Treasury department may be responsible for managing the long-term and short-term borrowing of the entity, the investment of short-term surplus cash, the management of the entity's cash, and managing financial risks such as exchange rate risks and interest rate risks.
- **Human resources management**: operations concerned with managing people – the employees of the entity.

For any area of operations subject to an operational internal audit assignment, the internal auditor needs to consider:

- the risks
- the control procedures for managing and limiting the risk, and whether these are adequate
- how the control procedures can be tested, to make sure that they are working effectively.

Each of the four areas of operations is considered in turn below.

2.4 Procurement operations

In many organisations, procurement is the specific responsibility of a buying department or purchasing department. Organising this activity in a centralised department should help to ensure that spending is managed and controlled.

The main risks with procurement are as follows:

- The entity may buy items that it does not really need or cannot afford.
- It may pay prices that are higher than necessary. Items might be available at a lower price.
- Some payments to suppliers may be fraudulent; for example, some suppliers may receive payments for items they have not supplied.
- The entity might pay suppliers the wrong amount.

- The entity may take too long to pay (longer than the time agreed in the terms of credit with the supplier). This could have an adverse effect on the business reputation of the entity.

Various controls can be applied to manage these risks:

- The entity might establish an authorised list of suppliers, and (as a matter of policy) goods and services can be purchased only from suppliers on the list. (There may be exceptions to the policy guidelines. For example, a company policy may be that a supplier must be on the authorised list if more than one purchase order is ever placed with the supplier, but for one-off purchases, a supplier does not need to be on the list.)
- There should be procedures for the requisition of goods and services, and procedures for the authorisation and approval of purchase orders. For example, requisitions to purchase store items may be generated by the store department's stock control system, and the authorisation for the purchase and the placing of the purchase order should be made by individuals at a suitable level of seniority, depending on the size and value of the order.
- There should be established policies and procedures in the buying department for negotiating favourable prices with suppliers.
- For very large purchase contracts, it may be a policy requirement that a system of tendering should be used, and more than one supplier should be asked to tender for the contract.
- Supplier performance should be monitored. Have they delivered goods on time and to the specified quality?
- The payments system should be subject to suitable controls. (These are largely financial controls and so should be subject to the annual external audit.)
- There should be a control reporting system that reports to management on supplier performance and any breach of purchasing policy guidelines and procedures.

To test the effectiveness of these policies, procedures and controls, the internal auditor should carry out a number of checks:

- He may carry out a check on a sample of purchase orders, tracing the order from the original purchase requisition, through authorisation and placing the order, to delivery, invoicing and payment. Were the correct procedures followed? Was the purchase authorised properly? Was the order placed with a supplier on the approved list? Was the pricing correct? Were the items delivered on time? Was the invoice correct? Was it paid within the allowed credit period?
- The internal auditor should also review the controls applied by management. If reports are provided to management about purchases that did not follow the approved procedures, what action did management take?

2.5 Marketing operations

Marketing can be a difficult area of operations for an operational internal audit assignment. This is partly because it is difficult to establish the effectiveness of some activities, such as advertising and branding; and some marketing activities may have a long-term impact but may not be effective in the short-term (such as using marketing to build a corporate image).

Marketing activities differ widely between different types of business. Some entities rely heavily on direct selling by sales representatives. Others rely more heavily on advertising. All entities should be trying to find out as much information as they can about what customers (and potential customers) are buying, and what they would like to buy.

However, marketing is much more than just selling and advertising and obtaining market research information. It is useful to think of marketing activities in terms of the 'four Ps':

- **Product**. The product itself (or service) is an aspect of marketing. Does it meet the needs of customers as effectively as it could? Product design and product quality have an important influence on the buying decisions of customers for many items. The 'product' also includes related services such as after-sales service (repairs and maintenance).
- **Place**. The delivery of the product to customers is an element of marketing. How does the product get to the customer? Where does the customer have to go to buy it? For example, consumer items may be sold by shops, supermarkets and general stores, or by specialised retail outlets. Many items can be purchased on the internet.
- **Price**. The price of the product is a key element of marketing, because customers will often make their buying decisions on the basis of price. Discounts and special price offers, for example, are a common feature of marketing consumer products in retail stores.
- **Promotion**. These are the activities that are probably most associated with marketing, such as market research activities, advertising, sales promotion, and direct selling.

The main risks in marketing operations are as follows:

- Market research is inadequate, and the entity fails to obtain enough information about what its customers want and what its competitors are doing.
- Marketing activities are ineffective because the four Ps of marketing are not planned in a co-ordinated way.
- Too much marketing spending achieves too few positive results.
- Marketing initiatives are not properly co-ordinated with other operations of the entity. For example, there is a risk that marketing campaigns to sell a particular product may fail because there is insufficient production capacity and stock to meet the anticipated increase in demand.
- In some cases, there may be the risk of adverse publicity, which could affect the reputation of the company and customer demand for its products.

Controls applied to the marketing operations are largely management controls, and there is a need to plan and co-ordinate marketing activities and to monitor and review their effectiveness. The key controls may therefore be as follows:

- There should be a marketing strategy, fully documented and approved at senior management level.

- There should be a system for preparing detailed and co-ordinated marketing plans, and for reviewing and updating plans.
- There should be systems in place for gathering market research information, and learning about customers' opinions.
- Planning should include procedures for assessing the cost-effectiveness of marketing activities.
- There should be procedures for inter-departmental co-ordination. For example, there should be procedures for co-ordinating marketing activities with the activities of other departments, such as production and warehousing.
- There should be a reporting system for monitoring the performance of marketing operations (including a system for reporting marketing spending and comparing this with budgeted spending levels) and for taking control action where performance is unsatisfactory.
- Marketing staff should be trained sufficiently to carry out their tasks efficiently and effectively.

Tests of these controls over marketing operations will consist mainly of reviewing the management systems:

- Is there a documented marketing strategy? How often is it reviewed? Does the strategy appear reasonable?
- Is there a system for preparing marketing plans over the short-term and the longer-term? Is planning well co-ordinated between different marketing activities, and between the marketing department and other departments?
- Do the systems for obtaining market research information provide the quality and amount of information required?
- Do the procedures for monitoring and controlling marketing performance appear to operate effectively?
- Are the programmes for training marketing staff adequate?

2.6 Treasury operations

Operational internal audits of Treasury operations can be difficult for internal auditors because of the specialised nature of some Treasury activities, such as trading in the financial markets, including trading in financial derivatives instruments.

The main risks in Treasury operations, for a large Treasury department, may be as follows:

- There is a risk that the Treasury department will raise finance for the entity in an inefficient or inappropriate way. For example, interest rates on borrowing may be higher than necessary. There may be too much short-term borrowing and not enough longer-term borrowing (or not enough short-term borrowing and too much long-term borrowing). The balance between equity finance and debt may be inappropriate, resulting in a high cost of capital for the entity.
- The Treasury department may fail to manage the financial risks of the entity sufficiently. For example, it might make insufficient use of forward contracts (for

foreign exchange) and may fail to manage interest rate risk using derivatives such as swaps.

- The Treasury department may employ 'dealers' for foreign exchange or investing surplus funds. Dealers may exceed their trading limits. They may make mistakes when dealing, such as buying when they ought to sell, or making a mistake when agreeing the price or the quantity for a transaction. Dealers may also fail to record/document their transactions properly.
- The Treasury department may earn only a low return on their investment of surplus funds.

Controls over Treasury activities may therefore include the following:

- There should be a Treasury policy, set at the highest management level, about the capital structure of the entity. Treasury activities should be carried out within the overall financing policy guidelines.
- There should be regular reports from the Treasury department to a senior financial manager (such as the finance director) on the activities of the department, including the costs of its borrowing and the returns on investment of surplus cash.
- There should be Treasury policy guidelines on the use of financial instruments (such as forward contracts and financial derivatives) for hedging exposures to financial risks.
- There should be controls over dealers, such as dealing limits. The activities of dealers should be closely supervised and monitored. Regular audits of dealers' transactions may be an appropriate form of control. There should be a segregation of duties between dealing (buying and selling in the financial markets) and settlement (payments and receipts of money in relation to deals).

An operational internal audit should check the effectiveness of these controls:

- The internal auditor may look at the performance of the Treasury department, and analyse the effectiveness of its borrowing (the cost of borrowing) and its investment activities.
- The internal auditor should also look at the finance raised by the Treasury department for the entity, and check that it is consistent with the entity's policy guidelines.
- The use of financial instruments to hedge exposures to financial risk should also be checked. The internal auditor should assess whether the Treasury department has obtained sufficient protection against financial risks, or whether the entity has been over-exposed to the risks.
- The controls over dealing should be checked through normal auditing techniques of observing and:
  - checking samples of transactions (the size and nature of the transactions, the price for the transaction, documentation and settlement), and
  - making checks on dealers' trading positions and whether these have been properly supervised and have remained within limits

2.7 Human resources management

There are several aspects to the management of human resources. These include:

- Recruitment and selection
- Pay and terms and conditions of employment
- Training and development
- Disciplinary and grievance procedures
- The management of redundancy arrangements and other leaving arrangements
- Maintaining employee records.

The main risks associated with human resources are as follows:

- Not having enough employees to achieve the objectives of the entity.
- Failing to recruit employees with the required skills
- Failing to train employees to the required standards and failing to develop individuals for advancement to more senior positions within the organisation
- Failing to comply with employment legislation
- Paying more for employees, in terms of salaries and other benefits, than the entity can or should afford
- Failure to monitor the performance of employees, and failing to get efficient and effective performance from employees.

For each of these aspects of human relations management, there should be systems and controls:

- There should be a human resources strategy, linked to the overall strategy of the entity. There should also be a detailed human resources plan, setting out the required numbers and skills of employees, and policies for making sure that these staffing levels are achieved.
- Within the overall human relations plan, there should be plans for recruitment and for training and development.
- There should be formal procedures for dealing with disciplinary matters and for dealing with grievances from employees. These must conform to the requirements of UK laws and regulations.
- Similarly, there must be established procedures for dealing with redundancies, that must comply with relevant legislation.
- There should be a system for the regular monitoring of employee performance, and for maintaining records of performance reviews.
- Labour costs should be monitored at appropriate levels of management (by the board of directors, and also by managers at departmental level).

An operational internal audit into human relations activities will seek to establish whether these controls are efficient and effective, and so whether they achieve their objectives.

- The internal auditor may carry out some analytical procedures (covered in a later chapter), to assess:
  - the level of spending on employment costs (for example, have there been any significant changes in the ratio of employment costs to total expenditure?), or
  - the level of labour turnover, and whether the entity is failing to retain sufficient staff with the skills and experience that the entity needs
  - where analytical procedures indicate something unusual, such as steeply-rising labour costs or a high rate of labour turnover, the auditor should investigate the reasons.
- The internal auditor should also review the various human resources plans (the overall plan, and plans for recruitment and for training and development).
- Some tests can be carried out into the effectiveness of implementing plans.
  - For example, the internal auditor can look at a sample of recruitment activities, to find out whether the attempt to recruit a new employee was successful, how long it took and how much it cost, and whether the entity was able to recruit its first-choice applicant.
  - Similarly, the internal auditor could look at a sample of training programmes, and assess their purpose and whether each programme achieved this purpose, in terms of the numbers trained, the cost of the training and the resulting improvement in skills.
- The internal auditor can also look at a sample of cases involving disciplinary procedures, grievance procedures or redundancies, to make sure that the correct procedures were followed.
- The internal auditor could also check a sample of employee records, to make sure that these are being properly maintained and are up-to-date.

Nature and purpose of other internal audit assignments

3 Nature and purpose of other internal audit assignments

3.1 Introduction

The internal auditors work on behalf of management and report to management. The type of work they do will therefore be dictated by what management wants them to do. However, it is possible to list the other work that might be done by internal auditors under the following broad headings:

- Value for money audits
- Best value audits
- Financial audits
- Information technology (IT) audits.

3.2 Value for money audits

The value for money (VFM) audit originated in public sector organisations as a way of assessing financial performance. In public sector organisations, conventional profit-based measures are not appropriate because the objectives of these organisations are not usually to make a profit. The concept of value for money and the VFM audit has now been widely adopted by commercial organisations as a means of assessing performance on a broader basis than just profit.

Value for money, as the term suggests, means getting good value from the money that an entity spends. Value for money is obtained from a combination of the '3Es':

- economy
- efficiency
- effectiveness.

Economy means not spending more than is necessary to obtain the required resources. At a very basic level, it means buying supplies from the cheapest suppliers of materials of the desired quality, avoiding excessive salary payments to employees and avoiding unnecessary spending on other items of cost.

Efficiency means getting a high volume of output from the resources that are used. The efficiency of employees is often referred to as 'productivity'. Efficiency can be achieved by making better use of equipment and machines (reducing non-use time), improving employee productivity, making better use of available accommodation or getting better use out of marketing spending, and so on.

Effectiveness means achieving the objectives of the entity with the resources that it uses. Using resources efficiently has no value if the resources are not used in a way that achieves objectives. For example, a manufacturing company may improve efficiency and produce a larger quantity of output with its available machines. However, if the extra output cannot be sold, the organisation will not achieve its objective of increasing profit.

The 3Es are summarised in the table below:

	Meaning	**Measurement**
Economy	'Doing it cheaply'	Compare money spent with inputs acquired
Efficiency	'Doing it well'	Compare inputs used with output achieved
Effectiveness	'Doing the right thing'	Compare output achieved with objectives

Measuring the 3Es is important for the purpose of a VFM audit. The internal auditor should measure each of the three Es in order to assess whether sufficient value for money is being achieved, or whether improvements can be made.

The right hand column of the table shows that there are four variables involved in the measurement of value for money:

- the money spent
- inputs acquired with the money spent, and inputs used
- output produced with the inputs used
- objectives achieved.

Overall, VFM therefore provides a link between **money spent** and **objectives achieved**.

Good overall performance is dependent on a high level of achievement on all of the 3Es. For example, it is no good saving money by purchasing low grade materials (good economy) if those materials break and are wasted in the production process (poor efficiency).

VFM audits focus on the organisation's performance in a given area by looking at each of the 3Es with the objective of identifying areas where VFM might be improved. The internal auditor can then make suitable recommendations to management.

Example

Consider a VFM audit approach to employee and payroll costs. Questions which the auditor could consider in this area might include the following:

- Does the organisation recruit staff with a sufficient, but not excessive level of competence for the tasks which they will be performing?
- Do staff go through appropriate training and development programmes?
- Are staff rewarded and motivated in an appropriate way?
- Are staff effectively supervised and managed in their day-to-day work?

The VFM audit will consider these issues in terms of achieving value for money:

- Are employment costs unnecessarily high?
- Are employees sufficiently productive in the work that they do?
- Does the work done by employees enable the entity to achieve the purposes for which they are employed?

3.3 Problems with VFM audits

The VFM concept and VFM audits have proved to be a useful tool in assessing organisational performance, but there are problems involved in applying the principles in practice. These include the following:

Measurement difficulties

It is not always possible to measure efficiency or effectiveness. Whereas it is relatively easy to measure the output of a manufacturing activity, it is not so easy to measure the output of a service department in an organisation, such as the human resources department, the training department or even the internal audit department itself.

Some functions in an organisation may not have quantified objectives. Again, this is typically a problem with service departments. Without clear objectives, it is not possible to measure effectiveness.

Possible over-emphasis on cost savings

VFM audits often focus on ways of reducing costs. It is often possible to reduce costs by finding ways to improve economy and possibly efficiency. However, this is likely to lead to a quality problem. Effectiveness may be overlooked. By cutting costs, the quality of output may fall, and customers may stop buying the products that the entity makes.

Calculating VFM measures

VFM auditors may assess economy, efficiency and effectiveness by making comparisons with other organisations, or with other departments in the same organisation. In order to have meaning, all performance measures should be calculated on a comparable basis. Whereas the calculation of profit is tightly regulated by accounting standards, there are no regulations about the measurement of the 3Es. This can make it difficult to undertake meaningful performance comparisons between organisations and possibly between units in the same organisation.

3.4 Best value audits

'Best value' is a relatively new concept, introduced into local government authorities by the UK government. There is some evidence that the concept of best value is now used by some private sector organisations as a means of measuring performance.

The fundamental concept of best value is 'continuous improvement'. Organisations can attempt to achieve continuous improvement by focusing on the '4Cs', as set out below:

- **Challenge** – Ask how a service is provided and, more importantly, why it is provided. If there is no satisfactory answer to these questions, consider withdrawing the service. In other words, challenge the need to provide any service and challenge the way in which it is provided.
- **Compare** – Make comparisons with other (similar) organisations. Use comparisons to look for ways of improving.
- **Consult** – Discuss the services provided with the users of those services. Meet with your customers. Make sure that the services provided meet the needs of their users.
- **Compete** – Use fair competition as a means of improving performance. For example, when two companies would like to provide a service, use fair competition between the two companies to obtain best value. The two companies may be asked to tender for the work, and the contract should be awarded to the company offering the best value (which may be the lower price).

The internal auditor's role in best value auditing is to establish:

- whether the organisation has best value procedures in place, and
- whether those procedures are achieving their objective of promoting continuous improvement.

3.5 Financial audits

Performing financial audits is the traditional role of the internal auditor. Internal auditors may be asked by management to review accounting records and other records to substantiate figures appearing in financial statements and management accounts.

This work overlaps with the work of the external auditor. Consequently this aspect of internal audit work is now seen as a relatively minor part of the total work of an internal audit department.

However, it is important to remember that by performing financial audits, the internal auditor is able to look at the internal controls that are in place to minimise risks, to identify weaknesses and to recommend improvements in the internal control system.

3.6 Information technology (IT) audits

IT audits are a specific application of one of the key roles of the internal audit function, which is to assess internal controls. In the case of IT audits, the controls involved are those that operate within the organisation's computer systems.

IT systems are a key aspect of the modern business environment, and assessing and monitoring computer controls is often a key role for the internal auditor. Organisations may employ one or more computer specialists in their internal audit department to perform this role.

The general audit approach to computer-based systems is covered in a later chapter.

Internal audit reports

- Status of internal audit reports
- Structure of the internal audit report

4 Internal audit reports

4.1 Status of internal audit reports

Internal auditors are normally employees of the entity, who therefore work on behalf of management. When they prepare an audit report, they report their findings to management.

Reports by auditors to management are sometimes called 'private reports'. There are no legal requirements or other formal requirements regulating internal audit reports. A report from the internal auditors may therefore take any appropriate form. Internal audit reports should be prepared in the same way as any other internal business report.

4.2 Structure of the internal audit report

A possible structure for an internal audit report is the same as for any other business report, and may therefore be as follows:

- Introductory items
  - Title of the report
  - The person or group of people to whom the report is addressed
  - The person or department that has prepared the report (the internal auditor)
  - Date of the report
  - Possibly its status (for example, 'Confidential')
- Executive summary. The executive summary of a report sets out the purpose of the report, the main points in the report, and the conclusions and recommendations.

  For example, an internal audit report should set out the purpose of the report. This will involve an explanation of the purpose of the audit. It should then go on to describe how the audit was conducted, in order to achieve its objective. The main findings of the audit should be explained, together with any conclusions the auditor reached and recommendations about what should be done as a result of those conclusions.

  The purpose of an executive summary is that any person reading the report should be able to understand the main content of the report by reading the summary. This means that a 'busy executive' can save time and does not have to read the entire detail of the report in full.

  Another reason for having an executive summary is that a person intending to read the report in full can get an idea about what the main part of the report will contain. This can make it easier to understand the detail of the report, because the executive summary puts the detail of the report into a structured context.

- Main text of the report. The main text of the report follows the executive summary. This goes into more detail than the executive summary, and so is longer. However, it should be structured in the same way as the executive summary, presenting findings and conclusions in the same order.

  The main part of the report should avoid excessive detail. Supplementary details should be provided in appendices.

- Appendices. Appendices provide additional detailed information and analysis that the reader of the report can refer to if he or she wishes. Appendices may include valuable detailed information, but should not contain vital information that is not also included in the main body of the report and the executive summary.

Regulation and ethics of internal audit

- Regulation of internal audit
- Ethics of internal audit

5 Regulation and ethics of internal audit

5.1 Regulation of internal audit

There are no specific legal requirements regulating the internal audit process. Rather than being controlled by statute, internal audit is controlled by management in the same way that other functional departments in the organisation are controlled by management.

ISAs do not have mandatory authority for internal auditors. However, they can be seen as indicative of good audit practice, and are therefore frequently adopted by internal audit departments.

Internal auditors are not required to be a member of a regulatory body such as the ACCA. However, in recruiting internal auditors, management will often look for qualified accountants (or will expect recruits to the internal audit department to become student members of an accountancy body and obtain a professional qualification).

The Institute of Internal Auditors (IIA) is a global body to which internal auditors may belong. However, membership is not mandatory.

5.2 Ethics of internal audit

All members of the ACCA are bound by its ethical guidelines. Therefore, matters such as objectivity and confidentiality are just as important to an ACCA member working as an internal auditor as they are to a member acting as an external auditor.

Clearly, there is a potential problem with objectivity and independence in the case of an internal auditor, because he is (usually) an employee of the company.

In order to operate effectively, internal auditors need a degree of independence within the structure of the organisation. This may be achieved in any of the following ways:

- The internal audit department should be responsible to and accountable to members of senior management who have no financial responsibilities. For example, the internal audit function might report directly to the audit committee. Alternatively, the internal audit department may report to a senior executive manager such as the finance director, but in addition should be required to report periodically to the audit committee.
- Internal auditors should not be involved in carrying out non-audit tasks. Their independence can be protected to some extent by making them audit specialists.

- Internal auditors should have unrestricted access to the information necessary to their audit work.
- The internal audit department should have the support of management at all levels.

The IIA has issued ethical guidance for its members that are broadly similar to the guidance issued by the ACCA.

Outsourcing internal audit

- The nature of outsourcing
- Benefits of outsourcing
- Possible problems of outsourcing

6 Outsourcing internal audit

6.1 The nature of outsourcing

In some circumstances, a company may decide to **outsource** its internal audit function. Outsourcing means giving the work that was previously done by the entity's own employees to an external entity. When internal audit work is outsourced, the work is usually given to the audit firm that does the external audit for the company, or to another firm of accountants.

The main reasons for outsourcing internal audit work are as follows:

- The cost of maintaining a permanent internal audit function may be very high.
- Smaller companies may have a need for an internal audit function, but not on a permanent basis.

6.2 Benefits of outsourcing

There are several advantages of outsourcing internal audit work:

- There is no need for the company to recruit and train its own internal audit staff. An internal audit function can therefore be instantly available.
- The outside supplier is likely to have specialist staff available, such as computer audit experts. Internal auditors with an IT specialisation may be difficult to recruit as full-time employees.
- The cost of the internal audit function is a variable cost rather than a fixed cost. A company therefore only pays for the internal audit time that it uses.

6.3 Possible problems of outsourcing

If internal audit work is outsourced to the company's external auditors, independence problems may arise for the external auditor. These should be assessed and managed in accordance with the ethical rules described in an earlier chapter.

CHAPTER 6

Audit planning and risk assessment

Contents

Planning an audit: ISA 300

- The purpose of an audit plan
- Professional scepticism
- Introduction to ISA 300
- Contents of the overall audit strategy and the audit plan

1 Planning an audit: ISA 300

1.1 The purpose of an audit plan

A plan sets out what needs to be done to achieve an objective. In the case of an external or internal audit, the objective is the production of an audit report containing an opinion on the information subject to audit. An audit plan should be prepared as a means of achieving this objective efficiently and effectively.

Content of an audit plan

Preparing an audit plan is the first stage in the conduct of an audit engagement. The plan sets out answers to three main questions (the '3Ws'):

- **Who** will perform the audit work? (Staffing)
- **When** will the work be done? (Timing)
- **What** work is to be done? (The scope of the audit)

Risk assessment and the audit plan

To prepare a suitable audit plan, the auditor needs to have an in-depth knowledge and understanding of:

- the entity to be audited, and
- the environment in which the entity operates.

The auditor needs this knowledge and understanding in order to assess the risk attached to the audit. **Risk assessment** is a key feature of the audit planning process and the assessment of risk in the audit will affect:

- the amount of audit work performed in general, and
- the areas on which the auditor will focus his attention.

The planning process is essential to **all** audits, both internal and external. It is equally important to other assurance engagements such as a 'review' assignment.

1.2 Professional scepticism

When planning and performing an audit it is important that the auditor adopts an attitude of **professional scepticism**. This does not mean that the auditors should disbelieve everything they are told, but they should view what they are told with a questioning attitude, and consider whether it appears reasonable and whether it conflicts with any other evidence. In other words, they must not simply believe everything management tells them.

The idea of approaching work with an attitude of professional scepticism was included in the principle of **rigour** as set out in the *Auditors' Code* (covered in a previous chapter). It is also a requirement of ISA 200.

1.3 Introduction to ISA 300

ISA 300 *Planning an audit of financial statements* requires the auditor to plan the audit so that the engagement will be performed **in an effective manner.**

Adequate planning **benefits** the audit by:

- helping the auditor to devote appropriate attention to important areas of the audit
- helping the auditor to identify and resolve potential problems
- helping the auditor organise and manage the audit engagement so that it is performed in an effective and efficient manner
- assisting in the selection of staff with appropriate experience and the proper assignment of work to them
- allowing for the direction and supervision of staff and review of their work.

ISA 300 requires the auditor to:

- **plan** the audit work so that the audit will be performed in an effective manner
- establish an **overall strategy** for the audit
- develop an **audit plan** in order to reduce audit risk (see Section 3 below) to an acceptably low level
- **document** the overall audit strategy and the audit plan, including any significant changes made during the audit.

The documented strategy and plan will set out a general approach to the audit, and should include:

- the general 'direction' of the audit and what it is aiming to achieve
- the scope of the audit coverage
- the basis for drawing up the audit programmes. (Audit programmes are sets of instructions to the audit team, specifying the audit procedures that should be performed in each area of the audit.)

The plan should be discussed with the members of the audit team and also with the client.

1.4 Contents of the overall audit strategy and the audit plan

The overall audit strategy

The overall audit strategy sets the **scope, timing and direction of the audit and guides the development of the more detailed audit plan.** The establishment of the overall audit strategy involves the following:

- Determining the characteristics of the engagement that define its **scope** such as:
  - the financial reporting framework used (for example, international financial reporting standards)
  - any industry specific reporting requirements
  - the location of the components of the entity (for example, there might be overseas branches).
- Ascertaining the **reporting objectives** of the engagement, such as reporting deadlines and the nature of communications required.
- Considering **important factors** which will determine the focus of the audit team's efforts, such as:
  - materiality thresholds
  - high risk areas of the audit
  - the audit approach (for example, whether the auditor is planning to rely on the entity's internal controls)
  - any recent developments in relation to the entity, the industry or financial reporting requirements.

The above will then allow the auditor to decide on the **nature, extent and timing of resources** needed to perform the engagement. In particular the auditor should consider:

- where experienced members of staff may be needed (for example, on high risk areas)
- the number of staff to be allocated to specific areas (for example, extra staff may be needed for attendance at the year-end stock count)
- when the resources are needed (for example, are more staff needed at the final audit than at the interim audit*)
- how such resources are to be managed, directed and supervised (for example, the timing of team briefing meetings and manager and partner reviews of work performed by other members of the audit team).

*Most large audits will be split into two phases. Much of the systems assessment work and transaction testing will be carried out on the **interim audit** (taking place perhaps two-thirds of the way through the year) with the balance of the work and testing of balance sheet items taking place at the **final audit** shortly after the year end.

The audit plan

Once the overall audit strategy has been established the auditor can develop the more detailed audit plan.

The audit plan includes the **nature, timing and extent of audit procedures** to be performed by audit team members in order to:

- obtain sufficient appropriate audit evidence, to
- reduce audit risk to an acceptably low level.

Audit risk is considered in detail in the next section. What constitutes "sufficient appropriate audit evidence" is considered in a later chapter.

The plan will set out:

- the procedures to be used in order to assess the risk of misstatement in the entity's accounting records/financial statements, and
- planned further audit procedures for each material audit area.

These procedures will be set out, as discussed above, in a series of **audit programmes.**

Understanding the business and materiality: ISAs 250, 315 and 320

- Understanding the entity and its environment
- Understanding the accounting and internal control systems
- Risk and materiality
- Compliance with laws and regulations: ISA 250

2 Understanding the business and materiality: ISAs 250, 315 and 320

2.1 Understanding the entity and its environment

As has been seen above, in preparing an audit plan, the auditor should consider matters such as:

- the state of the economy
- the industry in which the entity operates
- the nature and competence of its management
- its current financial performance
- reporting requirements and deadlines
- any recent developments.

This is a requirement of ISA 315 *Understanding the entity and its environment and assessing the risks of material misstatement*. ISA 315 states that the auditor should:

- obtain an understanding of the entity and its environment, including its internal controls, that is
- sufficient to identify and assess the **risks of material misstatement**.

The auditor should look for factors that could be significant and to which particular attention should be given by the audit team. For example, the auditor may be aware that there is a recession in the industry in which the client company operates, but that rising commodity prices have forced companies to raise the prices of their products and so pass on the higher costs to customers. In addition, the auditor may also be aware that the client company has a poor track record in collecting trade debtors. This knowledge of the business might make the auditor reach the conclusion that the audit should give particular attention to the measurement of trade debtors, and the estimates for bad and doubtful debts.

The necessary knowledge and understanding of the business and its environment will be obtained by the following procedures and methods:

- observation and inspection
- asking questions (and getting answers from the management of the client company, and others)

- analytical procedures, which involves the study of ratios and trends (information technology may be of use here in calculating changes to balances in the financial statements from previous years and graphing trends).

Each of these procedures or methods will be described in more detail in later chapters that deal with the techniques of gathering audit evidence. However, they are all used at this stage to help the auditor identify areas of risk and to plan his audit approach. In addition, the use of analytical procedures is **required** by ISA 520 *Analytical procedures* at the planning stage of the audit.

With regard to the entity and its environment the auditor should obtain an understanding of the following (requirements in respect of internal controls are considered below):

- Relevant industry, regulatory and other external factors, including the applicable financial reporting framework.
- The nature of the entity, including its operations, ownership and management structures.
- The entity's selection and application of accounting polices, including whether they are appropriate for its business and consistent with the industry and the applicable financial reporting framework.
- The entity's objectives and strategies and those related business risks that may result in risks of material misstatement.
- The measurement and review of the entity's financial performance.

When the auditor draws on knowledge he has gained from audits of the client in previous years, it is important that he should take into account any significant changes in circumstances, or changes in the general environment. He should not routinely follow the same plan as in the previous year, because a significant change in circumstances may mean that the audit plan used in the previous year is no longer appropriate.

Business risks are defined by ISA 315 as risks resulting from "significant conditions, events, circumstances, actions or inactions that could adversely affect the entity's ability to achieve its objectives and execute its strategies, or through the setting of inappropriate objectives and strategies".

2.2 Understanding the accounting and internal control systems

ISA 315 requires the auditor to **obtain an understanding of internal controls relevant to the audit**. Although most of the entity's internal controls will relate to financial reporting, not all will be relevant to the audit.

The auditor should try to reach a judgement about how strong (or weak) the internal controls are, in order to make a decision about the amount of testing that should be carried out in the audit. He should consider:

- his previous knowledge of the client company
- any recent changes
- any known problems in the internal controls of the client
- the effect of any new auditing or accounting requirements.

The auditor's assessment of the entity's internal control systems is dealt with in more detail in later chapters.

2.3 Risk and materiality

The auditor is required by ISA 315 to identify and assess the **risks of material misstatement** at both the financial statement and assertion levels.

The **financial statement level** refers to risks which are pervasive to the financial statements as a whole and which potentially affect many assertions (see below). An example might be if management have a tendency to override internal controls – this would affect all areas of the accounting systems.

The **assertion level** refers to specific objectives of the financial statements, for example, that all liabilities have been recorded and that recorded assets exist. The use of financial statement assertions is considered in detail in a later chapter.

Risk assessment is an important aspect of planning an audit. Issues to consider are:

- the areas where risk of misstatement (error) appears to exist, and the nature of the risk
- when an error should be considered material, and when it may be ignored
- what aspects of the audit will be the most difficult to plan because of the high risk of misstatement.

The auditor should consider:

- assessments of **inherent** risks and **control** risks, and the identification of significant audit areas
- setting materiality levels
- the possibility of material misstatements, including those arising because of fraud (rather than unintentional error)
- the identification of complex accounting areas, particularly those involving accounting estimates. (Areas of accounting where the estimates used will be more difficult to audit.)

The auditor will then focus his work on balances in the financial statements where he considers there is a **material risk of misstatement**. High risk/material items will be audited in detail, but low risk/immaterial items will receive less attention. Inherent risk, control risk and risk assessment are explained in detail later in this chapter.

This **audit risk approach** was developed in the 1980s. Previous approaches included the following:

- The **substantive approach** whereby every item in the financial statements is tested and vouched to supporting documents. This approach is still sometimes used for small entities where internal controls are weak and there are few transactions. It may be more efficient to just test everything (especially if the auditor is also providing accountancy services, where he will see all of the supporting documents in any case).

- The **systems approach** which was developed to avoid over-auditing. Under this method the underlying accounting systems were tested with less emphasis on the testing of individual transactions and balances. However, this approach could still lead to over-auditing as systems covering low-risk/immaterial areas were also tested.

Most firms now use a mixture of the audit risk approach and a systems-based approach.

Materiality and audit planning

Materiality is a fundamental concept in both auditing and accounting. It reflects the fact that the users of financial statements find the statements useful even if they are not 100% accurate. Financial statements will normally be useful provided they do not contain 'material' errors or misstatements.

An error or omission is material where it affects the decisions taken based on the information presented in the financial statements or elsewhere.

ISA 320 *Audit materiality* states that auditors should consider materiality at two stages of the audit:

- At the planning stage, when the auditor evaluates the nature, timing and extent of the planned audit procedures.
- At the reporting stage, when the auditor evaluates the effects of misstatements that have been discovered by the audit.

At the audit planning stage, risk and materiality are the two key factors which determine the auditor's answer to the 'what audit work is to be done?' question.

At the planning stage, the auditor will set a **materiality level** for use in evaluating errors or omissions that may be discovered during the audit work. An error or omission that is discovered that exceeds the materiality level will be considered significant.

The level of materiality that is chosen will be based on the concept of materiality given above, which relates to the effect of the error on the overall view presented by the financial statements and on the decisions that might be taken by users of the statements.

However, the level of materiality set at the audit planning stage should be constantly reviewed as the audit progresses, whenever significant new information arises.

Materiality levels

Materiality levels are often based on 'quantitative' factors, and expressed as a percentage of turnover, profit or asset values, such as 1% of revenue or 5% of post-tax profit. For example, the materiality level for stock valuation may be set at 5% of post-tax profit. If the auditor finds, as a result of audit tests, that his estimate of stock differs from the client's measurement by an amount that is more than 5% of post-tax profit, the error would be considered material.

However, it is important to bear in mind that 'qualitative' characteristics may also be taken into account. For example, many auditors would take the view that certain figures in financial statements should be absolutely correct and that **any** errors in those figures would be judged to be material. Examples might include a requirement for 100% accuracy in reporting issued share capital and directors' remuneration.

2.4 Compliance with laws and regulations: ISA 250

ISA 250 *Consideration of laws and regulations in an audit of financial statements* requires that the auditor should, when planning and performing an audit, recognise that non-compliance with appropriate laws and regulations may have a material impact on the information under audit.

This can be seen as part of the general requirement that, at the planning stage, the auditor must understand the environment – here, the legal environment – within which the entity operates. This might include such matters as employee rights legislation, health and safety law, consumer protection legislation or the current tough laws now in place in many countries relating to money laundering activities.

If the auditor identifies material areas of non-compliance, the following actions may be appropriate:

- The auditor should confirm his understanding of non-compliance.
- The law may require appropriate authorities to be notified.
- The non-compliance should be discussed with management. If a particular level of management is seen to be involved in the non-compliance, the matter should be discussed with management at a higher level. If executive management as a whole may be involved, non-executive directors should be informed.

Audit risk and sampling: ISAs 330 and 530

- Risk-based approach to auditing
- Responses to assessed risks: ISA 330
- The audit risk model
- The relationship between sampling and the audit risk model
- The nature of sampling
- Sampling risk and statistical sampling
- Sample design
- Evaluation of sample results

3 Risk and sampling: ISAs 330 and 530

3.1 Risk-based approach to auditing

As discussed above, a key feature of modern auditing is the 'risk-based' approach that is taken in most audits. At the planning stage, as required by ISAs 300 and 315, the auditor will identify and assess the main risks associated with the business to be audited and will prepare an overall audit strategy and an audit plan as required by ISA 300 to focus the audit work on the high risk areas.

This area of risk assessment in audit planning is also covered by ISA 330 *The auditor's procedures in response to assessed risks*. ISA 330 requires the auditor to:

- "determine overall responses to assessed risks at the financial statement level", and
- "design and perform further audit procedures to respond to assessed risk at the assertion level".

These "responses" are considered in the next section.

3.2 Responses to assessed risks: ISA 330

At the **financial statement level** these "responses" are overall ones, which may include:

- emphasising to the audit team the need to maintain an attitude of professional scepticism
- assigning more experienced staff or increased supervision of staff
- the use of experts
- changing the nature, timing and extent of audit procedures (for example, performing more substantive procedures at the final rather than at the interim audit, or obtaining more "persuasive" audit evidence).

The assessment of the risks at this level and therefore the auditor's response is very much affected by the auditor's assessment of the **control environment**. An effective control environment will be likely to increase the auditor's confidence in controls in all areas and allow him to carry out more procedures at the interim audit and to carry out less **tests of detail**. Both of these terms are considered in later chapters.

At the **assertion level** these "responses" take the form of further audit procedures, discussed in detail in later chapters. Audit procedures can take the form of **tests of controls** and/or **substantive procedures**. Again, these terms are covered in later chapters.

In summary, the auditor is required to:

- assess the risks involved in the audit
- plan the audit work so that any material misstatements are identified and corrected if necessary.

This should then ensure that a 'true and fair view' is presented by the financial statements.

3.3 The audit risk model

A standard audit risk model is available to help auditors identify and quantify the main elements making up overall audit risk.

Audit risk is the risk (chance) that the auditor reaches an inappropriate (wrong) conclusion on the area under audit. For example, if the audit risk is 5%, this means that the auditor accepts that there will be a 5% risk that the audited item will be misstated in the financial statements, and only a 95% probability that it is materially correct.

The audit risk model can be expressed as follows:

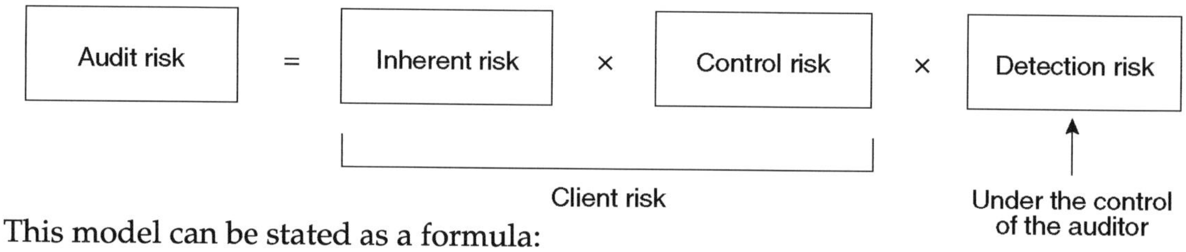

This model can be stated as a formula:

AR = IR × CR × DR

where:
AR = audit risk
IR = inherent risk
CR = control risk, and
DR = detection risk.

Risks are expressed as proportions, so a risk of 10% would be included in the formula as 0.10.

Inherent risk

Inherent risk is the risk that items may be misstated as a result of their inherent characteristics. Inherent risk may result from either:

- the nature of the items themselves. For example, estimated items are inherently risky because their measurement depends on an estimate rather than a precise measure; or
- the nature of the entity and the industry in which it operates. For example, a company in the construction industry operates in a volatile and high-risk environment, and items in its financial statements are more likely to be misstated than items in the financial statements of companies in a more low-risk environment, such as a manufacturer of food and drinks.

When inherent risk is high, this means that there is a high risk of misstatement of an item in the financial statements.

Inherent risk operates independently of controls. It cannot be controlled. The auditor must accept that the risk exists and will not 'go away'.

Control risk

Control risk is the risk that a misstatement would **not** be prevented or detected by the **internal control systems** that the client has in operation.

In preparing an audit plan, the auditor needs to make an assessment of control risk for different areas of the audit. Evidence about control risk can be obtained through 'tests of control'.

The initial assumption should be that control risk is very high, and that existing internal controls are insufficient to prevent the risk of material misstatement. However, tests of control may provide sufficient evidence to justify a reduction in the estimated control risk, for the purpose of audit planning. Tests of control are covered in detail in a later chapter.

Example

Your assurance firm is the auditor of Risky Sounds, a retailer selling hi-tech recording equipment. Risky Sounds was started up just under a year ago by its sole shareholder and director, Sam Smith. Sam has employed a series of book-keepers to help him with the accounting records and financial statements, and the most recent one has just left. In order to start up the business Sam re-mortgaged his house and, in addition, took out a business loan. As a condition of continuing to provide the loan, the bank has asked to be provided with a copy of the annual financial statements.

Required

Identify the risks in the above scenario and explain why they are risks.

Answer

Hi-tech recording equipment. Any hi-tech product is likely to become obsolete very quickly, as more advanced products come on to the market. There is therefore a risk of obsolete stock, which will need to be written down, and ultimately, if the entity cannot keep up with trends, the business may not be able to continue in existence.

Started up just under a year ago. Any start-up business is inherently risky, as many businesses fail in their first year. Also, this must mean that the first set of annual financial statements is due (a problem, given the lack of a bookkeeper). Also, this creates detection risk, as the assurance firm will also be unfamiliar with the business and no prior year figures will be available for comparison.

Sole shareholder and director. This may give Sam personal motivation to misstate the figures. There is also no other (perhaps, more experienced) director to keep Sam in check and ensure that he is making sound business decisions. This could increase the risk of business failure.

A series of book-keepers. This perhaps indicates that Sam is putting undue pressure on his book-keeper (perhaps to misstate the figures) or that the business is so chaotic that the book-keepers have perhaps all despaired of ever being able to put a decent accounting system in place. Either of the factors indicates a high risk of misstatement (intentional or otherwise).

The most recent bookkeeper has just left. Again, this indicates a high risk of misstatement in the financial statements as there is currently no book-keeper to prepare them. Even assuming that one is recruited, he will be unfamiliar with the business and any accounting systems.

Mortgage and bank loan. Both of these give Sam possible personal motivation to misstate the figures to ensure that the business does not go under and his home is safe from repossession.

Detection risk

Detection risk is the risk that the **audit testing procedures will fail to detect a misstatement** in a transaction or in an account balance. For example, if detection risk is 10%, this means that there is a 10% probability that the audit tests will fail to detect a material misstatement.

Detection risk can be lowered by carrying out more tests in the audit. For example, to reduce the detection risk from 10% to 5%, the auditor should carry out more tests.

In preparing an audit plan, the auditor will usually:

- **set** an overall level of audit risk which he judges to be acceptable for the particular audit
- **assess** the levels of inherent risk and control risk, and then
- **adjust** the level of detection risk in order to achieve the overall required level of risk in the audit.

In other words, the detection risk can be managed by the auditor in order to control the overall audit risk. Inherent risk cannot be controlled. Control risk can be reduced by improving the quality of internal controls. However, recommendations to the client about improvements in its internal controls can only affect control risk in the future, not control risk for the financial period that is subject to audit. However, audit risk can be reduced by increasing testing, and reducing detection risk.

e

Example

An auditor has set an overall level of acceptable audit risk in respect of a client of 10%. Inherent risk has been assessed at 50% and control risk at 80%.

Required

Explain:

(a) The meaning of a 10% level of audit risk

(b) What level of detection risk is implied by this information.

(c) If the level of audit risk were only 5%, how would this affect the level of detection risk and how would the audit work be affected by this change?

a

Answer

(a) A 10% level of audit risk means that the auditor will be 90% certain that his opinion on the financial statements is correct (**or** there is a 10% risk that his opinion will be incorrect).

(b) AR = IR × CR × DR

then DR = AR / (IR × CR)

DR = 0.10 / (0.50 × 0.80)

Therefore DR = 0.25 = 25%

(c) If AR is reduced to 5%, DR would now be 12.5%. More audit work will be needed to achieve this lower level of detection risk.

3.4 The relationship between sampling and the audit risk model

Auditors do not normally check 100% of transactions and balances that go into the production of financial statements. For example, they do not count every item of stock, and do not check 100% of customer balances in the trade debtors ledger. Instead, they select a sample of items for testing, and test the sample for accuracy/reliability.

Sampling is the application of audit procedures to less than 100% of items within a population, in order to draw conclusions about the population as a whole.

Detection risk is the risk of failure to detect a material misstatement of an item in the financial statements as a result of insufficient audit testing. It can be analysed into two sub-risks:

- **sampling risk**, and
- **non-sampling risk**.

Sampling risk is the risk that the sample is not representative of the population as a whole. If an auditor uses a sample that is not representative of the entire population, he will reach a conclusion about the accuracy of the client's financial statements that may be unjustified and incorrect. In order to decrease sampling risk, the auditor could select a larger sample. By the laws of probability, sampling risk should be lower when a larger sample is taken.

Non-sampling risk is the risk that auditors fail to detect a material error for reasons other than sampling risk. Because this could only occur due to factors involving errors by the auditors or incompetence of the audit team, or the need to work to very tight deadlines, in practice, the non-sampling risk will usually be set at zero.

In order to control detection risk, the auditor therefore needs to control the sampling risk. This means that detection risk is affected by the size of the sample and the way in which the sample is selected. The way in which the auditor selects his sample and evaluates the results of his testing of that sample is therefore fundamental to the risk-based audit.

3.5 The nature of sampling

Sampling is not always appropriate for auditing. For example, if a population consists of a small number of large items, it may well be appropriate to apply audit tests to the entire population. Also, sampling is only appropriate where the population is **homogeneous** (i.e. where all the items in the population share common characteristics). If this condition is not satisfied, it may be necessary for the auditor to test the entire population.

For example, suppose that a company owns just three very large machines, and each machine serves a different purpose. It would be appropriate to carry out audit tests on all three machines instead of testing just one or two machines as a 'sample' of the entire population of three machines.

As discussed above, sampling in auditing involves applying audit testing procedures to less than the entire population of items subject to audit. So, if a company has issued 1,000 sales invoices in a period and the auditor tests 999 of them, this is a sampling exercise – although the size of the sample would be very large, given the size of the total population!

The auditor is not interested in the results of the sample itself. The sample is used as a basis for reaching a conclusion on the entire population. For example, if an auditor tests 500 sales invoices out of a population of 1,000 invoices, the purpose of the audit test is to make a conclusion about all 1,000 invoices, not just the 500 that are tested.

It is therefore important that the sample chosen should be **representative** of the population, and should reflect the characteristics of the population as a whole. The larger the sample, the more likely it will be to be representative and to reflect the characteristics of the entire population. However, large samples are more time-consuming for the auditor to select and test. For reasons of time and cost, the auditor will want to test as small a sample as possible, consistent with the aim of achieving the required level of detection risk and limiting audit risk to a particular level.

3.6 Sampling risk and statistical sampling

The auditor can never be certain that a sample is fully representative of the population. Even if the auditor tests 999 out of 1,000 invoices and finds no audit problems, it could be that the remaining single invoice contains a material error or omission. This is the problem of **sampling risk**.

The usual technique for obtaining a representative sample is **random selection**. In this context, 'random' means that each item in the sample has an equal chance of selection, so that there is no bias in the sample selection process.

The use of sampling in auditing is covered by ISA 530 *Audit sampling and other means of testing*. ISA 530 distinguishes between statistical sampling and non-statistical sampling:

- **Statistical sampling** is any sampling approach that involves random selection and applies probability theory to the evaluation of the sample results.
- **Non-statistical sampling** (also known as **judgemental sampling**) is any sampling technique not based on probability theory. Instead, it is based on a judgemental opinion by the auditor about the results of the sample.

3.7 Sample design

If an audit sampling exercise is to be effective – if sampling risk is to be reduced and detection risk reduced – the sample must be designed in an appropriate way. Sample design involves the auditor making a number of key decisions:

- the sampling method to be used (statistical or non-statistical)
- the nature of the population from which the sample is to be drawn
- the sample selection method
- the 'tolerable error'
- the 'expected error'
- the sample size required.

Statistical sampling or non-statistical sampling?

Statistical sampling techniques are now widely used in auditing. However, not all audit practices are convinced of their value and worth.

The benefits of statistical sampling techniques are as follows:

- Statistical sampling provides an objective, mathematically precise basis for the sampling process.
- The required sample size can be calculated precisely (using statistical probability techniques).
- There may be circumstances where statistical sampling is the only means of auditing efficiently (for example, in the case of very large 'populations' of items).

The disadvantages of statistical sampling techniques are as follows:

- A degree of training and technical expertise is required if auditors are to use statistical sampling techniques effectively.
- This requires an investment in the necessary training for audit staff.
- Sample sizes may be larger than under a judgemental approach, thus increasing the time (and the cost) involved in the audit.
- Some auditors take the view that it is preferable to rely on the skill, experience and judgement of the auditor, rather than on mathematical/statistical models.

The nature of the population from which the sample is to be drawn

The population from which a sample is to be drawn should be appropriate for the audit objective to be achieved, and the population should be complete. (In other words, all relevant items must be included in the population.)

For example, if the objective of the audit testing is to confirm the accuracy of trade receivable balances, the population should include **all** trade debtors balances as at a specified date. Alternatively, the audit objective might be more limited in scope – perhaps to confirm the accuracy of those trade debtors balances in excess of £500,000. The population should then consist of all debtors balances over £500,000.

Each item in the population (trade debtors in the example above) is referred to as a **sampling unit**. It is important that all sampling units should be homogeneous, (have the same characteristics). In the example of the trade debtors balances above, the auditor would have to ensure that all the individual balances have been processed by the same accounting methods.

If this is not the case, the population may not be sufficiently homogeneous to allow a valid sample to be taken. However, it may be possible to turn a non-homogeneous population into two or more homogeneous populations and then sample from each of these.

For example, suppose that trade debtors balances have been processed through two different accounting systems (perhaps a computerised accounting system and a manual, paper-based system). The entire population of debtors could be divided into two segments (or **strata**) and a sample could be selected for testing from each segment. This technique is known as **stratified sampling**.

The sample selection method

ISA 530 requires auditors to select a sample in such a way that each item in the population (each 'sampling unit') has an equal chance of being selected.

A wide range of sample selection methods is available to the auditor:

- **Random sampling**: All items in the population have an equal chance of selection. This is typically achieved by the use of random numbers to select items for testing.
- **Systematic sampling**: With systematic sampling, a random starting point is chosen from the population and then items are selected with a standard gap

between them (for example, every 10th item). For example, suppose that a sample will be 10% of the items in a population and the items in the population can be arranged in a sequence, such as listed in invoice number order, or account number order or date order. A systematic sample would be to select one of the first 10 items in the list at random, and then to select every 10th item in the list for testing in order to obtain the 10% sample.

- **Haphazard sampling**: The auditor selects the sample on an arbitrary basis, for example, choosing any 100 invoices from a file. This is not a scientifically valid method and the resulting sample may contain a degree of bias. It is therefore not recommended for use with statistical sampling techniques.

Tolerable error

In taking a sample, the auditor must accept that there will be some sampling error, and that the estimates of the population that are made from the sample results may not be fully accurate. Tolerable error refers to the maximum error that the auditor is willing to accept. An error above this level would therefore constitute a 'problem'.

The smaller the tolerable error, the greater the required sample size.

If the auditor is willing to accept only a small error in, say, the amount reported on the balance sheet for trade debtors, he will need to audit a large proportion of the debtors balances in order to be able to reach his audit conclusion. Taking this to its extreme, if the auditor will accept no error at all in the debtors balances, he will need to test **all** the balances in order to reach his conclusion.

Expected error

The auditor will also need to form a judgement on the rate or amount of error that may be **expected** to arise in the population. If a higher error rate is expected, a larger sample size will be required if the auditor is to reach a valid conclusion on the population.

The rate of expected error may be based on such factors as:

- experience of the population from previous audits
- experiences from the current audit on areas relating to the population. For example, if the auditor has discovered inaccuracies in the client's sales invoicing procedures, the expected error rate relating to trade debtors will also be high.

3.8 Evaluation of sample results

When evaluating the results of a sample the auditor should consider:

- the nature of the error, and
- the projection of the sample results to make conclusions about the entire population.

The nature of the error

For each error discovered in the sample, the auditor must establish whether it is a 'true' error in the context of the objectives of the audit tests being performed.

For example, if the objective is to gain evidence on the accuracy of the balance sheet figure for trade debtors, an error involving the posting of an invoice to a wrong customer account does not affect the balance sheet total and has no impact on the objective of the testing. (The total trade debtors will not be wrong. Only the balances on the individual accounts of two customers will be wrong.)

However, this error may have an impact on other areas of the audit work. It should therefore be considered in this context.

Projection of the results of the sample to the entire population

The auditor wants to reach a conclusion about the population as a whole from the results of the sample. It is therefore necessary to use the sample results to estimate the likely error that exists in the population. This is done by extrapolating the error found in the sample over the whole population.

Example

The results of audit tests on a sample of debtors balances recorded as £2,000,000 indicate that the correct balances should be £1,950,000.

The total of balances for similar items have been recorded as £10,000,000.

Required

Explain:

(a) what the auditors might conclude about the size of the error in the population of trade debtors

(b) the relevance of the tolerable error concept in this situation.

Answer

(a) The error in the sample is £50,000 (£2,000,000 - £1,950,000).

The error rate in the sample is 2.5% (50,000/2,000,000). Extrapolating this over the population as a whole, it will be estimated that total trade debtors contain errors of £250,000 (£10,000,000 × 2.5%) and trade debtors should therefore be stated at £9,750,000 (£10,000,000 – £250,000).

(b) The auditor will compare the total estimated error in the population to his pre-set tolerable error. If the tolerable error in the population was, say, £300,000 then the error is, in effect, not material and could be ignored.

Fraud: ISA 240

- Fraud and the role of the external auditor
- The auditor's responsibilities relating to fraud: ISA 240

4 Fraud: ISA 240

4.1 Fraud and the role of the external auditor

Fraud is an **intentional act** by one or more persons, involving the use of deception, to gain an unjust or illegal advantage.

Fraud is distinguished from **error**. Error results from a genuine mistake or omission, and is **not intentional**.

The objective of a statutory audit (an external audit) is to express an opinion on the truth and fairness of the view presented by the financial statements. Its objective is **not** primarily the prevention or detection of fraud. The auditor will be concerned with fraud only to the extent that it might impact on the view shown by the financial statements. He will therefore be concerned with the risk of **material fraud**. This is discussed below in the context of ISA 240.

It is primarily the responsibility of management to establish systems and controls to prevent or detect fraud (and errors). These systems and controls may then be monitored by internal audit. Internal audit may also be required by management to specifically review the entity's exposure to error or fraud or to undertake a special investigation to look into suspected error or fraud.

4.2 The auditor's responsibilities relating to fraud: ISA 240

The role of the external auditor with regard to fraud is covered by ISA 240 *The auditor's responsibility to consider fraud in an audit of financial statements.*

The objectives of the auditor under ISA 240 are the same as for any other area: to identify and assess the risks of **material misstatement** and to obtain sufficient appropriate evidence about those risks through appropriate audit procedures.

However, it is particularly important in relation to fraud that the auditor maintains an attitude of **professional scepticism** as required by ISA 200 and the Auditors' Code.

Two types of fraud are identified by ISA 240 *Fraudulent financial reporting and misappropriation of assets.*

Fraudulent financial reporting includes:

- forging or altering accounting records or supporting documentation which form the basis of the financial statements

- misrepresenting or intentionally omitting events or transactions from the financial statements
- improperly applying accounting principles, intentionally.

Misappropriation of assets includes:

- embezzling receipts (for example, diverting them to personal bank accounts)
- stealing physical assets (such as stock) or intellectual property (for example, by selling "trade secrets" to a competitor)
- causing an entity to pay for goods and services not received (for example, by the creation of fictitious suppliers)
- using an entity's assets for personal use.

ISA 240 requires the auditor to perform the following procedures to identify the risks of material misstatement due to fraud:

- Make enquiries of management in respect of:
  - their assessment of the risk of material fraud
  - their process in place for identifying and responding to the risks of fraud
  - any specific risks of fraud identified or likely to exist
  - any communications within the entity in respect of fraud (including to employees regarding management's views on business practices and ethical behaviour).
- Make inquiries of management and others within the entity as to whether they have any knowledge of any actual, suspected or alleged frauds and to obtain views about the risks of fraud.
- Evaluate any unusual or unexpected relationships identified in performing analytical procedures (covered in a later chapter) which might indicate a risk of material fraud.
- Evaluate information obtained from other risk assessment procedures to see if any **fraud risk factors** are present.

Fraud risk factors might include the following:

- The need to meet the expectations of third parties (for example, the entity is trying to obtain additional finance).
- Management being remunerated via profit-related bonuses.
- An ineffective control environment (covered in a later chapter).
- The entity's profitability being under threat (for example, due to increased competition or rapid changes in technology).
- The nature of the industry or the entity's operations providing opportunities for fraud (for example, complex transactions or significant accounting estimates).
- Low morale amongst staff or poor communication and/or enforcement of ethical standards by management.
- Personal pressure on staff to misappropriate assets (for example, personal financial problems or the threat of redundancy).

- Opportunity to misappropriate assets (for example, large amounts of cash held or processed or highly portable or valuable stock).
- Poor internal controls over assets (for example, lack of segregation of duties – covered in a later chapter).

Having identified the risks of material misstatement due to fraud the auditor must then, per ISA 330, **design and perform further audit procedures** to address those risks.

If an external auditor discovers fraud, it must be **reported to an appropriate level of management** as soon as practicable. He must also consider whether there is any statutory duty to report to the authorities. This was considered in a previous chapter in the context of exceptions to the auditor's duty of confidentiality.

Internal audit and review planning

- Internal audit planning
- Review planning

5 Internal audit and review planning

5.1 Internal audit planning

Many of the factors to consider in preparing a plan for an internal audit have already been covered in the context of the external audit. These factors, including the benefits of audit planning and the importance of developing a thorough and up-to-date knowledge of the business, also apply to the internal audit planning process.

However, the timescale within which internal auditors operate are often different from the timescale for the external auditors:

- The external audit operates essentially on an annual cycle, linked to the entity's financial reporting date.
- Internal audit work is not linked precisely to the financial reporting date. As a result of this, internal audit departments have more flexibility in the timing of their work and have scope for operating over a longer time frame.

As a result, internal audit work plans may be prepared at three 'levels', each one reflecting a different time scale.

- **Strategic level**: A strategic plan for internal audit may cover a period of up to five years. During this period, the internal auditors will aim to test all the major systems and controls operating on all aspects of the business activities.
- **Periodic level**: At the periodic level, the internal audit plan will normally relate to the financial reporting period (the budget period) and will express key aspects of the strategic plan in terms of particular goals and targets for that period.
- **Operational level**: At an operational level, internal audit plans will set out day-to-day audit objectives and procedures for each particular audit assignment to be performed.

5.2 Review planning

As discussed in a previous chapter, a firm may be appointed to undertake an assurance engagement such as a 'review'. This is similar to an audit, but provides a lower level of assurance. Even so, planning procedures for a review assignment are similar to those for external and internal audits. Of particular importance are:

- the need for the assurance provider to have a clear understanding of the objectives of the review assignment (an engagement letter should be in place to clarify this)
- the need for the assurance provider to have a full and up-to-date knowledge of the business and its environment.

CHAPTER

7

Documentation, sources of evidence and reliance on the work of others

Contents

Audit evidence: ISA 500

- General principles of gathering audit evidence
- Sufficient and appropriate audit evidence
- The quality of audit evidence
- Procedures for generating audit evidence
- The financial statement assertions

1 Audit evidence: ISA 500

1.1 General principles of gathering audit evidence

Before moving on to chapters dealing with the practical processes involved in performing an audit, we need to consider the general principles behind the gathering of audit evidence.

- The **outcome** of an audit is a report, usually expressing an opinion.
- That report and opinion must be **supportable** by the auditor, if challenged.
- Therefore the auditor will collect **evidence** on which to base his report and opinion.
- The auditor carries out procedures known as '**audit tests**' in order to generate this evidence.
- These tests, the evidence and the conclusions drawn must be **documented** in the audit files.

1.2 Sufficient and appropriate audit evidence

ISA 500 *Audit evidence* requires auditors to:

- obtain **sufficient, appropriate** audit evidence
- in order to be able to draw reasonable conclusions
- as a basis for forming an audit opinion.

Sufficient relates to the **quantity** of evidence.

Appropriate relates to the **quality** (reliability) of the evidence.

The auditor will need to exercise professional judgement on both of these aspects, the quantity and the quality of evidence.

- When is there enough evidence to support a conclusion?
- What is the quality of a given piece of evidence, and is this sufficient to justify the audit opinion?

The two characteristics of quantity and quality are also inter-related.

- An auditor may be able to reach a conclusion based on a smaller quantity of high quality evidence,
- But a larger quantity of lower quality evidence may be required to reach the same conclusion.

1.3 The quality of audit evidence

There are a number of general principles to assist the auditor in assessing the quality of audit evidence. These can be summarised as follows.

- **Written evidence is of a higher quality than verbal evidence**. In addition, original documents rather than copies should be used whenever possible.
- **External evidence, arising from outside the entity under audit, is of a higher quality than internal evidence generated by the entity under audit**. ISA 500 requires that the auditor should be satisfied as to the accuracy and reliability of any internal evidence used in reaching a conclusion.
- **Evidence produced by the auditor is of a higher quality than evidence produced by others**.

1.4 Procedures for generating audit evidence

A number of audit testing procedures are available to the auditor as a means of generating audit evidence. Note that:

- more than one procedure may be used in collecting evidence in a particular area.
- not all procedures may be appropriate to a given objective of the audit.

The auditor should select the most appropriate procedures in each situation. There are five main testing procedures for gathering audit evidence:

- Inspection of an item
- Observation of a procedure
- Computation
- Enquiry
- Analytical procedures.

The table below summarises these five main audit testing procedures, and gives examples of how they are used and applied.

Procedure	**Explanation/application**
Inspection (looking at an item)	▪ Of assets ▪ Of entries in accounting records ▪ Of documents (e.g. invoices)
Observation (watching a procedure)	▪ Of physical stock counts ▪ Of distribution of wages

Procedure	Explanation/application
	▪ Of opening of mail
Computation	▪ Recomputing figures prepared by the client (e.g. recalculating depreciation)
Enquiry	▪ Asking questions, receiving answers and validating the answer
Analytical procedures	▪ The use of ratios and trends to assess the reasonableness of figures

Example

An auditor wishes to:

(a) test that the plant and equipment recorded in the financial statements of the client does actually exist

(b) confirm the accuracy of the figures for the directors' bonuses

(c) understand the nature of an unusual payment recorded in the cash book.

Required

State which of the audit testing procedures set out in the table above would be most useful to the auditor in each of the above contexts.

Answer

(a) (Physical) inspection. The best way of getting the evidence of fixed assets is to go and look at them.

(b) (Re)computation. The figures for bonuses computed by the client can be checked by re-calculating what they should be.

(c) Enquiry (of management). The auditor should ask management to explain the nature of the unusual item, and should expect a satisfactory answer.

1.5 The financial statement assertions

Modern auditing theory takes the view that the financial statements prepared by the directors comprise a number of '**assertions**' or representations.

The assertions contained in a set of financial statements are as follows:

- **Completeness**: There are no unrecorded assets, liabilities, transactions or other undisclosed items.
- **Occurrence**: Transactions and events recorded in the financial statements took place during the accounting period and relate to the entity.
- **Measurement**: A transaction or event is recorded at the proper amount.

- **Presentation and disclosure**: An item is disclosed, described and classified according to the appropriate accounting framework (for example, UK Financial Reporting Standards).
- **Carrying value**: Assets and liabilities are properly valued.
- **Rights and obligations**: Assets and liabilities represent rights (assets) and obligations (liabilities) of the entity at the reporting date.
- **Existence**: An asset or liability exists at the reporting date.

The auditor should therefore generate evidence designed to reach a conclusion on the reliability of each of these assertions.

Required

Using your accounting knowledge from Paper F3, apply the above assertions to the audit of sales.

Answer

Completeness: All goods despatched have been invoiced and all such sales invoices have been entered into the accounting records.
Occurrence: All sales invoices reflected in the accounting records relate to goods despatched by the entity during the current year.
Measurement All invoices have been correctly priced and discounts properly applied, and they have been accurately entered in the accounting records.
Presentation and disclosure: Sales have been disclosed as "Revenue" in the income statement for the current year.

Tutorial note: The other assertions relate to assets and liabilities and so are not relevant.

Audit documentation: ISA 230

- Audit working papers (audit file)
- The quality of audit working papers
- The form and content of audit working papers
- The use of computer-based audit working papers
- Ownership, custody and confidentiality

2 Audit documentation: ISA 230

2.1 Audit working papers (audit file)

All audit work must be properly documented in the form of **audit files** (also known as audit working papers). This documentation provides written evidence of the audit work done and of the conclusions reached.

This documentation will provide evidence that the audit was carried out in accordance with International Standards on Auditing.

2.2 The quality of audit working papers

ISA 230 requires high quality audit files. These should be sufficiently complete and detailed to provide an overall understanding of the audit. In particular, the working papers should enable an experienced auditor, with no previous connection with that audit, to understand the work that has been performed and the conclusions that have been reached.

High quality audit working papers have the following benefits:

- They provide a record for the future of work done, problems encountered and conclusions reached in the audit (in case the quality of the audit is subsequently questioned or to assist with next year's planning)..
- They help with the control of the audit, in particular the review process whereby senior members of the audit team (ultimately the engagement partner) review the work done by more junior members.
- They encourage those undertaking the audit work to adopt a systematic and methodical approach to the work, so that the documentation of the work can be done logically and so more easily.

2.3 The form and content of audit working papers

The precise contents of the audit files vary, depending on the nature and size of the client and the complexity of the audit processes required to reach a conclusion.

However, it is normal practice in the case of on-going audits to maintain two types of audit files:

- a permanent file, and
- a current file.

Permanent file

The permanent file records information that is likely to be of significance to **every** annual audit of that client. Examples of such information might include:

- the legal constitution of the company
- other important legal documents such as loan agreements
- a summary of the history, development and ownership of the business
- a summary of accounting systems and procedures
- copies of previous years' financial statements, together with key ratios and trends.

As such information is of continuing significance, it is important that the auditor reviews the contents of the permanent file regularly and updates it as appropriate.

Current file

The current file contains information of relevance to the **current** year's audit. This is the evidence arising from the conclusion arising from the current audit will be primarily based. Examples of the contents of a current audit file include the following:

- The final financial statements and audit report.
- A summary of audit adjustments, including those not included in the final reported figures.
- Audit planning material (the audit plan, materiality threshold calculations, risk assessments).
- Audit control material: (these are items used to control the progress of the audit, such as time budgets, review points, and points for consideration by the audit partner)
- Audit letters (audit letters are explained in a later chapter)
- For each audit area (for example, stock, debtors)
  - an audit programme (detailing the work to be done on that area)
  - details of items selected for testing, the tests performed, problems encountered (together with their resolution) and the conclusion reached on that area
  - 'lead schedules' giving the figures for the audit area, as they appear in the final financial statements, cross-referenced to relevant audit tests.

All audit working papers should clearly show the following (where relevant):

- The name of the client
- The accounting date
- A file reference
- The name of the person preparing the working paper
- The date the paper was prepared
- The name of any person reviewing the work
- The date of the review
- A key to 'audit ticks' or other symbols used in the papers
- A listing of any errors or omissions identified
- A conclusion on the area.

2.4 The use of computer-based audit working papers

One of the features of modern auditing is the use of computer packages (often used in conjunction with laptop computers) to make the preparation of audit working papers more efficient for the auditor. These packages can be used to help prepare:

- analysis schedules, especially where the firm uses standardised working papers
- lead schedules, and
- draft financial statements

These can usually be automatically cross-referenced and updated as the audit proceeds.

Using these packages has several advantages.

- The working papers are neat, easy to read and in a standard format.
- The risk of errors in processing adjustments (updates, amendments, corrections) is reduced.
- The review process can be carried out 'remotely', without it being necessary for the review to take place at the client's premises.
- Significant time saving may result from the automatic processing of adjustments.

2.5 Ownership, custody and confidentiality

Ownership of the audit working papers rests with the auditor. The working papers **do not** form part of the accounting records of the client, and do not belong to the client.

The auditor needs to decide how long to keep the audit files. The ACCA recommends a minimum period of **seven years**.

Auditing standards require the auditor to ensure that working papers are kept safe and their contents are kept **confidential**. Information should only be made available to third parties in accordance with ethical guidelines (described in an earlier chapter).

Reliance on the work of others

- Reliance on the work of others
- Using the work of internal auditors: ISA 610
- Using the work of an expert: ISA 620
- Use by the client of service organisations: ISA 402

3 Reliance on the work of others

3.1 Reliance on the work of others

This section deals primarily with the **external audit** function. However, the general principles set out here are also valid for other assurance work and for the work of the internal audit function.

One of the aspects involved in the planning stage of an audit is the consideration of staffing, and **who** will perform the audit work. This includes a need for the external auditor to consider using, as a possible source of audit evidence:

- work that has been performed by the client's internal auditors or
- 'experts'.

A very important principle to bear in mind here is that, although the auditor is relying on information from another party, the auditor remains fully responsible for the report that he prepares and the opinion that he gives in his report. It is therefore essential for the auditor to assess the quality of the information provided, before relying on it as audit evidence.

To reinforce this principle, the external auditor **should not refer** in his audit report to **reliance on the work of others** as this could be misunderstood as a division of responsibilities.

There are two principal reasons why the external auditor may wish to rely on work done by others:

- Internal auditors may recently have audited areas of relevance to the external audit. Using the work of the internal auditor (if appropriate) may make the external audit more efficient and cost-effective.
- There may be circumstances where the audit firm does not possess the level of technical knowledge needed to understand certain aspects of the client's transactions. This may apply, for example, to clients in high-technology or research and development-based businesses. Expert scientific help might be appropriate here. Another situation where information is often supplied by experts is in the area of revaluation of fixed assets, such as the revaluation of land and buildings.

3.2 Using the work of the internal auditors: ISA 610

ISA 610 *Considering the work of internal audit* requires that, at the planning stage of an external audit, the auditor must consider the work of the client's internal auditors and its effect, if any, on the external audit procedures.

This means that the external auditor will assess the **effectiveness** of the internal audit department and its procedures. A decision can then be taken as to whether the work of the internal auditors can be used as part of the evidence on which the external audit opinion will be based.

The table below summarises the criteria against which the effectiveness of the internal audit function will be assessed. These criteria are also relevant in the context of limitations of the internal audit function as discussed in a previous chapter.

Criterion	Comment
Organisational status	▪ Where does the internal audit function 'fit' into the organisation? ▪ To whom does it report? ▪ Does it have any operational responsibilities which may impair its independence?
Scope of work	▪ What is the extent and nature of the internal auditors' work? ▪ Is their scope unduly influenced or limited by management?
Technical competence	▪ What level of technical ability is demonstrated by internal audit staff? ▪ Do they undergo adequate, regular training?
Due professional care	▪ Is the internal audit work planned, documented and controlled to the same level as the external audit work?

In addition to the **general** assessment of the internal audit, ISA 610 also requires the external auditor to evaluate each **specific** piece of work performed by the internal auditors before it is used as external audit evidence.

The external auditor should review:

- the internal audit work programme
- the scope of the work performed and the conclusion reached
- the relevance of this conclusion to the objective of the external audit.

3.3 Using the work of an expert: ISA 620

The term 'expert' is used here in the sense of a person or an organisation that possesses specific technical skills or knowledge **in fields other than accounting and auditing.**

The auditor may use the work of an expert to provide knowledge relevant to the audit, which the audit firm itself does not possess. ISA 620: **Using the work of an expert** gives a number of examples where experts may be used by an auditor. These include:

- legal opinions
- specialist valuation areas, such as property or pension liabilities
- determination of the quantity or physical condition of assets (for example, complex stocks or work-in-progress).

Assessing the need for an expert

There is a cost attached to the use of an expert by the auditors. The expert will charge a fee for the professional service he provides. The use of an expert should therefore be evaluated on a cost/benefit basis.

The extent to which the external auditor will derive benefits from the use of an expert can be determined from such factors as:

- the materiality of the area in which the expert will be involved
- the level of audit risk attached to that area of the audit
- the amount of other audit evidence available in respect of that area, together with the quality of that evidence.

If the auditor judges that evidence from an expert is necessary, the matter should be discussed with the management of the client company, because it is the client company (either directly or through the audit fee) that will have to pay for the expert's services. In principle, the client company should engage an appropriate expert – if it is unwilling to do so, the expert should be engaged directly by the auditor.

Assessing the work of an expert

ISA 620 requires the auditor to apply the procedures set out below when using the work of an expert. The auditor should:

- assess the competence and independence of the expert
- ensure that the expert's work constitutes sufficient and appropriate audit evidence
- ensure that the scope of the work is appropriate to the objectives of the audit
- review the work of the expert for consistency with other audit evidence. Any inconsistencies should be discussed and resolved by the auditor.

This approach reinforces the point made earlier, that the auditor remains fully responsible for the report produced, even if evidence on which it is based was produced by others. The auditor therefore cannot simply accept work performed by experts. That work must be evaluated in the same way as any other audit evidence is evaluated.

3.4 Use by the client of service organisations: ISA 402

A client company may use service organisations to assist it in various areas of its operations, such as:

- information processing (for example, payroll processing)
- the maintenance of accounting records (for example, keeping the share register for a company with many shareholders)
- the maintenance of the safe custody of assets, such as investments.

The use of service organisations is often referred to as **outsourcing**.

Impact of outsourcing on the external auditor

ISA 402 *Audit considerations relating to entities using service organisations* requires the auditor to:

- consider the impact of the use of such organisations on the entity's system of internal control. (When work that is subject to audit is outsourced by the client, the client company relies on the internal controls of the entity to which the work has been given)
- assess the resultant risk of material mis-statement as a consequence of the control risk in the situation
- design and perform appropriate further audit procedures to obtain suitable audit evidence.

The external service organisation should be regarded by the auditor, for the purpose of the audit, as an extension of the client entity itself.

If the auditor uses the report of an auditor of a service organisation of the client company, he should assess the work of that auditor in a similar way to that in which he would assess the work of an internal auditor. For example he should:

- make enquiries as to the competence of that auditor
- consider the nature and content of his audit report.

CHAPTER

8

Internal control: ISA 315

Contents

The importance of internal control

- The auditor's assessment of internal controls
- The meaning of internal control
- How the auditor uses internal controls
- Summary of the audit approach: tests of controls or substantive tests?

1 The importance of internal control

1.1 The auditor's assessment of internal controls

As seen in previous chapters, the auditor is required by ISA 315 to **make an assessment of risk**. This is made at both the financial statement level and at the assertion level.

The auditor is then required by ISA 330 to **respond to those risks**. The overall responses in relation to the financial statement level risks were discussed in a previous chapter.

The responses at the assertion level involve the auditor selecting appropriate audit procedures. The choice of audit procedures will depend on the auditor's assessment of both:

- inherent risk, and
- control risk.

This chapter looks at this requirement in detail and considers how the auditor's assessment of internal controls will influence his selection of the approach to the audit.

1.2 The meaning of internal control

A formal definition of internal control is as follows:

'The process designed and implemented by those charged with the governance of the organisation and others to provide reasonable assurance about the achievement of objectives with regard to:

- *the reliability of financial reporting*
- *the effectiveness and efficiency of operations*
- *compliance with appropriate laws and regulations.*

Internal controls should be designed and implemented to address identified business risks that threaten the achievement of objectives.'

The following points should be noted from this definition:

- It is the responsibility of management to 'design' and put in place a suitable system of internal controls.
- Internal controls are designed to deal with financial risks, operational risks and compliance risks.
- Since internal controls are established by management, the auditor has to accept what controls there are. However, he can assess and evaluate the controls, and will plan his audit on the basis of his assessment.

1.3 How the auditor uses internal controls

Modern auditing is, wherever possible, based on a 'systems' based approach. With this approach, the auditor **relies** on the accounting systems and the related controls to ensure that transactions are properly recorded.

- His assumption is that if the systems and the internal controls are adequate, the transactions should be processed correctly.
- The audit emphasis is therefore, as much as possible, on the systems processing the transactions rather than on the transactions themselves.

Before the auditor can rely on the systems and controls that are in place, he must establish what those systems and controls are, and carry out an evaluation of the effectiveness of the controls.

In other words, the systems-based audit approach is that accounting systems and their related internal controls are sufficient to record transactions properly. However, the auditor should first test the controls, in order to satisfy himself that this approach to the audit is valid.

The degree of effectiveness of an internal control system will depend on the following two factors:

- The **design of the internal control system** and the individual internal controls. Is the control system able to prevent material misstatements, or is it able to detect and correct material misstatements if they occur?
- The proper **implementation of the controls**. Are the controls operated properly by the client's management and other employees?

The outcome of this evaluation helps the auditor to assess **control risk** – which is one of the key elements in the audit risk model (described in an earlier chapter).

1.4 Summary of the audit approach: tests of controls or substantive tests?

As far as possible, the auditor will **rely** on the internal controls that are in operation. However, all internal control systems have inherent limitations, and controls can never be 'perfect' and 100% certain to be effective. It will therefore never be possible for the auditor to rely on them completely.

This point is made in the Turnbull Report on Internal Control, which comments that:

'A sound system of internal control reduces, but cannot eliminate, the possibility of poor judgement in decision-making; human error; processes being deliberately circumvented by employees and others; management overriding controls; and the occurrence of unforeseeable circumstances.'

The auditor must therefore:

- test the underlying internal control systems themselves, using **tests of controls,**
- and, in addition, perform some tests on the transactions and balances in the financial statements.

These tests on transactions and balances are referred to as **substantive tests**:

- Where the auditor concludes that the system of controls is weak, and that the controls therefore cannot be relied on, he will have to do extensive substantive tests. When an audit relies heavily on substantive tests, the approach to the audit is called a **transactions-based approach**
- If the auditor judges that the internal controls are strong, he will carry out tests on the controls (in order to verify his opinion about them) and should need a smaller amount of substantive testing. When an audit is based mainly on a favourable assessment of the internal controls, the approach to the audit is called a **systems-based approach**.

The diagram below summarises the audit approach, which will be considered in more detail in later sections.

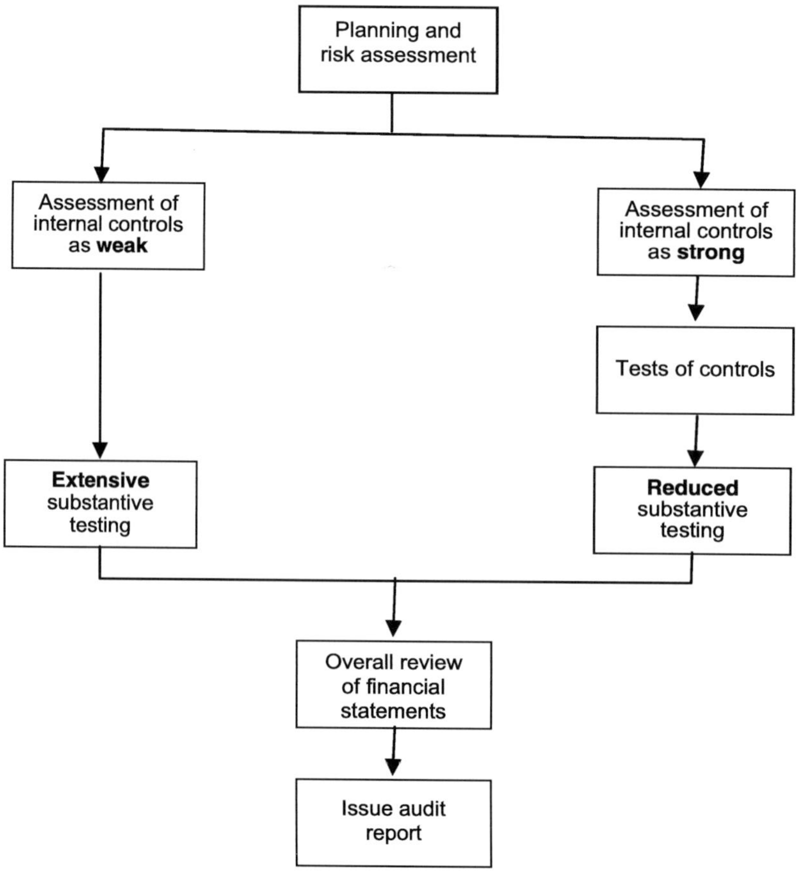

The elements of internal control

- Internal control system and internal controls
- The five elements of internal control
- The control environment
- The entity's risk assessment process
- The information system
- Control activities
- Monitoring of controls
- Understanding the control system: walk-through tests
- Specific IT controls

2 The elements of internal control

2.1 Internal control system and internal controls

A distinction should be made between:

- an internal control system, and
- internal controls.

The Turnbull Report on Internal Control defines an internal control system as follows:

'An internal control system encompasses the policies, processes, tasks, behaviours and other aspects of a company that, taken together:

- *facilitates its effective and efficient operation by enabling it to respond appropriately to significant business, operational, financial, compliance and other risks to achieving the company's objectives. This includes the safeguarding of assets from inappropriate use or from loss and fraud, and ensuring that liabilities are identified and managed;*
- *help ensure the quality of internal and external reporting. This requires the maintenance of proper records and processes that generate a flow of timely, relevant and reliable information from within and outside the organisation;*
- *help ensure compliance with applicable laws and regulations, and also with internal policies with respect to the conduct of business.'*

Internal controls are a part of the internal control system, but the internal control system is more than just the internal controls.

2.2 The five elements of internal control

ISA 315 identifies five elements which together make up the internal control system. These are:

(1) The control environment

(2) The entity's risk assessment process

(3) The information system

(4) Control activities (internal controls)

(5) Monitoring of controls

ISA 315 requires the auditor to:

- gain an understanding of each of these elements as part of his evaluation of the control systems operating within an entity
- document the relevant features of the control systems together with his evaluation of their effectiveness.

Once this understanding has been gained, the auditor should confirm that his understanding is correct by performing **'walk-through' tests** on each major transaction type (for example, sales, purchases, payroll).

Walk-through testing involves the auditor selecting a small sample of transactions and following them through the various stages in their processing in order to establish whether his understanding of the process is correct.

2.3 The control environment

The 'control environment' is often referred to as the general 'attitude' to internal control of management and employees in the organisation.

ISA 315 states that the control environment includes 'the attitudes, awareness and actions of management concerning the entity's internal control and its importance in the entity. The control environment also includes the governance and and management functions and sets the tone of an organisation, influencing the control consciousness of its people. It is the foundation for effective internal control, providing discipline and structure.'

The control environment includes the following elements:

- Communication and enforcement of integrity and ethical values
- Commitment to competence
- Participation of management
- Management's philosophy and operating style
- Organisational structure
- Assignment of authority and responsibility
- Human resource policies and practices

A strong control environment is typically one where management shows a high level of commitment to establishing and operating appropriate controls.

The existence of a strong control environment cannot guarantee that controls are operating effectively, but it is seen as a positive factor in the auditor's risk assessment process. Without a strong control environment, the control system as a whole is likely to be weak.

Evaluating the control environment

ISA 315 requires auditors to gain an understanding of the control environment. Part of this understanding involves the auditor evaluating the control environment, and assessing its effectiveness.

In evaluating the control environment, the auditor should consider such factors as:

- management participation in the control process, including participation by the board of directors
- management's commitment to a control culture
- the existence of an appropriate organisation structure with clear divisions of authority and responsibility
- an organisation culture that expects ethically-acceptable behaviour from its managers and employees
- appropriate human resources policies, covering recruitment, training, development and motivation, which reflect a commitment to quality and competence in the organisation.

2.4 The entity's risk assessment process

Within a strong system of internal control, management should identify, assess and manage business risks, on a continual basis. Significant business risks are any events or omissions that may prevent the entity from achieving its objectives.

Identifying risks means recognising the existence of risks or potential risks. Assessing the risks means deciding whether the risks are significant, and possibly ranking risks in order of significance. Managing risks means developing and implementing controls and other measures to deal with those risks.

ISA 315 requires the auditor to gain an understanding of these risk assessment processes used by the client company's management, to the extent that those risk assessment processes may affect the financial reporting process.

Risks can arise or change due to circumstances such as:

- changes in the entity's operating environment
- new personnel
- new or revamped information systems
- rapid growth
- new technology
- new business models, products or activities
- corporate restructurings
- expanded foreign operations
- new accounting pronouncements.

These are the sort of factors which the examiner might build into a scenario to see if you can identify such factors as potential risks.

The quality of the risk assessment and management process within the client company can be used by the auditor to assess the overall level of audit risk. If management has no such process in place, the auditor will need to do more work on this aspect of the audit planning.

2.5 The information system

An information system consists of:

- infrastructure (physical and hardware components)
- software
- people
- procedures, and
- data.

Infrastructure and software will be absent, or have less significance, in systems that are exclusively or primarily manual, as opposed to computerised. Since most modern systems, even in small entities, make extensive use of information technology (IT), most questions in the exam are likely to be based on computerised systems in some shape or form. It is important that you recognise this and ensure that any audit tests or controls you suggest for such a system are appropriate. For example, if orders are placed via a website there is no point in suggesting that staff are observed writing out order documents. The appropriate approach would be to place a "test" order via the website and ensure the order has been recorded in the system by viewing it on screen.

ISA 315 requires the auditor to gain an understanding of the business information systems (including the accounting systems) used by management to the extent that they may affect the financial reporting process.

This aspect of the auditor's work will involve identifying and understanding the following:

- the entity's principal business transactions
- how these transactions and other events relevant to the financial reporting process are 'captured' (identified and recorded) by the entity
- the processing methods, both manual and computerised, applied to those transactions
- the accounting records used, both manual and computerised, to support the figures appearing in the financial statements
- the processes used in the preparation of the financial statements.

2.6 Control activities

Control activities are the policies and procedures, other than the control environment, used to ensure that the entity's objectives are achieved. They are the application of internal controls.

Control activities are the specific procedures designed:

- to prevent errors that may arise in processing information, or
- to detect and correct errors that may arise in processing information.

Categories of control activities (internal controls)

ISA 315 categorises internal controls into the following types: (In the examination, if you are asked to suggest suitable internal controls within a given system this list should provide a useful checklist.)

- **Performance reviews.** These include reviews and analyses of actual performance against budgets, forecasts and prior period performance. Most of these control activities will be performed by management and are often referred to as **management controls**. They include supervision by management of the work of subordinates, management review of performance and control reporting (including management accounting techniques such as variance analysis).
- **Information processing.** A variety of controls are used to check the **accuracy, completeness and authorisation of transactions**. These controls are split into two broad groupings which are discussed further below:
    - **Application controls**
    - **General IT controls**
- **Physical controls**. These include controls over the physical security of **assets and records** to prevent unauthorised use, theft or damage. Examples include limiting access to stockholding areas to a restricted number of authorised personnel, and requiring authorisation for access to computer programs and data files.
- **Segregation of duties**. This control involves assigning different people the responsibilities of authorising and recording transactions and maintaining the custody of assets. This reduces the likelihood of an employee being able to both carry out and conceal errors or fraud. This type of control is explained further below.

General IT controls

General IT controls are polices and procedures that **relate to many applications** (such as sales, purchases, payroll etc). They support the effective functioning of application controls (see below) by ensuring the continued proper operation of IT systems.

Because these general IT controls will apply to most or all of the entity's IT applications, if general IT controls are weak, it is unlikely that the processing undertaken by the system will be complete and accurate.

The auditor will therefore firstly review and test the general IT controls, in order to reach a conclusion on their effectiveness. This will enable him to assess the control risk attached to the entity's IT systems as a whole. If control risk is assessed as low he will then move on and test application controls, in order to decide if he can rely on specific systems and reduce his substantive testing.

Many of the general controls apply to large computer systems that are written, developed and maintained by the client company. However, some general controls also apply to smaller entities and users of off-the-shelf accounting software.

The main categories of general controls that an auditor would expect to find in a computer-based information system are:

- controls over the development of new computer information systems and applications
- controls over the documentation and testing of changes to programs
- the prevention or detection of unauthorised changes to programs (for example, by an employee committing fraud or by a 'hacker' accessing the system)
- controls to prevent the use of incorrect data files or programs
- controls to prevent unauthorised amendments to data files
- controls to ensure that there will be continuity in computer operations (and that the system will not 'break down' and cease to be operational).

Examples of general controls

Examples of each of these categories of general controls are set out in the table below:

Control area	Controls
Development of computer based information systems and applications	New computer systems may be designed and developed for a 'computer user' (the client company) by an in-house IT department or by an external software company. ▪ Appropriate IT Standards should be used when designing, developing, programming and documenting a new computer system. ▪ There should be controls to ensure that tests are carried out on new systems before they are introduced. ▪ A new computer system design should be formally approved by the system 'user'. ▪ There should be a segregation of duties between the designers and testers of systems. ▪ Staff should be given training in the use of a new system before they use it for 'live' operations.

Table continues

Control area	Controls
Documentation and testing of program changes	▪ When a computer system is operational, it may be necessary to update and amend some of the programs in the system. There should be suitable general controls over the development of new versions of programs. ▪ There should be controls to ensure that formal testing procedures on new program versions before they are used for 'live' operations ▪ All new versions of programs must be authorised at an appropriate level of management. ▪ Staff should be given training, where appropriate, in the use of a new program version before they use it for 'live' operations.
Prevention or detection of unauthorised program changes	There is a risk that new programs will be introduced without proper authorisation. The risks are particularly serious in companies that have large purpose-written computer systems, and where the computer systems are operated on large computers (mainframe computers or minicomputers) in a centralised computer centre. ▪ There should be a segregation between the tasks of programmers (who write new programs) and computer operators (who use the programs). ▪ There should be full documentation of all program changes. ▪ There should be restricted access to programs (program files), and only authorised programmers should have access to them. ▪ Program logs should be maintained, to record which programs and which versions are used. ▪ There should be virus protection for programs (using anti-virus software) and there should be back-up copies of all programs (in the event of 'malicious' changes to programs used in operations).
Prevention of the use of Incorrect programs or data files	In large computer systems, there may be several versions of a program at any time, not just one 'current version'. For example, when a new version is written, the 'old' version may be kept. It is important to ensure that the correct version of the program is used. ▪ Computer operating staff should be suitably trained, and should follow standard operating procedures for checking the version of the program they are using. ▪ Job scheduling: there should be formal job scheduling in large computer centres, and a job schedule should specify the version of the program to be used. ▪ Supervision. Supervisors should monitor the activities of operating staff. ▪ Reviews by management. Management should carry out periodic reviews, to make sure that the correct versions of programs are being used.
Prevention of unauthorised amendments to data files	In addition to the risk that there may be unauthorised access to program files and unauthorised amendment of programs, there is also a risk that data files will be accessed without authorisation (by an employee or an external 'hacker'). ▪ Physical access to computer terminals may be restricted to authorised employees. ▪ Access to programs and data files may be restricted using passwords. There should be rigorous checks by management to ensure that a password system is being used effectively by employees (so that passwords are not easy to 'guess') ▪ Firewalls (software and hardware) can be used to prevent unauthorised external access via the internet.

Table continues

Control area	Controls
Ensuring continuity of operations	When problems occur in a computer system, the system may be at risk of ceasing to function. This could happen if there is physical damage to computer equipment or files, or if program files or data files are 'corrupted' or altered without authorisation. ▪ There should be controls over maintaining secure second copies of all programs and data files ('back-up copies'). The back-up copies can be used if the original copies are damaged or corrupted. ▪ There should be measures for the protection of equipment against fire, power failure and other hazards. ▪ The company should have disaster recovery plans, such as an agreement with another entity to make use of its computer centre in the event of a disaster such as a fire or flood. ▪ The company should make suitable maintenance and service agreements with software companies, to provide 'technical support' in the event of operating difficulties with the system.

Application controls

Application controls apply to the processing of **individual applications** (such as sales, purchases, payroll etc). These controls help to ensure that transactions occurred, are authorised and are completely and accurately recorded and processed. These controls could be manual or computerised, depending on the system in question. Examples include:

- All significant transactions being authorised at an appropriate level (**authorisation controls**).
- Checking the arithmetic accuracy of records. These are often referred to as **arithmetic controls**. These are checks on the arithmetical accuracy of processing. An example is checking invoices from suppliers, to make sure that the amount payable has been calculated correctly.
- Maintaining and reviewing accounts and trial balances. These are often referred to as **accounting controls**. These are controls that are provided within accounting procedures to ensure the accuracy or completeness of records. An example is the use of control account reconciliations to check the accuracy of total trade debtors or total trade creditors.
- IT controls such as edit checks of input data (see below)
- Numerical sequence checks
- Manual follow-up of exception reports

In a manual processing system, controls vary by application. For example, specific internal controls over stock are different from internal controls over payroll. Similarly, the application controls that should be used in an IT system will vary depending on the particular application.

However, in IT systems, application controls share a number of common features regardless of the particular application involved. These common features can be categorised as:

- input controls (controls over input data)

- processing controls
- data file controls
- controls over the output from the system (output controls).

Each of these areas is considered in turn below. Some of the IT terms which are used are explained in the last section below.

Control area	Controls
Input	Application controls should place a high degree of emphasis on controls over **input**: if the input is not correct, the output from the application cannot possibly be correct. **Authorisation controls** ▪ Data for input is authorised ▪ Data is input only by authorised personnel **Completeness controls** ▪ Document counts (for example, a physical count of the number of invoices input for processing) ▪ Control totals ▪ Checking output to input ▪ Review of output against expected values: check for reasonableness. (For example, is the total payroll cost broadly in line with expectations?) **Accuracy controls** (see below) ▪ Check digits ▪ Range checks (is a particular figure input value feasible?) ▪ Existence checks (does a customer reference number exist?) ▪ Use of control totals
Processing controls	These are controls to check that the correct number of transactions has been processed and that they have all been fully processed ▪ Control totals (see below) ▪ Batch totals (see below) ▪ Manual review ▪ Screen warning ('screen prompts') that processing is not complete
Controls over master files and standing data	These are controls to check that data held on master files and standing files is correct. For example there may be a check in the sales invoicing system to make sure that the price list for products is up-to-date. There may also be a check to make sure that the master file of customers seems complete, for example by looking at the total of records on file. ▪ Management review of master files and standing data ▪ Regular updates of master files ▪ Record counts
Output controls	▪ Only authorised personnel should have access to output from the system (for example, invoices or payroll details). ▪ Output can be checked visually for reasonableness.

Segregation of duties

Segregation of duties means dividing the work to be done between two or more individuals, so that the work done by one individual acts as a check on the work of the others. This reduces the risk of error or fraud.

- If several individuals are involved in the completion of an overall task, this increases the likelihood that errors will be detected when they are made. Individuals can often identify mistakes of other people more easily than they can identify their own.
- It is more difficult for a person to commit fraud, because a colleague may identify suspicious transactions by a colleague who is trying to commit a fraud.

Example

The purchasing of stock involves several different tasks. Someone has to initiate a purchase requisition for a new supply of stock. Someone has to place a purchase order with a supplier. Someone has to check that the items are delivered by the supplier. Someone has to record the amount payable in the accounting system, and someone has to make the payment at the appropriate time.

Control risks include the risks that stock will be ordered when it is not needed, that the supplier will not deliver any stock or will deliver the incorrect quantity, or that the supplier will be paid too much or will be paid for items that he has not delivered.

A segregation of duties can help to reduce these risks:

Transaction stage	Responsibility
Initiation – Replenishment of stock item is required	Warehouse staff/stores staff
Purchase order – Item ordered	Purchasing officer. The purchasing officer is able to check the materials requisition from the stores staff
Custody – Item received	Goods inwards officer. The items actually delivered are checked physically and counted. This is a check that items have actually been delivered in good condition, as stated in the supplier's delivery note

Table continued

Transaction stage	Responsibility
Recording – Invoice received, checked and processed	Accounts clerk. The invoice from the supplier is checked against the delivery note and the original purchase order. The amount payable is recorded in the accounts system.
Payment – Invoice is paid	Cashier. The amount payable to the supplier is eventually paid by a different person in the accounts department.

Additional controls will also be applied. For example, there should be authorisation controls, and both the placing of a purchase order with the supplier and the payment to the supplier should be authorised at an appropriate level of management.

2.7 Monitoring of controls

It is important within an internal control system that management should review and monitor the operation of the controls, on a systematic basis, to satisfy themselves that the controls remain adequate and that they are being applied properly. ISA 315 requires the auditor to obtain an understanding of this monitoring process.

2.8 Understanding the control system: walk-through tests

ISA 315 requires the auditor to:

- gain an understanding of each of the five elements of the client's internal control system, and
- document the relevant features of the control systems.

Once this understanding has been gained, the auditor should confirm that his understanding is correct by performing **'walk-through' tests** on each major type of transaction (for example, sales transactions, purchase transactions, payroll).

As explained earlier, walk-through testing involves the auditor selecting a small sample of transactions and following them through the various stages in their processing in order to establish whether his understanding of the process is correct.

If he understands the controls that are in place, the auditor can go on to assess their effectiveness, and the extent to which he can rely on those controls for the purpose of the audit.

2.9 Specific IT controls

You may not have been familiar with all the IT application controls set out above. Therefore, some of them are described in more detail below. The purpose of these controls is to reduce the risk of errors in transactions input to the computer for processing, or to make sure that all transactions are fully processed.

Control totals

Control totals may be used when several transactions are input for processing at the same time. A control total is a total value for all the transactions input. For example, an accounts clerk might be processing 20 purchase invoices. A control total for the

20 transactions can be calculated (manually, with a calculator): this may be a total, say, of the value of the 20 invoices. A manual record may be kept of the control total.

When the 20 transactions have been processed, the computer program may output its own control total for the value of the items processed. This can be checked against the control total taken manually, to make sure that they agree.

Check digits

Check digits are checks within a computer program on the validity of key numerical codes, such as customer codes, supplier codes and employee identification numbers.

When check digits are used, every code is given an extra digit, the check digit. This is a unique digit obtained from the other digits in the code.

An example might illustrate how check digits operate. In this example, a Modulus 11 check digit system is used, where the check digit can be any of 11 'numbers' – 0 to 9 or X (10).

The basic coding system is for a five-digit code, and a sixth digit (the check digit) will be added to complete the code. Suppose that a customer's five-digit code is 23467. The check digit is calculated as follows (in the Modulus 11 system).

Code digit	Weighting	
2	× 6	12
3	× 5	15
4	× 4	16
6	× 3	18
7	× 2	14
		75
Check digit = 2	× 1	2
		77

In a Modulus 11 system, the check digit is given a weighting of 1, and it is calculated so that the total of all the digits in the code multiplied by their weightings will add up to a multiple of 11. In this example, the multiple of 11 is 77, and the check digit 2 makes the total add up to 77.

The six-digit customer code is therefore 234672.

A computer program can carry out a mathematical check on the code for every transaction input for processing. The program will check that the total of the code digits, when weighted as shown above, is a multiple of 11.

If the weighted total is not a multiple of 11, there must be an error in the code. This means that the computer program will detect any errors in input data for the particular code, and will not process the transaction. Instead, the program will output an error report, so that the error can be investigated and corrected.

Range checks and existence checks

Range checks and existence checks are other examples of 'data validation checks' that can be written into a computer program to test the validity of input data. The program looks at the value for a particular item of data in the input transaction, and if it is invalid, it produces an error report and will not process the transaction.

- A **range check**. The value of an item of data might have to be within a particular range. For example, stock codes may be within the range 2000 – 3999. If so, the program can be written so that it checks the stock code for every transaction, and produces an error report if the code is not within that range.
- An **existence check** is similar, but the program checks the actual existence of a particular code. For example, in a payroll system, input transactions may include a department code for each employee. Department codes may be B, C and P. A program check can be carried out on the department code for all input transactions, and if the code is not B, C or P, an error report will be produced.

Batch totals

A batch total is a form of control total. Transaction data is input to the computer system in batches, and a control total is calculated. It may simply be a total of the number of transactions in the batch. The batch total is input to the computer system for processing, and the computer program will check the batch total that has been input with its own batch total count.

The program will report any discrepancy between the manually counted batch total and its own batch total, as an error report.

Batch totals can be useful in helping to make sure that every transaction in a batch is actually input for processing and is actually processed.

On-screen prompts

On-screen prompts are often used in computer systems where data is input by keyboard, mouse and computer screen, typically by the user's own accounts staff. The screen will display 'prompts', telling the user what to input next or what to do next. They help to make sure that transactions are fully processed, and that operators do not leave transactions only partly processed.

Example

One part of the sales system at Dolally operates as set out below:

- Orders are received by telephone. On receipt of an order a clerk enters the details into the system.
- The system checks that the goods are available and, if so, a despatch note is produced and e-mailed to the distribution centre.
- Distribution centre staff pack the goods and despatch them with two copies of the despatch note.
- On receipt of the goods the customer signs the despatch notes and one copy is returned to the accounts department at Dolally.

- The accounts department flag up the despatch note on the system to indicate that the goods have been delivered and the system automatically produces an invoice and e-mails it to the customer.
- An exception report of uninvoiced despatch notes is produced weekly.

Required

Set out an example of each of the above five types of control activities set out in ISA 315 as they might operate in Dolally's system.

Answer

Performance reviews: Management should compare budgeted sales to actual sales on a monthly basis (provided that the budgets are reliable, this would detect where significant sales had not been recorded).

Information processing – application: Manual follow up of the exception report of uninvoiced despatch notes.

Information processing – general IT: Controls over the development and testing of the sales system to ensure it will lead to accurate processing (such as documentation and testing of any changes to programs).

Physical controls: Access controls over the sales price master files such as access only being possible via a high-level password, known only to senior employees (such as the sales director) (as invoices are produced automatically by the system it is important that the integrity of this file is maintained).

Segregation of duties: Different employees should be responsible for taking and inputting orders, despatching goods and flagging up the despatch note.

Tutorial note: There are a number of other possible examples other than those set out above.

Limitations of internal control systems

- Reasons why internal controls may be ineffective
- Problems for small entities

3 Limitations of internal control systems

3.1 Reasons why internal controls may be ineffective

Internal control systems are never foolproof. All systems, no matter how effective they may appear to be, have several limitations:

- Human error may result in incomplete or inaccurate processing which may not be detected by control systems.
- It may not be cost-effective to establish certain types of controls within an organisation.
- Controls may be in place, but they may be ignored or overridden by employees or management.
- Collusion may mean that segregation of duties is ineffective. Collusion means that two or more people work together to avoid a control, possibly for the purpose of committing fraud.

Although modern auditing is based on testing the systems and controls rather than transactions, auditors will never rely solely on such tests in reaching a conclusion. This is because of the limitations inherent in **all** control systems. Auditors will always supplement their work on systems with some testing of transactions and balances themselves (substantive testing). The amount of substantive testing will depend on the auditor's evaluation of the effectiveness of the controls.

3.2 Problems for small entities

Many of the control activities that are typically found in a large company may be inappropriate for a small entity because they are too costly or impractical.

Segregation of duties is an obvious example of this. It is difficult to segregate duties in a small company with only a few employees. The same individual has to carry out a variety of different tasks.

Often, control systems in small entities are based on a high level of involvement by the directors or owners. Authorisation and performance review controls, with the owner or a senior director personally authorising many transactions, might therefore be a key feature of control systems in small entities.

However, the auditor will often see this management involvement as only a partial substitute for 'normal' control systems. The following problems may arise when control systems rely excessively on the involvement of senior management.

- There may be lack of evidence of controls. (How does the auditor know that the controls exist and are being applied?)
- Management may override other controls that are in place.
- Management may lack the expertise necessary to control the entity effectively.

When auditing a small entity, the auditor needs to understand and evaluate whatever controls are in place and plan his audit work accordingly. It is likely that a lower level of reliance will be placed on controls in a smaller entity, and that a large amount of substantive testing will therefore be required.

Recording internal control systems

- The need to record internal control systems
- Recording methods
- Questionnaires

4 Recording internal control systems

4.1 The need to record internal control systems

The auditor must gain an understanding of each of the five elements that make up the client's internal control system. This is to enable the auditor to carry out an evaluation of the systems and to conduct an audit risk assessment. The outcome of this assessment and evaluation will establish his overall approach to the audit – whether it will be systems-based or transactions-based.

The auditor's work on internal control is therefore an important element of gathering audit evidence, because it influences the direction that the audit work will take. As with all other significant audit evidence, it must be properly documented in the audit working papers – probably in the permanent audit file.

4.2 Recording methods

The principal methods available to the auditor for recording internal control systems are:

- narrative notes
- systems flowcharts
- questionnaires.

Narrative notes

Narrative notes are a written description of the control system and the controls that are in place. They are used mainly to make a record of the control activities involved in processing transactions.

Narrative notes are simple to prepare, but can become lengthy. They may be time-consuming to prepare initially. When narrative notes are long, it may also be time-consuming to update them when the system or the controls change.

Ideally, narrative notes should be written clearly, but should not be longer than necessary to provide a full description.

Systems flowcharts

Systems flowcharts provide a representation of accounting systems in the form of a diagram. For each type of transaction, they show the documents generated, the processes applied to the documents and the flow of the documents between the various departments involved. Flowcharts therefore show the flow of work by showing how documents are transferred within a system (and filed) and how they are used.

As they are in the form of a diagram, flowcharts present an immediate visual impact of the system. This can sometimes help the auditor to identify weaknesses in controls more easily than by reading narrative notes.

However, some expertise is needed to draw a good flowchart and to use it to assess the effectiveness of controls. In addition, although flowcharts work well with standard accounting systems and transactions, they may not be appropriate for documenting specialised areas of accounting.

4.3 Questionnaires

Questionnaires are widely used by auditors to document systems. Questionnaires can be prepared in advance as standard documents. They are also ideally suited for use by the auditor in an electronic form, which means that standard questionnaires are available and ready for use on the auditor's laptop computer.

A questionnaire is a list of questions about controls in a particular aspect of operations or accounting.

There are two main types of questionnaire. Each has a different objective. They are:

- the internal control questionnaire (ICQ)
- the internal control **evaluation** questionnaire (ICEQ).

Internal control questionnaire (ICQ)

An internal control questionnaire (ICQ) is designed to establish whether appropriate controls exist, that meet specific control objectives. Each question requires a 'Yes' or a 'No' answer, and deals with a particular type of control. The auditor has to establish the answer to each of the questions, and fill in the questionnaire.

ICQs are usually drawn up in such a way that:

- a 'Yes' answer to a question indicates a control strength, and
- a 'No' answer to a question indicates a control weakness.

For example, the following ICQ questions might be included in a questionnaire dealing with procedures for assessing the credit-worthiness of potential new customers:

Are credit references taken on all potential new customers?	YES/NO
Are credit limits set for customers?	YES/NO

Example

As part of his evaluation of internal controls, the auditor wishes to establish each of the following:

(a) That the correct product prices are charged on sales invoices to customers.

(b) That raw materials delivered are of the correct specification and in the correct quantity.

Required

Draft ICQ questions that could be used to establish the existence of appropriate controls.

Answer

(a)	**Is a check carried out to match the price on a sales invoice to the official price list?**	YES/NO
(b)	**Are raw materials counted and checked against the purchase order when the materials are delivered?**	YES/NO

An ICQ not only provides the auditor with a means of recording the system and its controls; it also assists with the evaluation process. The auditor can review the Yes/No answers to gain an overall picture of the reliability of the system under review.

The ICQ approach above has the advantage of producing a document that is relatively simple for the auditor to complete. So the questionnaire can often be completed by a relatively junior member of the audit team. However, the questionnaire can become lengthy (with a large number of questions) and so time-consuming to complete.

Internal control evaluation questionnaire (ICEQ)

In recent years the auditing profession has responded to this by developing a second type of questionnaire, the internal control evaluation questionnaire (ICEQ).

The idea behind the ICEQ is to draw up a small number of **key control questions** designed to establish whether major weaknesses may exist in a control system:

- Using an ICQ, the auditor is looking for 'good news' and expects to find particular controls in place.
- Using an ICEQ, the auditor is on the look-out for 'bad news' and the possibility that controls may be weak.

Like an ICQ, an ICEQ contains a (shorter) list of questions, for which the answer is Yes or No. A questionnaire is normally designed so that a Yes answer indicates good controls and a No answer indicates weak controls.

An earlier example showed how ICQ questions might be written, relating to controls over the creditworthiness of customers. An ICEQ approach in this same area might consider just one key control question, as follows:

Is there reasonable assurance that goods can only be despatched to authorised customers whose account balance is within their credit limit?	YES/NO

Although the ICEQ approach typically produces a document that is shorter than an ICQ, ICEQs may suffer from the disadvantage that the questions are less precise and may need more knowledge and experience on the part of the auditor to answer them.

Choosing which type of questionnaire to use is a matter of preference for the auditor or the audit firm.

As in the case of the ICQ, the ICEQ approach also serves a dual purpose for the auditor – both to record and to evaluate the internal control system.

Evaluation of controls and audit risk assessment

- The purpose of evaluating controls
- The evaluation process

5 Evaluation of controls and audit risk assessment

5.1 The purpose of evaluating controls

Having established the control systems that are in place, and having recorded them in the audit working papers, the auditor should now evaluate the controls and establish their effectiveness. The results of this evaluation will allow the auditor to identify the control risk (which is an element of audit risk). The auditor can then decide on a systems-based or a transactions-based approach to the audit.

The evaluation of accounting and control systems is a two-stage process. The auditor will need to establish:

- Whether controls are effective 'on paper'. This means that if it can be assumed that the controls are applied properly in practice, are they sufficient?
- Whether the controls are applied properly, and so whether they are actually working and operating effectively. Controls may be adequate if they are applied properly, but in practice they might not be applied as they should be. This aspect of the auditor's evaluation is described in more detail in a later chapter on **tests of controls**.

5.2 The evaluation process

The auditor should obtain a general picture of the effectiveness of the controls established by management, by reviewing his documentation of the internal control system. This is the evaluation of the controls 'on paper'.

If this 'paper' review of the controls indicates that major weaknesses exist, the auditor will probably take the view that the audit approach will have to focus on tests of transactions (substantive tests) rather than on tests of controls (a systems-based approach). A systems-based audit approach will not be appropriate if there is a high level of control risk.

If the auditor's initial assessment of the control systems shows that those systems are weak, then he will move straight to substantive testing and will not bother to carry out tests of controls.

Even if the controls appear to be acceptable on paper, the auditor cannot rely on them and perform a systems-based audit unless he is confident that the controls are actually working. In this situation, the next stage in the audit process is to carry out **tests of controls**.

If the outcome of the tests of controls indicates that controls are actually operating effectively, the audit can be systems based, with a reduced amount of substantive testing. Remember that the auditor will always need to perform **some** substantive testing – because of the inherent limitations in any system of internal controls.

In view of this ISA 330 requires that substantive procedures are carried out for each **material class of transactions, account balances and disclosure**. These terms are considered in a later chapter on substantive testing.

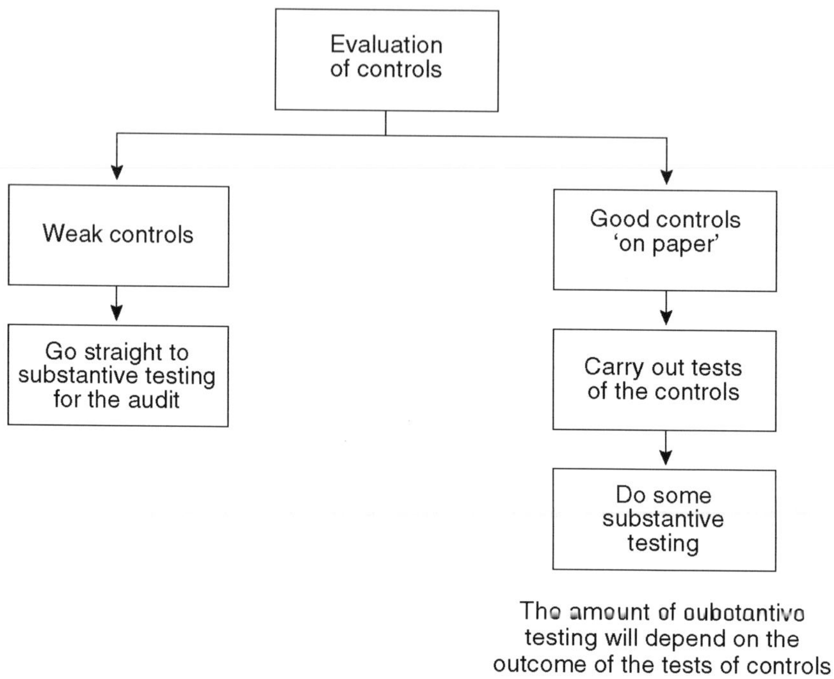

The risks of specialised IT systems

- Microcomputer systems
- Online systems
- Electronic data interchange (EDI) systems
- E-business: Bulletin 2001/3

6 The risks of specialised IT systems

When evaluating the general controls and application controls in a client's computer systems, the auditor needs to take account of the type of computer-based information system that the client is using.

The types of system may require special attention:

- microcomputer systems
- online systems
- electronic data interchange systems.

6.1 Microcomputer systems

This is not a precisely defined term. However, a microcomputer system is a system where the client company uses a number of 'desktop' computers located throughout the organisation, rather than a large 'centralised' computer-based information system with a mainframe computer or minicomputer.

Companies may use a microcomputer system because it is more efficient and cost-effective than a centralised system with a large single computer. Another commercial advantage of microcomputer systems is that the systems can often be operated (and possibly even programmed) by the user's operating staff (for example, accounts clerks) with little technical training.

Microcomputer systems may, however, generate problems of audit risk for the auditor, for the following reasons:

- It may be difficult to ensure adequate physical security of the equipment, because desktop computers for the system may be in many different locations.
- For similar reasons, there may be problems in connection with security of the data and storage media (disks of data files).
- The wide access available in most of these systems introduces problems of authorisation. There is the possibility of unauthorised amendments to programs or data files. The risks in this area can be minimised by the use of passwords to restrict access to certain files.
- Programs may be written or modified by the user (one of the potential attractions to the entity of the use of 'micros') but this may cause processing and software problems.

- The auditor should want to see adequate documentation for software systems. When software is purchased 'off-the-shelf' documentation should be provided by the software supplier.

6.2 Online systems

These are computer-based information systems that allow users direct access to centrally-held data and programs through remote terminals linked together in a network.

Companies use online systems because they can offer several benefits, such as:

- immediate entry of transactions into the system (for example, sales transactions in a retail outlet can be input from the check-out desk from 'electronic point of sale' terminals linked to a central computer in a network)
- immediate updating of master files (such as the immediate updating of stock records as soon as stock is requisitioned)
- enquiry systems (such as immediate answers to price enquiries from customers).

Again, although they can be efficient and effective for the client company, on-line systems can create concerns about audit risk for the auditor. Controls should be in place to minimise the risks that arise from the use of online processing systems by the client.

Controls in an online system are a mixture of general controls and application controls.

General controls in online systems

- Access controls need to be strong because transactions are processed immediately by online systems. It is therefore important that unauthorised access to the programs and data files should be prevented.
- Programming controls should be built in to prevent or detect unauthorised changes to programs or standing data.
- Transaction logs should be used to create an 'audit trail'. An **audit trail** refers to the ability of the auditor to trace a transaction through all its processing stages. An audit trail can be provided by a record ('log') of how the computer has processed any transaction. An audit trail may not exist in 'paper form' in an online system, but the computer program should be written so as to generate the audit trail on request for any transaction.
- Firewalls should be used. These are software or hardware devices that protect the network 'server' (computer) from unauthorised access via the internet.

Application controls in online systems

Applications systems that run on online computer systems should have application controls that are suitable for the nature of the processing system. For example:

- There should be pre-processing authorisation. This means that individuals should be required to log on to the system before they can use the program.

- Program checks (data validation checks) can be carried out on the input data. These include check digit checks, range checks, existence checks and completeness checks. These programmed checks help to ensure the completeness and accuracy of processing (for example, the correct number of digits in product codes).
- 'Balancing'. This is the immediate checking of control totals of data submitted from a remote terminal, before and after processing.

6.3 Electronic data interchange (EDI) systems

EDI systems are systems that allow the electronic transmission of business documents, such as purchase orders, invoices or payroll information.

EDI systems may operate:

- within the organisation (for example, the sales department may use an EDI system to send copies of customer orders to the accounting department), or
- externally (for example, a company may submit payroll data to an external agency or 'bureau' for processing, and a company may send a purchase order electronically to a supplier).

In an EDI system, the transmitted 'documents' are automatically entered into the (different) computer system of the receiver of the message. For example, a purchase order sent to a supplier by EDI is read automatically into the sales order computer system of the supplier, and so can be processed without the need for manual intervention.

Once again, although EDI systems may improve the operational efficiency of the organisation, they may create the following additional problems for the auditor:

- There is a lack of a paper audit trail. (A 'paper' audit trail is one where a transaction can be followed through the stages of its processing, by going from one paper document to another. With EDI, the system needs an electronic audit trail for transactions, and the computer system should be able to provide one.)
- There is an increased level of dependency on the computer systems of the organisation and possibly on outsiders. Any computer failure may therefore have an increased impact on the client's organisation. General controls for IT will therefore be extremely important.
- There is a risk of possible loss or corruption of data in the process of transmission.
- There are also security risks in the transmission of data. Unauthorised individuals may be able to read transmitted data.

Auditors should expect to see controls in place to minimise the risks inherent in EDI systems. Typically, controls will cover such matters as:

- controls over transmission of data (encryption, acknowledgement systems, authentication codes)
- monitoring and checking of output

- virus protection systems
- contingency plans and back up arrangements.

(Note: Authentication codes are used so that senders and receivers of transmitted data have to authenticate their identity before data is transmitted. Encryption involves translating data into 'coded' form for transmission, and then re-translating it at the recipient's end.)

6.4 E-business: Bulletin 2001/3

Guidance on this area is provided by APB Bulletin 2001/3 *E-business: identifying financial statement risks* which was developed in response to the growth in electronic commerce (usually referred to as e-commerce or e-business) in order to provide guidance on the impact of e-business on the auditor's risk assessment.

E-business is any commercial activity that takes place via connected computers overt a public network. The most common example is a mail order company, selling goods over the Internet.

The use of computer networks to conduct e-business is not a new development but the evolution of the Internet and associated systems has enabled e-business applications to be developed that are affordable to entities of all sizes. The basic principles and procedures underlying the audit of an entity conducting e-business will be no different to the audit of any other type of entity. However, e-business can have a significant impact on:

- the accounting and internal control systems (including possible reliance on automation of processing and on third parties such as payment collection businesses)
- the volume, speed and nature of transactions processed
- the taxation, legal and regulatory requirements the entity needs to comply with, and
- the accounting policies in respect of revenue and cost recognition and the capitalisation of development expenditure.

The statement focuses on the following areas:

- The **skills and knowledge** needed by the auditor to understand the effect of e-business on the entity's activities – the more complex the activities the greater the skills and knowledge required. Not only IT knowledge will be needed but also knowledge of relevant legal and regulatory requirements, in the different overseas jurisdictions in which the entity may do business. If necessary, the auditor may need to bring in external expertise.
- The extent of the **knowledge of the business** needed by the auditor. E-business may have a significant impact on the traditional business environment – increasing security risks and geographical markets. The auditor will also need to understand:
  - the overall e-business strategy and how that affects the position of the business

  - what e-business operations are undertaken and how e-business operations are likely to evolve – change may be rapid and an initially simple system may soon become a complex one
  - how the e-business operations may be supported by third parties
  - how the e-business operations interact with the entity's accounting and management information systems.
- **Additional risks** arising from e-business, such as:
  - loss of transaction integrity and security risks (especially where the e-business system is connected to the core operating and accounting systems)
  - going concern risks where the entity has made significant investment in e-business and/or conducts all of its business as e-business, especially if the entity is a new (start-up) entity
  - financing from third parties obtained on the basis of the number of "hits" on the entity's website over a specified period
  - the use of inappropriate accounting policies (e.g. in respect of the capitalisation of website development costs)
  - legal and regulatory risks.

CHAPTER 9

Tests of controls

Contents

Tests of controls and the main transaction cycles

- Planning tests of controls
- Computer-assisted audit techniques
- The major transaction cycles

1 Tests of controls and the main transaction cycles

1.1 Planning tests of controls

The auditor takes a systems-based approach wherever possible. He focuses on testing the systems and internal controls that produce the financial reporting figures, rather than the figures themselves. If the systems and the controls are satisfactory, the figures produced by the systems should be reliable.

Two conditions are necessary before the auditor can adopt a systems-based approach.

- The systems and controls in place should be **designed** to minimise the risks of mis-statements. The auditor carries out this check of controls in his procedures for the documentation and evaluation of the controls.
- The systems and controls should actually **operate** effectively. The auditor gains evidence that the controls operate in practice by performing **tests of control**.

A useful approach to examination questions dealing with tests of control is to consider the following:

- the objectives of the controls: what are the controls intended to achieve?
- the major controls which are in place (or should be in place): what specific controls will achieve the control objectives?
- the design of appropriate tests of control: what checks can be carried out to obtain evidence that the controls are actually operating in practice?

1.2 Computer-assisted audit techniques

Where systems are IT based, specialised techniques of obtaining audit evidence may be required. These are known as **computer-assisted audit techniques** (CAATs).

CAATs can be defined as any technique that enables the auditor to use IT systems as a source of generating audit evidence. They involve the use of computer techniques by the auditor to obtain audit evidence.

- CAATs are often necessary in the audit of IT systems because these systems may not provide an adequate audit trail.
- In addition, processing is 'invisible' because it is electronic. Therefore, the auditor needs to 'get inside the computer' to check the completeness and accuracy of the processing. CAATs allow the auditor to achieve this.

Two commonly-used types of CAATs are:

- audit software, and
- test data.

It is **test data** which is of most relevance to **tests of control**. The technique provides evidence of the operation of specific application controls in a given system. Audit software is more relevant to substantive testing and is therefore considered in a later chapter.

Test data

The use of test data involves the auditor processing a sample of data through the IT system and comparing the results obtained from the processing with pre-determined results.

A potential problem with using test data is that it will only give audit evidence at the time that test data is processed. Procedures may therefore be written into the client entity's computer information systems that will generate data for audit purposes **every time the process is run**. One way of achieving this without corrupting the client's data files with the test data is to establish an extra 'dummy' department, to which the test data results are allocated. Only the auditor should have access to the data stored in this dummy department.

Disadvantages of CAATs

CAATs give the auditor the ability to audit the processing of transactions in an IT system. However, there are some disadvantages with using CAATs. They can be expensive, and the use of CAATs should be evaluated on a cost benefit basis.

The costs related to the use of CAATs may include:

- purchasing or developing the programs
- keeping programs up-to-date for changes in hardware and software
- training audit staff in the use of computer systems to run the CAATs. CAATs are of no value unless auditors are properly trained in how to use them.

Example

Looking back to the system described in the previous chapter in relation to Dolally, set out four examples of how test data could be used to test that system. You need not restrict the controls you are testing to those in your previous answer.

Answer

1. Input a dummy order where you are aware that the goods are out of stock and ensure that the order does not lead to a despatch note being produced). (The system above did not specify how this situation would be dealt with. There would probably be some sort of pending orders file, checked against stock levels daily).

2. Input a dummy order where you know that the goods are in stock and ensure that a despatch note is produced. View the despatch note on screen and trace it through to the copy in the distribution centre.
3. Input dummy despatch notes without subsequently flagging them up for invoicing and ensure they appear on the exception report.
4. Flag up dummy despatch notes and check invoices are raised.

1.3 The major transaction cycles

The auditor will focus much of his audit work on the major '**transaction cycles**' which taken together cover the majority of the day-to-day transactions of the business.

The major transaction cycles are:

- sales,
- purchases, and
- payroll.

These three transaction cycles will have a direct effect on both the balance sheet and the profit and loss account. Tests of control are also applied to key balance sheet headings linking into the main transaction cycles:

- bank and cash
- stock, and
- revenue and capital expenditure (fixed assets).

Much of this chapter presents lists of control objectives, suitable controls and tests of controls, for different aspects of the main transaction cycles. These lists are not complete or comprehensive, instead they are intended to provide detailed guidance about how tests of control may be designed and applied.

In any examination question on tests of controls, you might find that this approach is helpful in constructing an answer.

The sales system

- Elements of the sales system
- Customer ordering
- Despatch of goods and invoicing
- Recording sales and accounting

2 The sales system

2.1 Elements of the sales system

Excluding the collection of payments from credit customers, the main elements of the sales accounting system may be classified as follows:

- Receiving orders from customers
- Despatching the goods and invoicing customers
- Recording sales and debtors in the accounts

For each of these elements of the system, we can identify control objectives, design internal controls and devise ways of checking whether the controls are applied in practice (tests of control).

2.2 Customer ordering

Control objectives

So what are the risks in a system of receiving and processing customer orders? The following list is not complete, but contains some of the risks:

- Orders may be accepted from new customers and new customers may be given credit, without checking the customer's references or without formal authorisation of a credit account for the customer with a credit limit.
- Orders may be accepted from existing customers that take them over their credit limit.
- Some orders are overlooked and are not processed. Some orders are processed twice.
- The customer is given discounts without proper authorisation.

Suitable control objectives may therefore be as follows:

- Giving credit to new customers and existing customers must be controlled, and must be consistent with company policy.
- All orders from customers are processed correctly.

Principal controls

Suitable controls may be as follows:

- There should be a segregation of duties, and the individuals who process orders from customers should not also carry out credit reference checks on new customers or credit limit checks on existing customers. The latter could be done manually by reference to a file of approved credit limits, or it could be a programmed control whereby the system will only accept an order if the customer will still be within his credit limit.
- All new customer accounts, and their credit limit, should be authorised.
- Orders should be recorded on sequentially-numbered documents or the system should allocate sequential numbers to documents.
- For every sales order, a despatch note should be produced (manually, or generated by the system from the order details). Goods should not be despatched to customers without a despatch note.

Tests of control

How might an auditor test whether these controls are actually applied in practice? The client can assist the auditor by collecting evidence that the controls have been applied. One way of doing this is to use the customer order document to record that checks have been completed; for example by providing space on the order form for individuals to sign their name or write their initials as confirmation that they have carried out a particular task.

Here are some suggested tests of control.

- The auditor can establish which individuals take orders and process them, and which individuals carry out credit reference checks on new customers and credit limit checks on existing customers. The auditor could observe these individuals to see if procedures are being properly followed. In an IT system he could use test data to check that orders which would take a customer over his credit limit would be rejected by the system.
- Further evidence that credit checks have been carried out can be checked by looking at the signatures or initials of credit checking staff on customer orders or by using test data as described above..
- Evidence that new customer accounts have been approved should be checked by looking for the signature of the manager giving the authorisation on the appropriate approval document.
- The auditor can look at lists of customer orders, sequentially numbered, and confirm that for every customer order there is a despatch note number. Alternatively, for an integrated IT system, he can follow test data through from order to despatch note and confirm that sequences are complete by viewing documents on screen.

It is important to remember that this list of controls and tests of controls is not complete, but it may help you to understand the process by which tests of control are carried out, and the way in which they should give the auditor the evidence that he needs for a systems-based approach to the audit. You need to take care in the exam that the controls or tests of controls you suggest are appropriate to the system described, taking careful note of which parts of the system are manual and which are IT based. The control objectives will be the same for both types of systems – it is the specific controls (and therefore also tests of controls) that will sometimes be different.

2.3 Despatch of goods and invoicing

The same approach can be applied to the despatch of goods and invoicing.

Control objectives

Here are some of the risks in this part of the sales system.

- For some customer orders, goods are not despatched, or the goods are despatched twice.
- Invoices are not produced for goods that have been despatched to some customers.
- Customers may claim that they did not receive the goods that have actually been delivered to them.
- Returns from customers are not properly recorded, so that the client company does not know the correct figure for sales net of sales returns.

Control objectives may therefore be as follows:

- Goods should be despatched for every authorised customer order.
- Customers should acknowledge the receipt of goods.
- For every despatch note, there must be an invoice.
- Invoices should be for the correct amount.
- For all goods returned by customers, there must be an authorised credit note.

Principal controls

Suitable controls may be as follows:

- Despatch notes should be numbered sequentially, and should be attached to a copy of a specific customer order.
- Customers should sign a delivery note for the receipt of goods.
- The signed delivery note should be attached to a copy of the despatch note and customer order.
- Invoices should be sequentially numbered or the system should allocate sequential numbers to documents..
- Each invoice should be linked to a copy of the despatch note and customer order or produced automatically from them.
- There should be a segregation of duties, and the individuals who despatch goods should not be the same as those who prepare invoices or process the customer orders.
- Credit notes should be sequentially numbered and authorised.
- There should be periodic checks by someone in the accounts staff on the accuracy of invoices or strong IT controls to ensure the accuracy of invoices.

Tests of control

Here are some suggested tests of control.

- The auditor can check that the segregation of duties does exist.
- The auditor should check that (sequential) lists of invoices show a customer order number and a despatch note number.
- The auditor should check a list of credit notes to make sure that they cross-refer to a sales invoice number.
- Credit notes should be checked to make sure that they contain the authorisation signature of the appropriate manager or have been raised, on the computer, only by a member of staff with authority to do so.
- Some delivery notes should be checked to confirm that customers do sign them.
- There should be documentary evidence that a member of the accounts staff has carried out arithmetical checks on the accuracy of invoices. Alternatively, the auditor may prove that there are strong IT controls which will ensure the accuracy of invoices by checking the calculations himself.

2.4 Recording sales and accounting

Again, a similar approach can be taken in identifying tests of control for the recording of sales in the accounting system.

Control objectives

Here are some of the risks and control objectives in this part of the sales system.

- There is a risk that invoices and credit notes may not be recorded in the accounting system. A control objective is to ensure that they are all recorded.
- There is a risk that invoices and credit notes are recorded in the wrong customer accounts. A control objective is to prevent this from happening, or to detect errors when they do occur.
- There is a risk that debts may be written off as uncollectable ('bad') without proper consideration. A control objective is to make sure that this does not happen.

Principal controls

Suitable controls may be as follows:

- Invoices and credit notes should be sequentially numbered.
- Regular statements should be sent to customers.
- Control account reconciliations should be carried out on trade debtors.
- Bad debts must be authorised.
- There are procedures for identification and follow-up of overdue accounts and unpaid invoices.

Tests of control

Here are some suggested tests of control.

- Lists of invoices and credit notes can be checked to make sure that there is sequential numbering or documents can be viewed on screen.
- There should be a segregation of duties between the individuals who prepare and send out invoices, and individuals who collect payments, and individuals who follow up late payments.
- The auditor can check that statements are produced and despatched to customers.
- The auditor can look for documentary evidence that control total checks have been made.
- There should be documentary evidence that proper authorisation is given for a debt to be written off as bad.
- There should be individuals responsible for collecting overdue debts, and evidence of their work. Alternatively the auditor might check that an exception report is regularly produced by the system, listing all overdue debts, and look for evidence that this is followed up.

The purchases and expenses system

- Elements of the purchases and expenses system
- Placing orders
- Receiving goods and invoices
- Recording and accounting for purchases and expenses

3 The purchases and expenses system

3.1 Elements of the purchases and expenses system

Excluding the procedures for making payments to suppliers, the main elements of the accounting system for purchases and other expenses may be classified as follows:

- Placing orders
- Receiving goods (or services) and receiving invoices
- Recording and accounting for purchases and expenses.

The same basic approach to devising tests of control can be taken as for the sales system. The control objectives, controls and tests of control listed here are not comprehensive. They are intended to show you the approach that can be taken.

Again, the control objectives will be the same for all systems, but the controls and therefore tests of controls, are likely to differ to some extent between manual and IT systems.

3.2 Placing orders

Control objectives

So what are the risks in a system of ordering goods or services from suppliers? The following list is not complete, but contains some of the risks:

- Orders for goods or services are made without approval or authorisation.
- Orders may be placed with suppliers who are not on the 'approved list'.
- For large orders, suppliers are not asked to submit tenders. When suppliers are asked to tender, the order might not be given to the supplier quoting the lowest price.

Suitable control objectives may therefore be as follows:

- All purchase orders must be properly authorised.
- Orders should not be placed with 'non-approved' suppliers.
- Competitive price quotations should be obtained for all large orders.

Principal controls

Suitable controls may be as follows:

- There should be a segregation of duties. Individuals who make a requisition for new supplies of stock should not be the individuals who place the order with the supplier.
- Purchase orders should be sequentially numbered.
- There should be a procedure for placing suppliers on the 'approved list'. In an IT system, physical controls must exist over access to the master file of approved suppliers.
- All orders must be placed with suppliers on an approved list. The purchase order may include an 'approved supplier reference number'. In an IT system the system must only be able to address orders to approved suppliers as on the master file.
- Orders above a certain value must be authorised by a senior manager, who should confirm that competitive tenders have been obtained from suppliers.

Tests of control

Here are some suggested tests of control.

- The auditor can check that the segregation of duties does exist.
- The auditor can look at lists of sequentially-numbered purchase orders. or view documents on screen. Alternatively, he could submit test data in the form of an order and check it is allocated the next number in the sequence.
- The auditor should ask management to provide documentary evidence that the procedure for placing suppliers on the approved list operates as intended. . In an IT system, the controls over the master file of approved suppliers will need to be tested.
- Purchase orders can be checked to make sure that they contain an approved supplier reference number.
- Large orders can be checked for management authorisation.

3.3 Receiving goods and invoices

Control objectives

Here are some control objectives for this part of the purchases transaction cycle.

- Goods may be accepted from a supplier without having been ordered. Or suppliers may claim to have delivered goods, but may actually not have done so. A control objective is therefore to make sure that all receipts of goods are recorded and checked against a purchase order.
- A company may fail to claim discounts from suppliers for orders above a certain size, or as regular customers of the supplier. A control objective should be that discounts are given by suppliers where these are available.
- Suppliers may invoice for goods that have not actually been provided. A control objective is to prevent this from happening, or detect when it does happen.

Principal controls

In this area there is little difference between manual and IT systems as this part of an IT system will be dependent on controls over the physical receipt of goods and invoices, which will be carried out by employees as opposed to by a computer program. Suitable controls may be as follows:

- A copy of all delivery notes should be retained, with a signature of the member of staff who took receipt and checked the goods.
- Goods received notes should be produced for each delivery, from the delivery note or after a physical count of the items received.
- A member of the accounts staff or purchasing staff must be responsible for checking discounts allowed by suppliers.
- There should be a segregation of duties between the individuals who take delivery of goods, those who place the orders and those who record the purchase invoices in the accounting system.
- All purchase invoices should be checked against a purchase order and a goods received note.

Tests of control

Here are some suggested tests of control.

- The auditor should check that delivery notes, goods received notes and purchase invoices are matched with each other. There should be evidence that they have been checked against each other; for example, the person making the check should sign or initial the purchase invoice.
- The auditor should look for any evidence that invoices, purchase orders or goods received notes cannot be properly matched (indicating that the controls are not working in practice and a control objective is not being achieved).
- The auditor should look for documentary evidence that discounts are checked and claimed from suppliers when available.
- The auditor should check that the segregation of duties does exist.

3.4 Recording and accounting for purchases and expenses

Control objectives

Here are some control objectives for this part of the purchases transaction cycle.

- There is a risk that purchase invoices will be recorded for goods or services that were not provided. A control objective is to make sure that this does not happen.
- There is a risk that purchase invoices will be incorrectly recorded in the accounts of suppliers. A control objective is to identify and correct any such errors that may occur.
- There is a risk that credit will not be claimed from suppliers for goods returned. A control objective is to make sure that credit is taken for purchase returns.

Principal controls

Suitable controls may be as follows:

- Purchase invoices must be checked against purchase orders before they are recorded in the accounts. If the purchase order number is not printed on an invoice, it should be written on the invoice by the individual making the check or entered onto the system alongside the invoice details.
- Regular statements should be received from suppliers, and the balance on the statement should be checked against the account balance in the trade creditors ledger.
- There should be regular control account reconciliations for trade creditors.
- A debit note should be created each time that goods are returned to a supplier. Debit notes should be sequentially numbered and matched with the supplier's credit note when it is received. An IT system could produce a regular exception report of unmatched debit notes for follow up by an employee.

Tests of control

Here are some suggested tests of control.

- The auditor should look for evidence that purchase invoices are matched against purchase orders. Evidence may be provided by a signature or initials on the purchase invoice of the individual making the check or by checking references on screen.
- There should be evidence that statements from suppliers are checked and approved. Again, evidence may be provided by a signature or initials on statements of the individual making the check.
- The auditor should look for documentary evidence of control account reconciliations.
- The auditor should be able to check a list of sequentially-numbered debit notes, cross-referenced to a supplier's credit note.

The payroll system

- Elements of the payroll system
- Calculating gross wages and salaries
- The calculation of tax and other deductions
- Recording wages and salaries payable in the accounts
- Payment of wages and salaries

4 The payroll system

4.1 Elements of the payroll system

A similar approach can be taken to designing tests of controls in the payroll system. Elements of the payroll system may be classified as follows:

- Calculating gross wages and salaries
- Recording wages and salaries payable in the accounts
- The calculation of tax and other deductions from wages and salaries
- The payment of wages and salaries.

Some control objectives, principal controls and tests of control are suggested below for each element of the payroll transaction cycle. However, they are now presented in tabular form, for ease of reading.

4.2 Calculating gross wages and salaries

Examples of control objectives	Examples of principal controls	Tests of control
Wages and salaries should not be paid to individuals who are not employees, for example to former employees who have now left employment.	There should be a segregation of duties: the individual responsible for preparing wages and salaries should not be the person who actually pays them.	The auditor can check that the segregation of duties does exist.
Salaries should be calculated correctly.	There should be formal authorisation of new employees.	Documentation for authorising new employees and putting them on the payroll file (manual or computerised) should be checked.

Table continues

Examples of control objectives	Examples of principal controls	Tests of control
Employees paid time-based wages should only be paid for time they have worked.	There should be formal personnel records, giving details of each employee and his or her rate of pay, and dates of starting and leaving employment.	The payroll file should be checked.
	There should be time sheets for hourly-based employees, and these should be authorised by an appropriate supervisor. Alternatively, a clock card system might operate.	Time sheets can be checked. These should include the signature of the manager or supervisor confirming the hours worked by the individual employee. For a clock card system, the auditor will need to test the controls in operation (such as to ensure that employees cannot clock in for each other)
	A senior manager should check the total payroll cost each week or month, to make sure that the total amount does not appear excessive. In an IT system, exception reports might also be produced, for example, reporting gross wages over pre-set parameters and then followed up by management.	Authorised payroll lists should be checked. These should contain the signature or initials of the manager who checked the list. Test data could be used to check that the exception reporting system is working properly. Exception reports cold be reviewed for evidence of follow-up (e.g. annotated explanations).

4.3 The calculation of tax and other deductions

Examples of control objectives	Examples of principal controls	Tests of control
Taxation and other deductions from pay should be calculated correctly.	Payroll procedures (IT or manual) should provide for the deduction of all appropriate deductions, using up-to-date rates of tax.	The auditor can review any manual procedures for calculating deductions, and the tax rates used. In an IT system, general IT controls will be

		important to check that the system was properly developed, tested and implemented. Test data could be used and results compared to independently calculated figures.
Voluntary deductions from pay (for example, for pension contributions) should only be made with the consent of the employee.	Senior management should check the total amount of deductions each week or month.	The auditor can check that a senior manager has approved total deductions, evidenced by his or her signature on the appropriate document.
	All voluntary deductions must be authorised in writing by the employee, and this written authorisation should be kept in the payroll file.	The payroll file can be checked against the calculation of deductions in employee wages or salaries, to confirm that voluntary deductions are authorised.

4.4 Recording wages and salaries payable in the accounts

Examples of control objectives	Examples of principal controls	Tests of control
Gross pay, deductions and net pay should be properly and accurately recorded in the accounts.	The accounts are prepared from payroll data that has been approved by a senior manager.	There should be evidence that the payroll has been formally approved. (In an integrated IT system, the nominal ledger accounts will be automatically updated.)
	Accounting for payroll should be completed within a strict timescale.	There should be checks on the procedures for recording payroll and the time within which the work is done.
	There should be control accounts for payroll, with regular reconciliations between control totals and the payroll records of all individual employees.	There should be documentary evidence of control account reconciliations and review thereof.

4.5 Payment of wages and salaries

Examples of control objectives	Examples of principal controls	Tests of control
The correct amounts of net pay should be paid to employees.	When wages and salaries are paid by automated bank transfer, the list of payments should be authorised by an appropriate manager.	Authorised lists of payments can be checked.
The correct amount of deductions is paid to the appropriate authority (for example, the tax authority)	There should be formal procedures and a formal timetable for the payment of deductions, and recording payments in the accounts.	The procedures for payments of deductions and manual recording of payments in the accounts can be checked. (In an integrated IT system, the nominal ledger accounts will be automatically updated for deductions.)
Payments of net wages and salaries are made only to the proper person (the employee)	Bank statements should be used to check that payments have been properly recorded in the accounts.	Evidence of bank reconciliation checks can be obtained.
Payments are correctly recorded in the accounts.		The accounts can be checked to confirm that payrolls each week or month (total payable and total paid) are reconciled. Again, this will not be necessary in an integrated IT system, provided that the auditor is satisfied that the system is working properly, perhaps by processing a "dummy" payroll run.

Note: The suggested control objectives, controls and tests of control in the above table assume that all wages and salaries are paid by bank transfer. When payments of wages are in cash, or where casual labour is paid in cash, additional controls will be needed.

The bank and cash system

- Control objectives for the bank and cash system
- Principal controls and tests of control for bank and cash

5 The bank and cash system

5.1 Control objectives for the bank and cash system

Bank and cash is often one of the most sensitive areas of an audit, in the sense that it is the asset which is most likely to be misappropriated. However, it may not be an area of high audit risk in practice, because the client company should be aware of the potential high level of risk and should therefore set up appropriate control systems.

Auditors will be particularly interested in establishing that **all** receipts belonging to the organisation have been recorded – **completeness** is a key audit objective in the area of cash receipts.

The term 'cash' is used below to mean both notes and coins, and also money in a bank account. Many entities try to reduce the risks of misappropriation of cash (banknotes) by arranging receipts and payments through their bank.

Cash payments are also an area of potential risk. Payments might be made to unauthorised persons, or individuals might be paid more than they should be paid.

Some control objectives for cash might therefore be as follows:

- All money received is recorded.
- All money received is banked.
- All money held as cheques, notes and coins is properly safeguarded.
- All payments are properly authorised.

5.2 Principal controls and tests of control for bank and cash

Some of the principal controls for cash, and tests of those controls, are suggested below.

Control objectives	Principal controls	Tests of control
All money received is recorded	There should be segregation of duties. The handling of cash should be kept separate from other accounting functions.	Check that segregation of duties does exist.
	Controls over receipts by post There should be supervision of the opening of mail. There should be a listing of all money received. Mail and cheques should be date-stamped.	**Controls over receipts by post** Observe that mail opening and cash handling procedures are being followed. Check amounts recorded as receipts from customers against the remittance advices (document from the customer confirming the amount paid).
	Cash sales Only a restricted number of employees should be authorised to receive cash. Cash tills and till rolls should be used to record cash sales. Another person should check the actual cash received against the till roll total. Restrict the employees who are able to receive cash. If the till rolls are not produced, receipts should be given for cash receipts, and a copy of receipts retained. Receipts should be sequentially numbered.	**Cash sales** Check amounts in receipt books or on till rolls to paying-in slips, the cash book and bank statements. Check whether bankings are made daily. Check payments out of cash takings, if any. Check for evidence that till roll totals or receipts totals are checked against cash received by an authorised person.
All money received is banked	There should be daily banking if possible. The amount of cash payments received should be recorded, and subsequently checked against the amount banked.	Check the frequency of banking receipts. Check that receipts are recorded in the cash book and that the bank statement matches the cash receipts recorded on a daily basis.

Table continues

Control objectives	Principal controls	Tests of control
Proper safeguards should exist over money held	**Bank** There should be established procedures for opening new bank accounts. There should be restrictions on individuals authorised to prepare and hold cheques. There should be safe custody of cheque books. In a manual system there should be no pre-signed cheques. In an IT system there must be strong physical controls over access to pre-signed cheques, such as being kept in a safe until the next payment run and batch and control totals used over cheque numbers.	**Bank** Confirm that new bank accounts have only been opened under established procedures. Observe which individuals are involved with company cheques. Enquire as to custody of cheque books and check to see whether any cheques are blank and pre-signed. In an IT system, observe a payment run and that pre-signed cheques are removed from the safe immediately before being printed and returned immediately afterwards. Arrange for a cheque to be missed out of the run and ensure the system flags it up as missing.
	Cash Notes and coin should be kept in a secure place, such as a safe. Only a very limited number of employees should have access to the cash. Receipts of cash and payments of cash must be recorded.	**Cash** Review the nature of cash payments made. Observe cash custody procedures.
All payments should be properly authorised, made to the correct person and are properly recorded	**Cheque payments** Cheque requisition forms should be used to request payments, backed by supporting documentation. Cancellation of documentation once cheque has been prepared. There should be established authority levels	**Cheque payments** Review paid cheques for payee, date, amount and signature. Agree payments in the cheque book or BACS listing to entries in the accounting records, bank statements and supplier statements.

	for cheque signing (usually two signatures required for cheques above a certain amount). Payments must be recorded promptly. All cheques must be numbered sequentially.	Review the documents supporting requisitions for payment. Review the sequence of cheque numbers(see also above under safeguarding pre-signed cheques).

The stock system and fixed assets

- The stock system
- Fixed assets

6 The stock system and fixed assets

6.1 The stock system

Stock is often a 'material' aspect of the financial statements and can also be a relatively high risk area. Consequently, the auditor will usually want some assurance as to controls in place for stock.

The tests of control suggested below do **not** repeat tests which have been dealt with in respect of sales and purchases. The tests here focus on other aspects, primarily stock movements and security. Audit work on the valuation of stock is normally performed at the substantive testing stage and will be dealt with in a later chapter.

Control objectives	Principal controls	Tests of control
Recording stock		
Stock records should be complete, accurate and include only items belonging to the company. All stock movements should be recorded and authorised.	There should be segregation of duties (ordering goods, custody of goods, accounting for stocks). There should be proper documentation for all issues of stocks from the store. All goods received should be checked and recorded Appropriate stock records should be properly maintained.	The auditor can look for evidence that stock movements (as recorded in the stock department) agree with despatch documents and goods received documents. The auditor should look for documentation providing evidence that stock movements are properly authorised.
Physical safeguards		
Stock is protected against loss and damage.	There should be restricted access to storage areas. Regular stock counts should be performed using appropriate procedures.	The auditor should look for compliance with access restrictions. The auditor should obtain confirmation that periodic stock counts are performed, and that counts are checked against records of what stock levels should be.

Table continues

Control objectives	Principal controls	Tests of control
Valuation		
Stock should be correctly valued at the lower of cost and net realisable value.	SSAP 9 should be applied. There should be procedures for identifying obsolete and slow moving stock items.	The auditor should look for evidence of how stock valuations are reviewed, in order to apply the principles of SSAP 9.
Stock management		
Appropriate levels of stock should be held at all times.	There should be maximum and minimum stock levels for all stock items of value. There should be appropriate re-order levels and re-order quantities.	The auditor should carry out a review for excessive stock levels (possibly via exception reports in an IT system). (This check is often performed in conjunction with the stock count). The auditor should also monitor the frequency of out-of-stock situations.

6.2 Fixed assets

Control objectives	Principal controls	Tests of control
Authorisation		
All expenditure on fixed assets should be properly authorised.	Appropriate authorisation procedures should be in place. Documentation and analysis should be produced to support (capital) expenditure requests. There should be approval procedures for the payment of invoices to the suppliers of fixed assets.	Many tests of control for the purchase of fixed assets are similar to those for the purchase of stock items. The auditor should also look for documentary evidence of capital expenditure authorisations.
Recording		
All expenditure on fixed assets should be properly recorded. Expenditure should be properly analysed as capital or revenue.	Invoices must be analysed and account codes entered on the invoices. Management should review the analysis of purchased items as capital or revenue items, to ensure compliance with standard accounting practice.	The auditor should check the capital/revenue analysis of invoices. The auditor should check that entries are made in the fixed asset register.

Other issues with tests of controls

- Tests of controls in smaller entities
- An approach to examination questions on controls and tests of control

7 Other issues with tests of controls

7.1 Tests of controls in smaller entities

Control systems in smaller entities are often less sophisticated than those in larger organisations. This is largely due to a lack of resources. In particular, a proper segregation of duties is often very difficult in small entities. It is also likely in small entities that there will be extensive involvement in control activity by senior management or the entity's owner.

In the case of smaller entities, the auditor will look for the existence of 'minimum business controls'. The minimum business controls should be identified, recorded and tested, as in any other type of control system.

The auditor is unlikely to be able to use the controls existing in a small entity as a basis for using a systems-based approach to the audit; therefore a large amount of substantive testing is likely to be adopted. However, the auditor may be able to rely on the controls which are in place as a means of gaining assurance on certain aspects of the audit, for example on the completeness of the accounting records.

7.2 An approach to examination questions on controls and tests of control

Most of this chapter has presented lists of control objectives, internal controls and tests of control, for different aspects of business and accounting operations. You do not have to learn all these lists, because each accounting system and each business is different. Their control objectives and appropriate controls also differ.

What you need to be able to do in the examination is to apply general principles to any particular system or business described in an examination question.

The approach that we recommend is the approach illustrated in this chapter.

- Consider the things that could go wrong with the system. This should give you **control objectives**.
- Think of **controls** which would help to prevent or detect the problem. You may be able to base these on some of the examples given in this chapter. Alternatively, you may find it helpful to use the list of control activities from ISA 315 and their sub-types (performance reviews (including management controls), application controls (including authorisation, arithmetic and accounting controls), general IT controls, physical controls and segregation of duties).

- Design audit procedures to **test** the operation of the control. In doing this you may find it helpful to think of the key audit testing procedures – inspection, observation, enquiry and computation and to consider the use of test data.

Example

Your audit client operates a chain of fast-food restaurants. Six types of standard meals are available and are heated when customers place their orders. The meals are ordered weekly by the restaurant managers from the distribution centre at head office. At the end of each week, unused meals from the previous week are sent back to the distribution centre for disposal.

Required

List the controls which your client should have in operation to prevent losses to the entity as a result of the above system.

Answer

- Managers should be required to produce a monthly reconciliation of meals bought, meals sold and meals returned to head office.
- Meals sold per this reconciliation should be agreed to the monthly sales figure (a difference could indicate theft).
- Where returns are above a pre-determined level, management at head office should investigate to identify over-ordering or a downturn in demand.
- Where returns are very low, management at head office should investigate to ensure that customers have not been turned away due to a lack of stock.
- Strict physical controls should operate to ensure that stock is not damaged in transit (e.g. refrigerated lorries) or once at the branch (e.g. sufficient, properly working refrigerators).
- Authorisation limits should be set for the number of meals any branch can order (based on budgets and past usage).
- Head office should carry out surprise stock counts at branches.

As an alternative, the examiner might require you to identify the risks to which a business might be exposed as a result of poor internal controls. These risks are the same as the control objectives not being met (for example, for sales, the risk that not all goods despatched are invoiced). However, you could also be asked to set out the **consequences of those risks** and suggest **controls** which would address them.

Example

An entity selling goods on credit terms is exposed to the risk of invoicing errors.

Required

Set out the possible consequences of the above risk and suggest suitable internal controls which could be implemented to address the above risk.

a

Answer

Possible consequences

- Sales and debtors will be misstated.
- Customer goodwill may be lost if they are charged too high a price (especially if this happens repeatedly).
- The time taken to correct the errors will result in delays in the payment of invoices by customers and could lead to cash flow problems. (If customers have been undercharged the difference may never be recovered.)
- If process charged or quantities entered are too low goods could be despatched to customers who would have been over their credit limits if the correct price had been charged. Again, this may result in the non-recovery of debts.

Internal controls to address

- Invoice checked for accuracy with respect to despatch note details, price list and any discounts agreed with that customer (or generally available for bulk purchases) and casts checked.
- Or, in an IT system, invoice produced automatically with strong physical controls over master files and good general IT controls).
- Data entry edit controls (e.g. field and range checks) if invoices are raised individually but then put onto an IT system.
- Independent authorisation of amendments to customer details and price lists.
- Amendments to standing data printed out and reviewed.

e

Example

Using the list of internal controls in the example immediately above, set out the audit procedures you could use to test the operation of each of those controls.

a

Answer

- Select a sample of sales invoices, check casts and agree to details per despatch note, master price list and bulk/customer specific discounts.
- Input a sample of dummy despatch notes and ensure invoice generated by the system is accurate.
- Input a sample of dummy sales invoices, with prices/amounts outside the preset parameters and with incomplete files to ensure these are rejected by the system.
- Review amendment forms for customer details or prices and ensure properly authorised.
- Review print outs of standing data amendments for evidence of review.

CHAPTER 10

Introduction to substantive testing

Contents

The role of substantive testing

- The nature of substantive testing
- Financial statement assertions
- Devising substantive tests
- Use of audit software
- Methods of obtaining audit evidence
- Directional testing
- The significance of the audit of balance sheet items

1 The role of substantive testing

1.1 The nature of substantive testing

Previous chapters have dealt with the planning stage of the audit and with the auditor's work on understanding, evaluating and testing the accounting system and control systems in place.

In accordance with ISA 330, the auditor will also do some substantive testing. He may decide, as a result of his risk assessment, to adopt a systems-based audit approach to the audit. On the other hand, his assessment may lead him to adopt a transactions-based approach (a wholly substantive approach). No matter which approach he takes, systems-based or transactions-based, he will do some substantive testing.

Substantive tests are audit procedures performed to detect material misstatements in the figures reported in the financial statements.

- They are designed to generate evidence about the **financial statement assertions** (discussed in a previous chapter, as set out in ISA 500).
- They include:
  - **tests of detail** on the accuracy of transactions, accounting balances and disclosures, and
  - **analytical procedures**.

ISA 330 also requires that, whatever level of substantive procedures are carried out, the auditor must carry out the following procedures:

- Agree or reconcile the financial statements to the underlying accounting records.
- Examine material journal entries.
- Examine other adjustments made during the course of preparing the financial statements.

1.2 Financial statement assertions

Evidence is obtained by the auditor to enable him to form an opinion and prepare an audit report on the financial statements. In order to do this, the auditor has to look for evidence that supports the financial statement assertions. These are the assertions that are made in the financial statements by the directors of the company.

These assertions have been described in an earlier chapter, but it is important that you should be able to recognise and understand them.

Financial statement assertions fall into seven categories. Some relate to assets and liabilities (balances); others relate to transactions or disclosures in the notes to the financial statements.

The seven categories are as follows:

C Completeness
O Occurrence
M Measurement
P Presentation and disclosure
E Existence
R Rights and obligations
C Carrying value (valuation)

Completeness

In preparing their financial statements, the directors of a company are making the assertion that the financial statements are complete. No assets and liabilities, transactions or events have been omitted that should be included.

The assertion of completeness is therefore an assertion that **there is no understatement** of amounts in the financial statements.

Occurrence

Occurrence is the assertion that **transactions** included in the financial statements did actually occur during the financial period. The assertion of occurrence:

- relates to transactions, rather than assets and liabilities, and
- is an assertion that **there is no overstatement** of the amount of transactions reported in the financial statements.

Measurement

This is the assertion that transactions and events are recorded at their correct amount for the financial period; in other words their amount has been measured correctly.

This assertion relates to **transactions** in the profit and loss account, particularly the measurement of sales, purchases and other expenses.

Presentation and disclosure

The assertion relating to presentation and disclosure is that everything has been presented and disclosed in accordance with the relevant legislation and accounting standards.

Existence

This is the assertion that the assets and liabilities reported in the balance sheet did exist at the balance sheet date. The assertion of existence:

- relates to **assets and liabilities**, rather than transactions, and
- is an assertion that **there is no overstatement** of assets and liabilities in the balance sheet.

This assertion of existence is extremely important, and a large part of an audit is directed towards obtaining evidence that this assertion is correct.

Rights and obligations

The assertion of rights and obligations also relates to **assets and liabilities**.

- The reporting entity asserts that it has the rights to the assets reported in the balance sheet. These are often the legal right of ownership, but they could be other rights. (Leased assets, for example, are not legally owned by the lessee, but the lessee has economic rights over the leased asset.) For example, the auditor may need to check the legal ownership of stock that is held by a company: the company may have the legal title to the stock; on the other hand, the legal ownership may still belong to the supplier, who has provided the items of stock on a 'sale or return' basis.
- The reporting entity also asserts that it has obligations for the liabilities reported in the balance sheet.

Carrying amount (valuation)

This is the assertion that assets and liabilities are reported at an appropriate carrying amount or valuation in the balance sheet as at the balance sheet date. In other words, the assets and liabilities have been valued at their appropriate value.

For stock, the carrying amount is the lower of cost or net realisable value, where 'cost' has been measured using an appropriate costing method.

For tangible fixed assets valued by the cost method, the appropriate carrying amount is original cost, less accumulated depreciation and accumulated impairment losses.

1.3 Devising substantive tests

The following chapters describe a variety of substantive tests that an auditor might carry out. In your examination, you might be asked to suggest what substantive tests ought to be carried out in a particular situation. Each accounting system and business is different, and substantive tests that might be appropriate in one situation would be inappropriate in another. What you need to be able to do in the examination is apply general principles of substantive testing to the particular system or business described in the question.

One possible approach to devising substantive tests is as follows:

- **What am I being asked to test?** Start by asking what it is that you should be trying to test, and obtain evidence about. Usually you will be asked to test for any misstatement, but sometimes you might be asked to test only for:
  - overstatement (occurrence of transactions or existence of assets or liabilities) or
  - understatement (completeness), or
  - one particular aspect of an item (for example, the carrying value/valuation of an asset).

  To decide what you are testing for, think about the financial statement assertions. Which of these do you want to test?
- **How does the system operate and what documents exist?** You should think about the specific system described in the examination question, and write down some ideas at this stage.
- **What special tests are used for this area?** There may be some audit tests that are particularly relevant to the system described in the question. Certain balance sheet items have specific tests, such as a year-end stock count for stock (that the auditor can attend) or 'direct confirmation' as a method of verifying debtors' balances.
- **What tests can I think of?** To devise substantive tests, you should think about what method or methods are appropriate for gathering the evidence you are looking for. For example, in an IT system, the auditor will need to consider the use of audit software (see below).

1.4 Use of audit software

In a previous chapter, the use of computer-assisted audit techniques (CAATs) was introduced. There are two types of CAATs: test data and audit software. Test data is primarily used in the testing of controls. **Audit software** is primarily used for **substantive testing**.

Audit software is computer programs used by the auditor to extract information from a computer-based information system, for use in the audit. The main types of audit software include:

- interrogation programs, to access the client's files and records and extract data for auditing
- interactive software, for use in interrogation of on-line IT systems
- 'resident code' or 'embedded' software, to monitor and review transactions as they are being processed by the client's programs. This type of software is called 'embedded audit facilities'.

e

Examples of the use of audit software

Audit software is used to extract and analyse information in the entity's IT systems for use in the audit work. Here are some examples:

- Account analysis. Audit software may be used to interrogate the client's data files for the general ledger, and extract from the files all items above £5,000 in the repairs expense account.
- Preparing an aged debtors list, if these are not already produced by the client as a matter of operational routine. The audit software can interrogate the trade debtors file, and produce a list and analysis in date order of unpaid invoices.
- Calculating ratios and making comparisons. Audit software can be used to assist the auditor with analytical procedures (which are described later in this chapter).

e

Example

You have been put in charge of the audit of stock at Kitchen Magic, a wholesaler of kitchen goods. Kitchen Magic keeps a permanent record of stock on its IT system and carries out a rolling programme of stock counts to check that the record on the system is reflected by actual goods held. The year-end stock will be listed for you, showing for each product: date of last purchase, date of last sale, cost, selling price, quantity and year-end valuation. This schedule will be available on the last day of the year.

Required

List the tests which could be performed by audit software which will assist you in your audit of stock. You will need to use your knowledge of SSAP9 *Stocks and long-term contracts* from Paper F3.

a

Answer

- Cast the year-end stock schedule.
- List out all items over a pre-set amount (at least the materiality threshold) (for subsequent physical verification).
- For each item on the schedule multiply the lower of cost and selling price x quantity and list out any items where this figure does not agree to the year-end valuation.
- Compare prices to those on the current sales price master file.
- List out any items where the date of the last purchase was more than, say, one month ago (as this may indicate that the product is obsolete/damaged/no longer in vogue and may need to be written down).
- List out any items where the date of the last sale was more than, say, one month ago (as, again, this may indicate that the product is obsolete/no longer in vogue and may need to be written down).
- List out any items which do not appear on the post year-end sales listing for the first, say, month of the year (again, may indicate that a provision is needed).

Tutorial note: If these tests were being carried out manually then only a sample would be checked. Due to the speed of computer software it is feasible to check all items.

Embedded audit facilities

Embedded audit facilities may also be called 'resident audit software' or an 'integrated audit module'. It is audit software that is built into the client's IT system, either temporarily or permanently.

The purpose of embedded audit facilities is to allow the audit to carry out tests at the time that transactions are being processed, in 'real time'.

This can be very useful for the audit of online systems where:

- data is continually processed and master files are being continually updated, and/or
- it is difficult, if not impossible, for the system to provide a satisfactory audit trail for following transactions through the system.

An embedded audit facility may also print out details of the transactions it has monitored, or copy them to a computer file, so that the auditor can study the transactions.

1.5 Methods of obtaining audit evidence

The methods of obtaining audit evidence have been described in an earlier chapter. It is important that you should know what they are, and be familiar with them. They are:

- **Inspection**. Obtain evidence about an item by going to look at it. For example, an auditor can obtain evidence about the existence of tangible fixed assets by going to look at them.
- **Observation**. The auditor can obtain evidence by watching a procedure and seeing how it is carried out.
- **Computation**. Obtain evidence by carrying out numerical checks.
- **Enquiry**. Evidence can be obtained by asking questions. For example, evidence about the existence of trade debtors can be obtained by asking customers on the list of trade debtors to confirm that they do owe the amount of money that the client company asserts.
- **Analytical procedures**. These are described in more detail later in this chapter.

Example

Continuing with the example above concerning the audit of year-end stock at Kitchen Goods.

Required

Describe a test using each of the above procedures (with the exception of analytical procedures).

Answer

Inspection: Trace items from the year-end stock schedule to the actual goods.

Observation: Observe counting of stock during the year to gain evidence as to the accuracy of the stock records.

Computation: Use audit software to cast the year-end stock schedule.

Enquiry: Enquire of management as to the need for a year-end stock provision.

How reliable is audit evidence?

To reach an opinion about the financial statements, the auditor needs to obtain sufficient, appropriate audit evidence.

This has already been explained in the context of audit evidence and the auditor's assessment of the internal controls and their effectiveness. Where inherent risk and control risk are high, the auditor needs more evidence from substantive testing, to reduce the detection risk.

But how reliable is the evidence obtained from substantive testing? The following general guidelines may be useful:

- Evidence obtained from sources outside the client company ('external sources') is more reliable than evidence obtained from the client company's own records. For example, an auditor may receive written confirmation from a customer of the client that the customer is a trade debtor owing a stated amount of money. This is more reliable than evidence in the form of a copy of the invoice in the files of the client company.
- Evidence obtained from the client company's own records is more reliable when the internal control systems of the client company operate effectively.
- Evidence obtained by the auditors themselves, for example through inspection and analytical procedures, is more reliable than evidence obtained from the client company's staff or records.
- Documentary evidence is more reliable than evidence obtained orally (for example as answers to questions).

These are guidelines about the reliability of audit evidence, not rules. An auditor must use his judgement in deciding whether the evidence he has obtained is sufficient and appropriate, so that it can be treated as reliable. Where evidence is not sufficient or appropriate, the auditor should look for more evidence; otherwise, his eventual audit opinion will be affected.

Reliability of documentary evidence

It follows that the reliability of documentary evidence depends on its source.

- The least reliable documentary evidence is documents held within the client company that the client has created itself, such as sales invoices.
- Documentary evidence is more reliable when it is held within the client company but has been created by an external entity, such as suppliers' invoices or a bank statement.

- The most reliable documentary evidence is a document obtained from an external entity and held by the auditor. An example is a written confirmation by a customer of the client about the amount of money that it owes.

1.6 Directional testing

With substantive testing, the auditor is normally interested in detecting two main types of misstatement:

- **errors** which may result in **either under or overstatement** of figures
- **omissions,** which result in **understatement**.

Understatement is much more difficult to detect than overstatement. This is because when he is looking for under-statement of items in the financial statements, the auditor is trying to audit something that isn't there – he is checking for **completeness**. With over-statement, he is checking that what is there is valid, and this is a check for **existence** or **occurrence**.

Directional testing is used by the auditor to detect both over and understatements. This technique is based on double entry principles.

The basic principle of directional testing takes as a starting point that the trial balance of the client entity balances, and that therefore the total of debit balances in the general ledger equals the total of credit balances. Finding one material error in the balances means that there must also be at least one other error somewhere in the balances.

The following conclusions can therefore be made when the auditor finds an error with substantive testing:

- If the auditor finds, say, an overstatement of a debit entry, there must also be a corresponding understatement of another debit entry or an overstatement of a credit entry. (Otherwise, the trial balance totals of debits and credits would not be equal.)
- Similarly, if the auditor finds an understatement of a credit balance for one item, there must be either an overstatement of another credit balance or an understatement of a debit balance.

This approach also allows the auditor to work in a cost-effective and efficient way. Using directional testing:

- **the auditor tests debit items (assets and expenses) for overstatement only**
- **he tests credit items (liabilities, income and equity) for understatement only**.

For directional testing to be effective, it is important that the auditor selects the correct starting point for the test.

- If the auditor is carrying out tests to detect **overstatement**, the starting point should be the figures **in the accounting records**.
- If the auditor is carrying out tests to detect **understatement**, the starting point should be a source **outside the accounting records**.

Examples

Testing trade debtors balances for overstatement/existence

A starting point for testing will be the entity's list of debtors balances (the list of customers owing money as at the balance sheet date). The auditor wants to check that these debtor balances do in fact exist. One way of doing this is to write directly to customers on the list asking them to confirm the amount that they owe the entity.

Alternatively, if the auditor is checking documentation within the client entity, he can take a sample of debtor balances from the list of balances, and trace their existence back through the accounting records, from sales ledger to sales day book to invoice.

Testing trade creditors balances for understatement/completeness

To test creditors for completeness, there is no point in taking as a starting point the entity's list of creditors balances – because this may not be complete, and the auditor is testing for completeness.

Instead the auditor may write to regular suppliers who might possibly be year-end creditors, based on the total amount of purchases from the supplier during the year. If the supplier is not on the list of trade creditors, or is listed as a creditor for only a small amount, the auditor can ask the supplier to confirm this fact. This is often referred to as testing the '**reciprocal population**'.

Alternatively, if the auditor is checking documentation within the client entity, he may take as a starting point a sample of documents indicating that goods have been purchased or received – such as a sample of goods received notes – and then trace the purchase through the system from purchase invoice to purchases day book to creditors ledger.

1.7 The significance of the audit of balance sheet items

The auditor will usually pay more attention to the balance sheet than to the profit and loss account. The reason for this is that if the current balance sheet is 'correct' and if the previous balance sheet was correct, then the profit figure linking the two balance sheets must also be correct.

The emphasis of the balance sheet audit will be on the verification of assets and liabilities, rather than the verification of equity. If assets and liabilities are correctly stated, equity (assets minus liabilities) will also be correctly stated.

This is all a question of emphasis – the auditor will not ignore the profit and loss account or equity, but these items will generally receive a lower level of audit attention (and audit time and resources) than assets and liabilities.

The auditor will carry out tests to gain evidence on all the relevant financial statement assertions, but to make the audit as efficient as possible, the emphasis of the audit will be focused as follows:

- Assets:
  - existence
  - rights and obligations (ownership) and
  - carrying value (valuation)
- Liabilities:
  - completeness and
  - carrying value (valuation).

Analytical procedures: ISA 520

- Using analytical procedures
- The nature of analytical procedures
- Analytical procedures in substantive testing
- Investigation of fluctuations and relationships
- Common ratios

2 Analytical procedures: ISA 520

2.1 Using analytical procedures

Analytical procedures were referred to earlier as one of the procedures for generating audit evidence.

ISA 520 *Analytical procedures* **requires** the auditor to apply analytical procedures at two stages of the audit:

- the planning stage (to identify areas of high audit risk), and
- the overall review stage (to assess the reasonableness of the reported figures).

In addition, the auditor **may** also use analytical procedures as a substantive audit testing procedure.

2.2 The nature of analytical procedures

Analytical procedures consist of analysing financial and non-financial information in financial statements, to identify relationships and trends. Much of the analysis consists of measuring ratios, and comparing the ratios obtained from the current year's financial results with:

- expected ratios, and
- ratios from previous financial periods.

If key ratios are close to what they are expected to be, the auditor may take this as evidence that the relevant balances or transaction amounts are reliable and 'accurate'. If a ratio is very different from what is expected, the auditor should investigate the reason for the variation. There may be a good reason why a ratio differs from its expected value. On the other hand, a ratio might have an unusual value because there is a misstatement in the financial statements.

Comparisons

The essential feature of analytical procedures in auditing is 'comparison'. The auditor will calculate key relationships between figures (non-financial figures as well as financial figures) and then compare the results with:

- prior periods (to establish patterns and trends)
- expected results (based on prior periods or budgets and forecasts)
- industry average results (from available financial information services)
- results for other comparable parts of the business (for example, other divisions or branches of the same entity).

Once the calculations have been performed, the auditor will then examine them for unexpected or unusual relationships. The auditor will then make enquiries of management in order to establish explanations for the relationships revealed.

Many of the accounting ratios used in analytical procedures may be familiar to you already from your other studies. If you have not as yet studied ratios then some common ratios are set out for you below. You should ensure you are familiar with these as you could be required to both **compute and interpret** key ratios in the exam.

Remember that ratio analysis is subject to limitations:

- Its usefulness depends on the quality of the underlying financial information. It is usual for the auditor to calculate financial ratios from the client's management accounts, which are more detailed than financial statements and can provide a source of more and better information.
- For comparison purposes, the information must be calculated on a consistent basis.
- The two figures used to calculate a ratio must be logically related.
- The auditor needs to understand the client's business, so that he is able to understand the potential significance of ratios, or reasons for differences (for example, differences between one year and the next).

Examples

Here are just a few of the ratios that an auditor might use. More are set out at the end of this section.

Payroll costs

Ratios can be used to assess whether the total recorded amount for payroll costs appear to be reasonable.

- One way of doing this is to look at the total payroll costs each month, and in each month of previous years. Changes in the total payroll cost should be reasonable, allowing for increases in wages and salaries, and for changes in the composition of the work force, and for leavers and starters in the period. Monthly payroll costs should be consistent with each other and reasonable.
- Another way of assessing payroll costs would be to measure the average monthly or annual pay per employee, and compare this with other months or previous years. Any unexpected changes should be investigated.

Other expenses

Another simple ratio that can be useful for an auditor is the ratio of expenses to annual sales income. Unusual changes in any ratio, such as the ratio of cost of sales to sales (and so gross profit to sales) should be investigated. Similarly, ratios of distribution costs, selling costs and administration costs to sales can also be measured and compared.

Working capital ratios

Working capital ratios, such as days' sales outstanding and the average stock turnover period, can be used to assess whether the total balance for trade debtors or stock is reasonable (or whether the figures for sales income and purchases appear reasonable).

2.3 Analytical procedures in substantive testing

ISA 520 requires auditors to decide whether the use of analytical procedures in substantive testing, as a means of reducing detection risk, will be:

- effective (Will it work?), and
- efficient (Is it cost-effective?)

In making a decision on the use of analytical procedures as a substantive testing technique ISA 520 requires the auditor to consider the following matters:

- The objective of the audit testing.
- The availability of relevant information.
- The reliability of that information as audit evidence, including the source of the information.
- The comparability of the information.
- The auditor's knowledge gained from previous audits.

The auditor will normally use analytical procedures to obtain **supplementary** audit evidence. It would not normally be appropriate to base the audit conclusion on analytical procedures alone. Analytical procedures are therefore designed to provide evidence that supports (or possibly contradicts) the outcome of other, more specific, audit testing procedures.

2.4 Investigation of fluctuations and relationships

The calculations performed in analytical procedures are only a part of the process. They are used to indicate areas where further audit work may be required.

If, for example, the gross profit percentage this year is the same as in previous years (and the auditor expected this to be the case), no further investigation should be necessary.

However, if the gross profit percentage is the same as in previous years, but the auditor knows that there have been significant changes in the nature of the business that should affect the gross profit percentage, he will need to make further enquiries.

These enquiries following analytical procedures will involve:

- using other audit evidence to help explain the ratios obtained from analytical procedures, and their unexpected and unusual value
- asking management for explanations of the unusual/unexpected ratios. Since explanations from management are being obtained as audit evidence, and oral evidence is not particularly reliable, they should be confirmed by further audit work.

Example

You are currently planning the audit of Numero for the year ended 31st December 20X3. You are aware that revenue was budgeted to fall by 20% from last year. The following information has been made available to you:

Sales £400,000 (20X2 £500,000)

Cost of sales £300,000 (20X2 £300,000)

Expenses £20,000 (20X2 £50,000)

Trade debtors £60,000 (20X2 £30,000)

Required

Explain which of the above amounts you believe might need further investigation and why.

Answer

Cost of sales has remained constant and yet sales have fallen by the anticipated 20%. Cost of sales would generally be expected to move in line with sales. *(Tutorial note: An alternative comment would be that the gross profit percentage has fallen from 40% to 25%.)*

Expenses have increased by 60%. This could be due to the fall in sales or it could indicate a misallocation between cost of sales and expenses.

Trade debtors days have increased from 22 days to 55 days. This may indicate a change in credit terms (to attract new/large customers in the light of falling sales) or that not all debts are recoverable and that a write-down is needed.

2.5 Common ratios

Profitability ratios

$$\text{ROCE} = \frac{\text{Profit before interest and taxation}}{\text{Share capital and reserves + Long - term debt capital}} \times 100\%$$

$$\text{Profit/sales ratio} = \frac{\text{Proft}}{\text{Sales}} \times 100\%$$

This could be calculated as a **net profit ratio** or a **gross profit ratio** (commonly referred to as the "gross profit percentage).

$$\text{Asset turnover ratio} = \frac{\text{Sales}}{\text{Share capital and reserves + Long - term debt capital}}$$

Working capital efficiency ratios

$$\text{Average days to collect} = \frac{\text{Trade debtors}}{\text{Sales}} \times 365 \text{ days}$$

$$\text{Inventory turnover} = \frac{\text{Stock}}{\text{Cost of sales}} \times 365 \text{ days}$$

$$\text{Average time to pay} = \frac{\text{Trade creditors}}{\text{Cost of purchases}} \times 365 \text{ days}$$

Liquidity ratios

$$\text{Current ratio} = \frac{\text{Current assets}}{\text{Current liabilities}}$$

$$\text{Quick ratio} = \frac{\text{Current assets excluding stock}}{\text{Current liabilities}}$$

Debt ratios

$$\text{Gearing} = \frac{\text{Long - term debt}}{\text{Share capital and reserves}} \times 100\%$$

$$\text{Interest cover} = \frac{\text{Profit before interest and tax}}{\text{Interest charges in the year}}$$

Investor ratios

$$\text{Earnings per share} = \frac{\text{Profits attributable to ordinary shareholders}}{\text{No. of shares}}$$

$$\text{P/E ratio} = \frac{\text{Current market price per share}}{\text{Earnings per share}}$$

$$\text{Dividend yield} = \frac{\text{Dividend per share}}{\text{Current market price per share}} \times 100\%$$

$$\text{Dividend cover} = \frac{\text{Earnings per share}}{\text{Dividend per share}} \text{ or } \frac{\text{Profit before dividends}}{\text{Dividends}}$$

The audit of accounting estimates: ISA 540

- The nature of accounting estimates and the audit problem
- ISA 540: Audit of accounting estimates

3 The audit of accounting estimates: ISA 540

3.1 The nature of accounting estimates and the audit problem

In the financial statements, estimated figures are used in situations where it is not practical or not possible to obtain a more precise measurement of an item. ISA 540 defines an audit estimate as: 'an approximation of the amount of an item in the absence of a precise means of measurement.' Accruals, prepayments and depreciation are all examples of areas where estimates are widely used. Other examples are the estimation of deferred tax, the estimate of losses or profits on long-term construction contracts, and provisions for the settlement of unfinished legal disputes.

Estimates are made for the financial statements by the management of the entity, using their judgement. The audit problem is therefore fairly clear. How does the auditor satisfy himself that the estimates made by management for inclusion in the financial statements are reasonable? The audit risk can be high.

3.2 ISA 540: Audit of accounting estimates

ISA 540 *Audit of accounting estimates* requires that auditors should obtain sufficient, appropriate audit evidence relating to accounting estimates.

The ISA gives the following examples of accounting estimates:

- Accrued revenue
- Provisions for claims under law suits
- Losses on construction contracts
- Depreciation
- Write down of current assets to estimated realisable value
- Provisions for warranty claims.

Audit evidence relating to such estimates is often of relatively poor quality, because of the nature of the items involved. This means that the auditor will require a higher volume of this lower quality evidence, particularly where the estimated item may be material or the audit risk is relatively high.

Audit work on accounting estimates (either during audit planning and the review of systems and internal controls, or at the stage of substantive testing) may include the following.

- Identify the company's procedures for establishing estimated amounts for the financial statements.
- Review and test the operation of these procedures.
- The auditor should consider preparing his own estimates or obtaining estimates from independent outsiders, and he should compare these 'independent' estimates with those by the client. If the differences are material, he should seek explanations for the material differences.
- Review events after the balance sheet date. Events since the balance sheet date may help to confirm the reasonableness of the estimates made at the balance sheet date.
- Consider using analytical procedures as a source of evidence on estimated amounts.

Opening balances and prior period comparatives: ISAs 510 and 710

- Auditing a client's financial statements for the first time
- ISA 510: Initial engagements – opening balance and continuing engagements – opening balances
- ISA 710: Comparatives

4 Opening balances and prior period comparatives: ISAs 510 and 710

4.1 Auditing a client's financial statements for the first time

When an audit firm has been auditing the financial statements of a client for a number of years, the auditor will become familiar with the client's systems and controls and will build up an audit file for the client. He will also have audited the previous year's financial statements, and will have given an audit opinion on the financial position of the client entity as at the end of the period.

Since the auditor will have audited the previous year's financial statements, he should therefore have obtained sufficient and appropriate evidence of the balances on the client's accounts at the beginning of the next financial period.

A different situation arises when an audit firm is carrying out an audit of a client for the first time.

For example, an auditor may be appointed to carry out his first audit of the financial statements for the year to 31st December 20X6. To do this, the auditor cannot ignore the opening balance sheet, as at 31st December 20X5.

- The figures in the closing balance sheet for the previous period will be presented as prior period comparative figures in the 20X6 financial statements. The new auditor is therefore giving an audit opinion on published financial statements that include the previous year's closing balances.
- Errors in the opening balances may affect the figures for the current financial period. For example, if opening stock is misstated and is overvalued, the cost of sales in the current period may also be misstated (too high).

4.2 ISA 510: Initial engagements – opening balances and continuing engagements – opening balances

ISA 510 provides guidance on the auditor's responsibilities in this area where:

- the auditor is performing the audit for the first time, and
- another auditor has audited the financial statements for the previous period.

In these circumstances, the auditor should obtain audit evidence about the opening balances. He should obtain sufficient audit evidence to be able to conclude that:

- the opening balances do not include misstatements that materially affect the current period's financial statements
- opening balances have been brought forward correctly into the current period
- accounting policies have been consistently applied in the two periods.

Audit procedures to reach a conclusion on these objectives may include the following:

- A review of the audit report on the financial statements for the previous period. This may involve a review of the audit files of the previous auditor. (Permission should be obtained from the audit client and the previous auditor, whose files they are). If the opinion in this previous audit report was that the financial statements did not give a true and fair view, further investigation will be required.
- A review of the accounting policies adopted, to confirm consistency between the previous period and the current period.
- The auditor should carry out a detailed review of the opening balances, because any misstatement in them may have a material effect on the figures for the current financial period.
- Using information from the current financial period to substantiate some of the opening balance sheet figures. For example, cash received from customers in the current period gives evidence of the existence of a debtor at the opening balance sheet date.

As usual, the auditor will need to draw conclusions and make a judgement from the evidence he obtains. These conclusions will need to be considered together with the results of all of the other audit work carried out, in order to reach an opinion and prepare his audit report.

4.3 ISA 710: Comparatives

ISA 710 *Comparatives* also relates to a similar area of the audit work. It deals with audit work on corresponding amounts and other information for the preceding financial reporting period. The considerations in ISA 710 apply to all comparative figures, whereas ISA 510 focuses specifically on opening balances (comparative balance sheet figures).

Audit procedures carried out on comparative figures are significantly less than those carried out on the current year figures. They are normally limited to ensuring that comparative figures have been:

- correctly reported, and
- appropriately classified.

This involves the auditor evaluating whether:

- accounting policies have been consistently applied in the two periods
- comparative figures agree with the previous period.

This task should not present any problems where the auditor:

- also audited the client's financial statements in the previous financial period, and
- issued an audit report on those financial statements stating that they showed a true and fair view.

If he did not audit the prior period financial statements, then he should follow the guidance set out in ISA 510 (see above). If the prior period financial statements were not audited at all, the auditor should state this fact in his report.

If the auditor did **not** issue a **clean** audit report for the previous financial period (if he was not able to say that the financial statements showed a true and fair view) and if the problem remains unresolved, then he will need to **modify** this year's audit report. Even if the matter was resolved in the current financial year, the auditor may need to add an **'emphasis of matter paragraph'** to this year's audit report. These terms are explained in a later chapter.

CHAPTER 11

Substantive testing: fixed assets

Contents

Tangible fixed assets

- Tangible fixed assets: the information subject to audit
- Principal internal controls
- Substantive testing procedures for tangible fixed assets
- Substantive testing procedures – additions and disposals

1 Tangible fixed assets

1.1 Tangible fixed assets: the information subject to audit

Before looking at substantive tests for tangible fixed assets, it may be useful to remind yourself of the information about these assets that is presented in the financial statements.

The figures in the balance sheet itself are supplemented by a note to the accounts, which may be presented as follows:

	Land and buildings	Plant, equipment, fixtures and fittings and motor vehicles	Total
	£	£	£
Cost			
At 31st December 20X6	X	X	X
Additions	X	X	X
Acquisitions through business combinations	X	X	X
Classified as held for sale	(X)	(X)	(X)
Disposals	(X)	(X)	(X)
At 31st December 20X7	X	X	X
Accumulated depreciation and impairment losses			
At 31st December 20X6	X	X	X
Depreciation charge for the year	X	X	X
Classified as held for sale	(X)	(X)	(X)
Disposals	(X)	(X)	(X)
Impairment losses	X	X	X
Reversal of impairment losses	(X)	(X)	(X)
At 31st December 20X7	X	X	X
Net carrying value			
At 31st December 20X6	X	X	X
At 31st December 20X7	X	X	X

When tangible fixed assets are included in the balance sheet at a valuation, a note should disclose:

- the basis used to revalue the assets
- the date when the assets were revalued
- whether an independent valuer was involved in the revaluation, and
- the nature of any cost index that was used as a basis for calculating replacement cost
- the carrying amount of each class of assets that would have been reported if the assets had been reported using the cost method (and so if the assets had been valued at cost minus accumulated depreciation)
- the revaluation surplus, and any movements in this surplus during the financial period.

In addition, a note should disclose the basis used for the depreciation of each class of assets.

When assets are disposed of, the gain or loss on disposal is the difference between the proceeds from the disposal and the carrying value (net book value) of the asset at the date of disposal.

When fixed assets are a significant item in the balance sheet of a company, the disclosures relating to them are therefore both extensive and of some significance in terms of obtaining audit evidence.

1.2 Principal internal controls

Although they are not a part of substantive testing, it is useful to remember the key internal controls that normally should apply to tangible fixed assets.

- An accurate and up-to-date fixed asset register should be maintained, showing the tangible fixed assets of the entity. This register should help the auditor to establish that all tangible fixed assets have been recorded in the financial statements (completeness).
- There should be formal authorisation procedures in respect of additions and disposals.
- There should be suitable physical controls over fixed assets: these should provide for both physical security and proper maintenance of the assets.
- There should be a regular management review of depreciation rates, asset lives and residual values.

1.3 Substantive testing procedures for tangible fixed assets

The substantive tests used by an auditor for tangible fixed assets will be designed to obtain sufficient and appropriate evidence about the assertions in the financial statements with regard to these assets. The tests will therefore be directed mainly to:

- completeness (no under-statement)
- existence (no overstatement)

- carrying amount or valuation and
- rights and obligations.

Possible tests to obtain this evidence are listed below.

Completeness

- Obtain or prepare a schedule of tangible fixed assets, showing cost or valuation, depreciation and net book value.
- Reconcile this list with the corresponding opening balances (see the notes below on substantive tests for additions and disposals).
- Select a sample of assets that physically exist (and whose existence has been verified, possibly by means of inspection by the auditor) and trace these assets to the fixed asset register.
- Obtain or prepare a reconciliation of ledger balances for tangible fixed assets with the fixed asset register and investigate any differences.

Existence

- Select a sample of assets from the fixed asset register and physically inspect them. During the inspection, note whether the asset is in use and the condition that it is in. For an asset register held on an IT system, audit software could be used to assist in the selection of a sample.
- Establish and investigate the reasons for any assets in the sample that are not found by the auditor

Carrying value/valuation

At cost

- **Land and buildings**: Confirm the figures for cost with the purchase contract for the asset and the invoices for associated costs (such as professional fees). Check that the purchase expenditure is analysed reasonably between land, buildings and equipment.
- **Equipment and vehicles**: Check the cost in the financial statements against the purchase invoices for the assets.
- Review the allocation of total expenditure on fixed assets between capital and revenue amounts.

At valuation

- Verify amounts in the financial statements with the valuer's report.
- Consider the reasonableness of the valuation.
- Check that valuations are regularly updated.
- Check the accounting for the rise or fall in value on revaluation.

Depreciation and impairment

- Review depreciation rates for reasonableness in the light of the nature of the asset, its estimated useful life and residual value.
- Ensure that consistent depreciation methods are in use.
- Review gains or losses on disposal (and the accumulated depreciation and impairment at the time of disposal).
- Consider the possibility that assets are obsolete or suffering impairment. This matter may have to be discussed with the directors of the client company.
- Check the depreciation calculations for accuracy, using the entity's stated policy. Again, in an IT system, audit software could be used to check these calculations.
- Ensure that fully-depreciated assets are not subject to further depreciation.
- Perform analytical procedures to verify the total charge for depreciation (for example, by taking the ratio of depreciation to total asset value, and comparing this with the ratio in previous years).
- Confirm that the entity has adequate insurance for its assets.

Rights and obligations (ownership)

- **Land and buildings**: Verify legal title to the assets by inspecting appropriate documents (such as legal documents of ownership, or lease agreements).
- **Vehicles**: Examine vehicle registration documents or similar documentation giving evidence of title.
- **Other assets**: Examine invoices or other documents transferring title.
- Ensure that documents are in the name of the entity (the client company).
- Review legal documents, bank documents and other documents for evidence of any loans that are secured by charges on assets.

1.4 Substantive testing procedures – additions and disposals

In the interests of audit efficiency, auditors will pay particular attention to substantive testing of additions and disposals of tangible fixed assets. These transactions, together with the depreciation charge for the year, will normally account for most of the changes between the valuations in the opening and closing balance sheets. Typical substantive testing procedures in these areas are listed below.

Additions

- Obtain/prepare a schedule of additions for the period.
- Check the authorisation of the expenditure to purchase these additions.
- Confirm that the total additions reconcile with the movement between the opening and closing balances in the note to the financial statements.
- Inspect a purchase invoice or other document as evidence of the cost of any addition, and confirm that these documents are in the company name.

- Verify the existence of the acquired fixed assets, by means of physical inspection where appropriate.
- Check that the entries in the accounting records are correct, confirming the allocation of total expenditure between capital and revenue expenditure.

Disposals

- Obtain/prepare a schedule of disposals for the period.
- Check the authorisation of the disposals.
- Verify that the cost and related accumulated depreciation have been removed from the accounting records.
- Verify the calculation of the figure for the gain or loss on disposal, and verify that this figure has been correctly recorded in the ledger.
- Discuss with management (including non-financial management) the possibility of unrecorded disposals of assets.

As always, the precise nature of substantive tests by the auditor must reflect the circumstances involved. This is mirrored in the exam by the particular scenarios set. For example, an entity may construct its own fixed assets rather than buy them from an outside supplier. In this event, the audit testing procedures will focus on confirming that internal costs (materials, labour, other direct expenses and overheads) have been properly accounted for as capital expenditure.

Example

During the year ended 30th June 20X6, Constructico acquired freehold land at a cost of £500,000 and built a distribution centre on it, using a mixture of sub-contract and own labour. The distribution centre cost a total of £200,000 to construct. The construction was completed by the end of April.

Required

Set out the audit objectives in respect of the above and the audit procedures you would carry out to achieve those objectives.

Answer

The land and the distribution centre exist at 30th June 20X6

- Visit site and confirm that the distribution centre has been built and is in use.

Constructico own the land and the distribution centre at 30th June 20X6

- Inspect the land registry certificate or write to third party for confirmation (e.g. bank or solicitor).
- Inspect correspondence confirming that local planning permission was granted and ensure any conditions were met.

Expenditure capitalised in respect of the distribution centre is <u>complete</u>

- Discuss with management their policy for capitalising expenditure incurred in building the distribution centre.
- If a formal system is in place for the identification and capitalisation of construction expenses, test that system.
- Review a sample of invoices not capitalised during the period and ensure treatment was correct.

The land and the distribution centre are appropriately <u>valued</u> at cost

- Inspect completion statement for purchase of land.
- Obtain an analysis of costs of building the distribution centre. Inspect:
  - purchase invoices for a sample of raw material and sub-contract costs
  - time records for a sample of internal labour costs
  - evidence in respect of any overheads capitalised.
- Recalculate the depreciation charge for the year, taking into account that the distribution centre was not completed until the end of April.

Intangible fixed assets

- Substantive tests for intangible assets
- Tests for purchased goodwill
- Tests for other intangibles

2 Intangible fixed assets

2.1 Substantive tests for intangible assets

The audit procedures relating to intangible assets such as goodwill and brands should be similar to those set out above in respect of tangible assets. The emphasis of the substantive tests will be on:

- existence and
- valuation.

Remember that the most common intangible assets that are recognised in the balance sheet are:

- purchased goodwill
- intangibles having a readily ascertainable market value, and
- development costs, subject to the conditions set out in the accounting standard SSAP 13.

There should therefore be adequate audit evidence available to enable a conclusion to be reached on these assets.

The main audit procedures are listed below.

2.2 Tests for purchased goodwill

The tests listed below relate mainly to the valuation of purchased goodwill:

- Confirm that a business was acquired and confirm the consideration paid for the business acquired. (This is a measure required to check the existence of purchased goodwill as well as to confirm its valuation.)
- Review the reasonableness of the valuation placed on the net assets acquired.
- Check the calculation of the purchased goodwill (as the difference between the consideration paid and the fair value of the net assets acquired).
- Review for the possibility of an impairment having arisen.
- Ensure that any impairment loss has been correctly calculated and recorded in the ledger.

2.3 Tests for other intangibles

The tests for other intangible assets, other than development costs, are similar to those that may be applied to tangible fixed assets.

- The auditor should confirm the existence, the cost and the client entity's legal rights to the acquired assets, by looking at the purchase documentation.
- Check the amortisation calculations for accuracy, using the entity's stated policy.
- Consider the possibility that the assets are suffering impairment. This matter may have to be discussed with the directors of the client company.
- Ensure that any impairment has been correctly dealt with in the ledger.

CHAPTER 12

Substantive testing: stock

Contents

Introduction to substantive testing for stock

- The importance of closing stock for audit testing
- Principal internal controls for stock
- Audit of stock: checking the valuation of items and stock quantities

1 Introduction to substantive testing for stock

1.1 The importance of closing stock for audit testing

For many businesses (although service organisations are often an exception) stock is one of the areas needing most attention from the auditor. The reasons for the importance of closing stock for the auditor include the following:

- Stock is often a material item in the financial statements.
- Stock may be a high risk area, involving a high degree of judgement in areas such as valuation. For example, judgement may be needed to estimate the stage of completion of work in progress.
- Stock may suffer from deterioration, loss or theft that may not be recognised in the client company's financial statements.
- Stock may be highly technical in nature. Where stock is complex, the auditor may need to consider whether to rely on the work of an expert.
- Establishing a closing stock figure may be a lengthy and complex process for the client, with a high risk of error.
- Closing stock is often not part of the double entry system, so directional testing (tests on other areas and other balances) may not reveal misstatements in stock.

Audit work on stock is often given to more experienced members of the audit team. The work will typically be subject to a process of rigorous review and quality control. In addition, analytical procedures are widely used to obtain evidence to supplement the detailed substantive testing on stock in the audit.

1.2 Principal internal controls for stock

Before going on to look at typical substantive tests, it may be useful to consider the main control objectives and the nature of internal controls for stock. The auditor has to evaluate the systems and controls in order to decide on the extent of substantive testing required to limit the audit risk to an acceptable level.

The main control objectives for stock are typically as follows:

- Stock should be correctly valued in the balance sheet, without material misstatement.
- Procedures for accounting for stock should be reliable, and accounting records for stock should be reliable with regard to the quantity of items held and their valuation.
- Stock should be kept physically secure, protected from theft, loss or deterioration in quality.

Suitable internal controls may therefore relate to the following areas:

- Accurate, up-to-date stock records should be maintained.
- There should be regular stock counts. After each count of stock, the current valuation of stock in the accounts (where the entity maintains continuous stock records) should be adjusted to agree with quantities counted. Significant differences between the accounting records and the physical count should be investigated.
- There should be established policies on stock valuation.
- There should be formal procedures for identifying each year any stock whose net realisable value may be below cost, and for adjusting the valuation to net realisable value when this is less than cost.
- There must be suitable physical controls over stock, to protect it from theft, loss and deterioration in quality.

1.3 Audit of stocks: checking the valuation of items and stock quantities

The figure for stock in the financial statements reflects:

- the **quantity** of stock on hand at the balance sheet date, and
- the **value** of each item of that stock.

Substantive tests for stocks will therefore focus largely on:

- the existence of the stock, and
- its carrying value

Valuation of stock

- SSAP 9: valuation of stock
- Substantive testing procedures
- Cost or net realisable value?

2 Valuation of stock

2.1 SSAP 9: valuation of stock

SSAP 9 requires that stock should be valued at the lower of cost or net realisable value, on an item-by-item basis.

- **Cost** includes the costs of purchase and all other costs incurred in bringing stocks to their present location and condition. In the case of work-in-progress and manufactured finished goods, this includes an amount for production overheads. (The absorption rate for production overheads should be based on normal levels of activity). Cost can be estimated by using a number of methods (such as first-in-first-out or average cost). The method chosen should provide a close approximation to the actual cost of the stock.
- **Net realisable value** (NRV) is the estimated selling price of the stock in the ordinary course of business, minus (1) any estimated costs to complete the items (and make them available for sale) and (2) the estimated costs of making the sale.

2.2 Substantive testing procedures

The substantive work on stock should be designed to allow for the nature of the stock and the nature of the situation that the auditor is facing.

- If the entity is a retailing organisation, the only major component of the cost of stock is likely to be the purchase cost of the goods for resale.
- If the entity is involved in manufacturing or processing, the cost of stock will include an amount for direct labour and production overhead, in addition to the cost of the raw materials and components.

Substantive testing procedures for the valuation of stock items are suggested below. In the exam, which procedures are the most appropriate will depend on the particular scenario given.

Cost of raw materials or the cost of goods purchased for resale

For raw materials and goods held for resale, the cost of stock will be the actual purchase cost of the items (plus any costs of delivery that the entity may have had to pay). The auditor should carry out the following tests for valuation.

- Confirm the approach adopted by the client company to estimate the cost of materials or goods used/sold (for example first-in-first-out, or weighted average cost).
- Check the figures for the cost of stock by comparing them with prices in purchase invoices or official supplier price lists.

Cost of manufactured goods and work in progress

For work-in-progress and items of finished (manufactured) goods, the auditor needs to check each of the elements in the cost: direct materials, direct labour and production overheads. He should therefore carry out the following tests:

- Obtain schedules showing the make-up of the cost figures for each item of work-in-progress and finished goods.
- Check the accuracy of the calculations.
- Materials
  - Perform the same substantive tests as for raw materials, shown above.
  - Check that the correct **quantity** of materials has been used in the valuation.
- Labour
  - Check pay rates for direct labour cost against payroll/personnel records for the employees who produced the work-in-progress or finished goods items.
  - Check the hours worked (and used to calculate labour costs in the stock) with the time records for the employees concerned.
- Production overheads
  - Confirm that only production overheads (as opposed to selling and administration overheads) are included in the valuation.
  - Confirm that overhead absorption rates are based on **normal levels of output**.
- Work in progress: in addition to the above tests, the auditor may also need to check the stage of completion of the work in progress, in respect of both materials and conversion costs (labour and overheads).

2.3 Cost or net realisable value?

In his substantive testing of stock, the auditor should also look at the procedures of the client entity for deciding whether each item of stock should be valued at cost or at net realisable value (NRV). The auditor may therefore carry out the following tests:

- Review and test the procedures in place for comparing NRV with cost for each item of stock.
- Follow up any information obtained from other audit work suggesting that for certain items of stock, NRV may be lower than cost. Information may be obtained from the physical stock count (where the auditor has observed evidence of deterioration of the stock) or from the amount of returns and allowances granted to customers.
- Review stock records and order books for evidence of slow-moving items, whose selling price might need to be reduced and whose NRV may therefore be less than cost.
- Review prices at which goods have been sold after the balance sheet date, for evidence that NRV is higher than cost

- In the case of work in progress, compare costs incurred to date with selling price minus costs to complete (NRV). Estimated costs to complete may be assessed by the auditor from the client's management accounts.

As discussed in a previous chapter, where the client has an IT system in place over stock, audit software may be used to improve the efficiency and accuracy of audit testing in this area.

Stock quantity: the physical stock count and ISA 501

- Physical stock counts: purpose and responsibilities
- Timing of the count
- Counting procedures
- Cut-off
- Audit work relating to the stock count
- Audit work before the count: planning
- Audit work during the count: observing and recording
- Audit work after the count: follow up

3 Stock quantity: the physical stock count and ISA 501

3.1 Physical stock counts: purpose and responsibilities

Many organisations rely on a physical stock count at the end of their financial year in order to arrive at a figure for stock in their financial statements. Even if an entity maintains 'sophisticated' stock records, with continuous accounting records for stocks, the accuracy of these records should be checked by means of regular physical counts of stock.

There are several reasons for physical counts of stock.

- Physical counts may be fairly easy to arrange, particularly where most items of stock are held in a limited number of physical locations.
- Physical counts provide evidence of the actual existence of the stock. This evidence is important to the client company (for preparing the financial statements) as well as for the auditor (for checking the reliability of those statements).
- Physical counts can be used by the entity to check the accuracy of its stock records, where it maintains continuous stock records.
- Where the entity does not have continuous stock records, a physical count of stock is probably the only way of establishing the quantity of stock at the year-end.
- Discrepancies between the physical count of stock and the entity's stock records may indicate weaknesses in physical controls over stocks, and losses due to theft or for losses from other causes.
- A physical count of stock can also be used to check the physical condition of stock, and whether there has been any deterioration in condition.

It is important to appreciate the relative responsibilities of management and auditors with respect to stock counts.

- It is the responsibility of management to arrange for physical counts to be made and to establish appropriate procedures for counting, to ensure that a complete and accurate count is taken. (It is the responsibility of the company's directors to ensure that the valuation of stock in the financial statements is reliable.)
- It is the responsibility of the auditor to gather evidence from which he can reach a conclusion on the figure for stock in the financial statements. Observation and other audit procedures performed by the auditor at the stock count will provide some of this audit evidence.

The auditor's attendance at the physical stock count is covered by ISA 501: **Audit evidence – Additional considerations for specific items**. ISA 501 states as a principle of auditing that: 'When inventory is material to the financial statements, the auditor should obtain sufficient appropriate audit evidence regarding its **existence** and **condition** by **attendance at physical inventory counting** unless impracticable.'

In the UK, the APB has also issued PN12 *Attendance at stocktaking*. The following sections are in line with PN12, which is more detailed than ISA 501.

3.2 Timing of the count

An entity can take any of three different approaches to the **timing** of the physical stock count: These are:

- an annual count at the balance sheet date (periodical counting)
- an annual count shortly before or after the balance sheet date (periodical counting)
- 'continuous counts' at a variety of dates during the period (perpetual counting).

Annual count at the balance sheet date

An annual count at the balance sheet date is the 'traditional' approach to the physical stock count. As the term suggests, all stock is counted on the balance sheet date.

The annual stock count may be a lengthy process, involving many staff. In order to count all of the stock on the balance sheet date, it may therefore be necessary for the entity to close down its production facility. This will ensure an accurate physical count, by making sure that no items of stock are produced or used, from the balance sheet date until the physical count has ended.

Annual count shortly before or after the balance sheet date

Companies often hold their 'year end' counts shortly before or shortly after the balance sheet date. There are usually practical reasons for this.

- The count may be held early to allow extra time for management to process the information from the stock count (and put their valuation to closing stock) before the audit begins.
- The balance sheet date may fall at an inconvenient time. In the UK the financial year end for many companies is 31st December, which is a time when many staff are on holiday.
- It may be convenient to hold the count on a Saturday or Sunday when business activity is at a lower level, and when the count can therefore be completed more quickly. The chosen Saturday or Sunday may be just before or just after the end of the financial year.

Timing the annual count to take place just before or just after the balance sheet date is acceptable for audit purposes, provided that the accounting records are sufficiently adequate to allow the auditor to check the changes in stocks between the date the count took place and the balance sheet date.

Continuous counting: counts take place at a variety of dates during the financial period

An entity may decide to hold several physical counts of stock throughout the financial year, in order to avoid the potential disruption of an annual count at the balance sheet date. This involves counting certain items of stock at different dates during the financial year.

This system is acceptable for audit purposes, provided that certain conditions are satisfied. The main conditions are as follows:

- The entity should have a system for maintaining accurate and up-to-date stock records. This is because the figure in financial statements for stock at the balance sheet date will be based on these records. Only a portion of the entity's stock will be physically counted at the balance sheet date.
- Every item should be counted at least once a year.
- Counting should be systematic, and properly organised and controlled.
- Counts must be fully documented and reviewed by management. Any differences between stock records and the figures from the physical stock counts must be investigated.

3.3 Counting procedures

It is the responsibility of management to arrange the stock count and to establish effective procedures to ensure that a complete and accurate count is taken. The auditor attends the count as a means of obtaining audit evidence. This evidence will be used, together with other appropriate evidence, to reach a conclusion on the value of stock in the financial statements.

It is important that the auditor should be confident that the stock counting procedures organised by the client's management will ensure a complete and accurate count.

The following procedures should therefore be in place:

- The directors of the client entity should issue written instructions for the stock count, well in advance of the count.
- The instructions should be reviewed by the auditor before the count takes place.
- The auditor needs to be satisfied that the instructions for the count are such that a complete and accurate count will be taken.
- If the auditor is not confident in the instructions, the matter should be brought to the attention of management, and suitable amendments to the counting procedures should be requested.

The instructions issued by management for the stock count should cover the following areas:

	Area	Comments
(1)	Adequate planning of the count.	Planning must be sufficient to ensure that the work will be carried out precisely and systematically. The planning should provide for the following: ▪ The early issue of counting instructions to the staff who will do the counting. There should be arrangements for the staff to comment on the instructions and discuss them with management, and for suitable amendments to be made to the instructions if appropriate. ▪ Deciding the date of the count. ▪ Identifying the locations at which stock is held. ▪ Ensuring that sufficient staff are available to conduct the count. ▪ There should be procedures for identifying high-value items (for which accurate counting is essential). ▪ There should be procedures to control or stop production and the movement of stocks during the count, in order to make sure that all stock is counted. ▪ There should be procedures for ensuring a clean stock **cut-off** (see below).
(2)	The stock should be divided into manageable sections for the purpose of controlling the count.	

Table continues

	Area	Comments
(3)	There should be proper instructions for counting, weighing, measuring, and checking.	The instructions should give clear guidance about the units of measurement that should be used for the count; for example, single units, units of 100, units of 1,000 etc, measurement by weight, and so on. Counting should be carried out by teams of two (one person to act as counter and the other person to act as a checker).
(4)	There should be procedures for identifying stock on the entity's premises that is owned by third parties.	This stock should be excluded from the stock valuation for the balance sheet. For example, stock may be supplied to the entity on a sale or return basis; this is legally owned by the supplier.
(5)	There should be procedures for identification of defective, damaged, obsolete and slow moving stocks.	These procedures are necessary in order to identify stock whose NRV may be below cost.
(6)	There must be appropriate documentation for recording the count.	Pre-numbered documents should be used. Typically, these are tags for attaching to counted stock items (containing details of the counted items) and sequentially-numbered sheets on which details from the tags are summarised, with the tags listed in numerical order. Controls over documentation should include keeping records of the tags and sheets that have been used, and accounting for all these documents at the end of the count. Records should be kept of the documentation issued.
(7)	There should be procedures for identifying and quantifying stocks belonging to the client but held by other entities.	For example, the entity may supply goods to customers on a sale or return basis. The auditor will probably seek to verify the quantity and value of these items of stock by writing to the other entities concerned and asking them for written confirmation of the amount of the client's stock that they are holding.

3.4 Cut-off

Cut-off is the process of ensuring that all transactions are **fully recorded in the correct accounting period**. Unless a correct ('clean') cut-off is achieved, there can be significant distortions in the figures reported for **two** consecutive financial periods.

Cut-off affects many areas of the financial statements:

- stock
- sales revenue recognition
- cost of sales
- debtors
- creditors.

Sales cut-off

Cut-off is concerned with making sure that sales are recorded in the correct accounting period. For example, sales that occur around the end of the financial year should be recognised in the appropriate year. This in turn affects the recording of debtors and stocks at the year-end.

For example, if a sale is recorded in the year to 31st December 20X6, the following should also be recorded in that period:

- a debtors balance
- the goods must be removed from stocks
- a cost of sales entry.

This is an example of **sales cut-off**. In particular it is important to ensure that the same item is not reflected as both a debtor balance and a stock item.

Purchases cut-off

Similarly, all purchases that occur around the end of the year should be recorded in the correct financial year. This in turn will affect the recording of creditors and stock in the year-end balance sheet.

For **purchases cut-off**, if goods are received in the year ended 31st December 20X6 and included in closing stock, the following entries should also be recorded in that period:

- a stock purchase
- a creditors balance.

It is important to ensure that if an asset (stock) is recorded, a corresponding liability (a trade creditor) must also be recorded.

The auditor's work should include substantive testing on cut-off. This is described below.

3.5 Audit work relating to the stock count

The main financial statement assertion addressed by the auditor's attendance at the stock count is **existence**. However, the audit work at the count (and after the count) will also generate evidence relating to:

- valuation, and
- ownership (rights and obligations).

It is convenient to deal with the auditor's work on the stock count under three headings:

- before the count: **planning**
- during the count: **observing and recording**
- after the count: '**follow up**'.

3.6 Audit work before the count: planning

The auditor should carry out the following planning tasks before the stock count:

- Establish the date, time and location of the count.
- Decide which counts at which locations will be observed by the audit team(s).
- Decide whether written confirmation is needed in respect of stocks held by third parties.
- Make arrangements with a local firm of auditors to attend a physical count location if the audit firm's own auditors are unable to do so.
- Consider the possible use of the client's internal audit department, which may be involved in checking stock counts.
- The auditor in charge should make a requisition for the appropriate number and grade of audit staff to observe the stock counts.
- The auditor should review (for adequacy) the instructions for the count that have been prepared by the client entity's management. He should suggest appropriate changes if necessary.
- He may also circulate these instructions to members of the audit team and invite their comments.
- He should become familiar with the client's stocks. He should give particular attention to high value or complex stock items.
- He should decide the scope of the audit testing to be performed during the count, based on materiality and risk considerations.
- He should consider whether there is a need to use an expert to assist with the count of complex items.
- He should read the audit files for previous years, to find out whether problems were encountered with the stock count on previous audits. If so, he should plan to make sure that similar problems do not occur again this year.

3.7 Audit work during the count: observing and recording

During the physical stock count, the auditor should observe the count and make his own records.

Observe

During the count, the auditor should:

- Observe whether or not the count is being conducted in accordance with the written instructions of the client's management

- Observe the condition of the stock, in order to identify items where NRV might be below cost (and in particular, stock that seems to have deteriorated in condition)
- Observe whether or not stock not owned by the client entity is properly identified and labelled (for example, stock owned by customers but held on the entity's premises)
- Observe whether or not, during the count, production of new stock and the movement of stock are controlled and properly documented, in accordance with management's instructions for the count
- At the end of the count, observe whether or not all stock items have been counted and tagged accordingly.

It is normal practice for the auditor to prepare a **stock count memorandum** recording his observations in the audit files. The memorandum should include a conclusion on the effectiveness of the count procedures.

Record

The auditor should also prepare some records relating to the stock count.

- The auditor should carry out a sample of **test counts**. Audit staff will count items of stock selected for the sample and compare the quantity they have counted with the quantity recorded by the client's staff. Any differences should be discussed with the client and resolved. The results of the test counts should be recorded.
- The auditor should make a record of the sequence numbers of the last tags and summary sheets used during the count. This record will be used after the count to confirm that all stock items are included in the client's stock list.
- The auditor should also record cut-off information. Typically he will record details of the last few goods received notes issued before the count and the first few goods received notes issued after the count. Similar information should be recorded relating to despatch notes. This helps to establish the financial year in which stock items were physically received or physically despatched so that the auditor can subsequently check sales and purchases cut-off.
- The auditor should record details of slow-moving or obsolete stock, or stock in poor condition, observed during the count.

3.8 Audit work after the count: follow up

The final audit work on stocks may take place several weeks after the stock count itself. In the intervening period the client should have calculated a final stock figure for the financial statements.

One of the main objectives of the audit work on stock quantity at this stage is to ensure that the stock quantities that existed at the count date are properly reflected in the final stock figure in the financial statements. (Note: At this stage, the auditor should also carry out his checks on the valuation of stock items, as described earlier.)

The audit work involved in verifying stock **quantities** will include the following:

- Obtaining the final stock sheets that were prepared by the client's staff during their stock count.
- Check the numerical sequence of the sheets and the auditor's record of the last sheet number, to confirm that no sheets are missing.
- Check the numerical sequence of tag numbers listed on the sheets and the auditor's record of the final tag number, to confirm that no stock items are missing from the sheets.
- Check the arithmetical accuracy of the calculations on the sheets.
- Confirm that stock records have been amended as appropriate. For some stock items, there is likely to be a difference between the physical count numbers and the quantity of stock shown in the client's stock records (where a continuous recording system is used). In these situations, the client's stock records will be incorrect. The auditor should therefore check that the stock records were amended.
- Confirm that stock belonging to the client, but held by third parties, is included on the stock sheets.
- Confirm that stock belonging to third parties, but on the client's premises at the date of the count, is not included on the stock sheets.
- Check that cut-off is correct. This is done by reference to the cut-off information recorded at the time of the count.

Having done all this work, the auditor should be able to reach a final conclusion on the quantity of stocks held at the balance sheet date.

Example

You are the senior in charge of the audit of stock at Spares R Us. Stock is comprised of large quantities of spare parts for the car industry. Spares R Us operates a perpetual stock recording system, backed up by a rolling programme of physical counts throughout the year. There is no year-end physical stock count and the amount for stock in the year-end financial statements is based on the computer records.

Required

Briefly summarise the audit procedures that you would undertake to obtain evidence on the amount for stock in the year-end financial statements.

Answer

- Carry out spot checks during the year.
- Conduct sample counts at the yare end, compare to perpetual records and investigate any differences.
- Review the results of the rolling counts and ensure any differences from book to actual are investigated and adjusted for.

- Check a sample of cost prices to purchase invoices.
- Assess obsolesce.
- Consider the use of audit software on the year-end stock file.

CHAPTER 13

Substantive testing: other current assets

Contents

Substantive testing: trade debtors and prepayments

- Confirmation of debtors balances
- ISA 505: External confirmations
- Planning the confirmation exercise
- Positive or negative confirmation?
- Sample selection and performing the confirmation exercise
- Audit procedures following the receipt of replies (with positive confirmation)
- Preparing a summary and reaching a conclusion
- Other audit procedures for debtors
- The audit of prepayments

1 Substantive testing: trade debtors and prepayments

1.1 Confirmation of debtors balances

The balance for trade debtors is usually a material amount in a company's balance sheet. A significant amount of audit work on trade debtors is therefore likely to be needed to check the reliability of this amount.

The main **financial statement assertions** which are relevant to the audit of trade debtors (an asset) are:

- existence
- rights and obligations (ownership), and
- carrying value (valuation).

An important audit technique for trade debtors is **direct confirmation of balances** with customers. This is sometimes known as a '**debtors circularisation**'.

Direct confirmation involves asking customers to provide written confirmation, direct to the auditors, of their account balance with the client entity. Written confirmation by customers can normally be taken as high-quality audit evidence because it is a strong source of written, external audit evidence.

However, the reliability of this evidence depends on two factors that are not entirely within the auditor's control:

- A large proportion of the customers who are asked to provide written confirmation should do so. Customers are not obliged to provide confirmation, and some time and effort may be required to get some customers to provide the information required.
- Some customers may provide written confirmation without properly checking the details.

The auditor will be concerned to check that the balance for trade debtors is not overstated. (The problem is not one of completeness and understatement.) The confirmation process is therefore based on the company's own list of debtors ledger balances (customer account balances). This is the main accounting record used in this part of the audit.

Principal control objectives and internal controls for debtors

The main control objectives for trade debtors are as follows:

- The amount of credit given to customers should be consistent with company policy.
- Customers should not take more credit (including a longer time to pay) than they are allowed by their terms of credit.
- Trade debtors should be recorded accurately in the accounts.
- There should be suitable controls over decisions to write off bad debts.

The main internal controls over trade debtors should be directed towards the achievement of these control objectives. The main control procedures will relate to the following matters:

- Credit checks on customers
- Establishment and operation of credit limits
- Follow-up procedures for overdue accounts (customers who have not paid what they owe on time, within the credit period allowed)
- Authorisation of the write-off of bad debts
- Regular reconciliation of customer account balances in the debtors ledger with the total balance for debtors in the debtors control account in the main ledger
- Regular preparation and review of aged listings of debtors balances ('aged debtors lists').

1.2 ISA 505: External confirmations

The confirmation process is covered by ISA 505 *External confirmations*.

ISA 505 states that, where it is reasonable to expect customers to respond to requests for confirmation of their balance, the auditor **should plan** to receive direct confirmation of account balances. In other words, direct confirmation of balances **should be a part of the substantive testing process** for trade debtors.

The letter to customers is sent out by the auditor, but must contain the authorisation from the client entity's management for the customer to provide the required information direct to the auditor. (An example of the form that this letter might take is shown later.)

Audit procedures relating to confirmation of debtors balances are summarised below, under the following headings:

- Planning
- Positive or negative confirmation?

- Sample selection and performing the confirmation exercise
- Audit procedures following the receipt of replies (with positive confirmation)
- Preparing a summary and reaching a conclusion

1.3 Planning the confirmation exercise

The auditor needs to plan the exercise for the confirmation of balances.

- **Decide on the timing of the confirmation**. Ideally the confirmation of balances should take place after the balance sheet date, and should be based on customers' account balances as at the balance sheet date. However, to reduce the time pressure at the final audit stage, the confirmation process is often based on balances at an interim date before the end of the financial year (normally no more than three months before the balance sheet date). In this case, the auditor will need to check the changes in the debtors balances between the confirmation date and the balance sheet date. This check will consist mainly of checking entries in the debtors control account with the transactions entered in the books of prime entry during the same period.
- **Decide on the number of customer balances to be confirmed**. The confirmation process is normally based on a sampling approach. There are often many customers and the time and effort required to obtain a confirmation from all of them is not worth the benefit obtained. The auditor should be able to reach a reasonable conclusion from a representative sample of accounts.
- **Decide on the confirmation method to be used**. This will be **positive** or **negative** confirmation. These methods are explained below.

1.4 Positive or negative confirmation?

The confirmation will be either positive or negative. The auditor should decide which type of confirmation to obtain.

Positive confirmation

A **positive external confirmation** asks the customer to reply to the auditor **whether or not he agrees with the balance** on his account that is in the client company's accounting records (debtors ledger) as at the date selected for the confirmation. Positive confirmation can be obtained in either of two ways:

- **Method 1**. By providing the customer with details of the balance on his account, and asking him to indicate his agreement that this information is correct, or to indicate that it is wrong.
- **Method 2**. By asking the respondent to provide details of his balance at the selected date, but not providing any details of the balance in the client company's debtors ledger.

This should provide reliable audit evidence. However, there is a risk with Method 1 that a customer may reply to a confirmation request without checking that the information is correct. This risk can be reduced by using Method 2. However, with Method 2 there may be a lower response rate from customers, because they are being asked to do more work to provide the confirmation.

Negative confirmation

A **negative external confirmation** asks the customer to reply to the auditor **only where he disagrees** with the balance recorded by the company. If no reply is received, there is no explicit audit evidence in respect of the customer's balance. The absence of a reply could mean that the customer agrees with the balance, but is not required to provide written evidence. On the other hand, the absence of a reply could mean that the customer has not carried out any check of the balance at all.
The use of negative confirmation therefore provides audit evidence that is **less reliable** than evidence obtained with positive confirmation requests.

Example: request for a confirmation of balance (positive confirmation)

A sample letter to a customer asking for confirmation of the outstanding balance, using the positive confirmation method, is shown below.

Note that it appears to be written by the management of the client company. In practice, this provides authorisation for the customer to provide the required information direct to the auditor. The letter will also be sent out to customers by the auditor (to make sure that the letters are actually sent to the customers in the selected sample). Replies should go directly to the auditor.

A COMPANY
25 South Street
Anytown

Customer's name and address

Date ....

Dear ....

In accordance with the request of our auditors, Arthur Dailey and Co we ask that you kindly confirm to them directly your indebtedness to us at (*insert date*) which, according to our records, amounted to £............... as shown by the enclosed statement.

If the above amount is in agreement with your records, please sign in the space provided below and return this letter **direct to our auditors** in the enclosed stamped addressed envelope.

If the amount is not in agreement with your records, please notify our auditors **directly** of the amount shown by your records, and if possible detail on the reverse of this letter full particulars of the difference.

Yours faithfully,

A COMPANY

Confirmation No ....

The amount shown above is/is not* in agreement with our records as at ....

Account No .... Signature ....

Date ....

Title or position ....

* the position according to our records is attached

1.5 Sample selection and performing the confirmation exercise

The auditor will normally select a sample of customers who will be asked to provide a confirmation of the balance on their account with the client company. The audit procedures for selecting the sample and for the confirmation process are as follows:

- Obtain or prepare an aged listing of debtors ledger balances at the chosen date.
- If the list is prepared by the client, check the completeness and accuracy of the list of balances and the total of the balances in the list. This can be done by checking the list against (1) the total balance for trade debtors in the debtors control account in the main ledger and (2) a sample of customers' account balances in the debtors ledger.
- As with all sampling, a selection process should be undertaken which, as far as possible, ensures that the sample is representative of the population.
- If the 'population' of debtors ledger balances is not homogeneous, stratified sampling might be used. (Stratified sampling was explained in an earlier chapter.)
- In selecting the sample, certain types of account should be considered for inclusion:
  - overdue accounts
  - credit balances (accounts where the client entity owes money to its customer, having issued credit notes to the customer)
  - accounts on which round sum payments are received (for example, where the customer makes payments of £500, or £1,000 or £3,000, instead of paying specific invoices)
  - nil balances. (A check on nil balances provides a check on the completeness of trade debtors.)

  In an IT system, with many year-end balances audit software can be used to help select the sample (eg by selecting every 500th £ for MUS sampling or selecting all balances over a certain amount, as well as nil and credit balances.
- In the case of an external audit, the confirmation requests are issued **by the auditor**, not by the client, and replies are sent directly to the auditor. However, the request will need to contain **management's authorisation** to the customer to disclose the necessary information. Should the client refuse to give permission for a confirmation letter to be sent to a particular customer, the auditor should look for a reason for the refusal. As that customer has been included in the sample selection, the auditor will need to carry out alternative audit work (see below) to verify that customer balance.
- With requests for positive confirmation, if the auditor does not receive a reply from a customer within a reasonable period of time, follow-up procedures should be initiated. For example, second request and third request letters could be sent, or the client could be asked to contact the customer and ask for a reply.

1.6 Audit procedures following the receipt of replies (with positive confirmation)

On receipt of the replies from customers, the auditor should check that the letters are signed by a responsible official. The replies are filed in the debtors section of the current audit file. The current audit file should classify the customers in the sample as follows:

- **Balance agreed**. The customer has replied and agrees with the balance in the client entity's accounting records (or has provided a balance that corresponds with the entity's accounting records – depending on whether Method 1 or Method 2 of positive confirmation is used). No further audit work is required.
- **Balance not agreed**. The customer has replied but does not agree with the balance in the client entity's accounting records. The auditor should ask the client to review the replies and try to reconcile the balance in their records with the balance confirmed by the customer. The auditor should then check the reconciliation, looking for evidence of errors in the client company's figures which may represent misstatements of their debtors' balances. However, many of the reconciling items will often be '**timing differences**' – invoices, credit notes or cash may be recorded in the accounts of one party (the customer or the client entity) but not yet recorded by the other. Provided that the auditor is confident that the difference in the balances is due to timing differences, they should not be seen as evidence of errors in debtors balances.
- **No reply received**. No reply has been received from the customer. The auditor cannot ignore these customer accounts. They have been chosen as part of a representative sample and the auditor needs to reach a conclusion on the accuracy of the balances on **all** the accounts included in the sample for the confirmation process.

Further checking where no reply is received

Where no reply has been received, the auditor should therefore perform alternative procedures in order to obtain evidence to confirm the customer's balance.

- If the customer has subsequently paid all of the amount due at the confirmation date, this is strong evidence of the validity of the debt.
- If no payment (or only part-payment) has been received, all the relevant documentation supporting the amount still due should be examined. For each invoice outstanding at the confirmation date, the auditor should examine:
  - a signed customer purchase order
  - signed delivery documentation (the customer's signature on the delivery note)
  - a sales invoice addressed to the customer.

1.7 Preparing a summary and reaching a conclusion

On completion of the confirmation exercise, the auditor should produce a **summary** of the responses. This should clearly indicate the amounts of the balances subject to confirmation for which the auditor has not been able to establish supporting evidence. These amounts indicate misstatement of debtors balances. In particular, they may indicate the existence of bad debts.

As always with a sampling exercise, the auditor should draw a **conclusion** on the likely level of misstatement in the total population of debtors balances based on the result of the sample, and whether this is material.
Such a summary might be prepared as follows:

	Value of balances	% of total
	£	
Replies received and agreed	465,600	80.3
Replies received and reconciled	56,400	9.7
Non-replies agreed using alternative procedures	43,200	7.5
Balances still unresolved	14,300	2.5
	579,500	100

Total value of debtors = £1,248,900.

Extrapolation of potential error = £1,248,900 × 2.5% = £31,222 – Transferred to the cumulative errors schedule

Note: The cumulative errors schedule is a list of items where the auditor's view of the amount of the item differs from the amount in the client company's accounting records/draft financial statements. The auditor builds up this schedule as the audit progresses, and will use it when reaching his final audit opinion.

1.8 Other audit procedures for debtors

In addition to the confirmation process, the auditor should consider the following additional audit procedures in respect of debtors:

Bad debts

The auditor needs to be satisfied that the amount of bad debts written off and the amount of the provision (or allowance) for doubtful debts are reliable. These will affect the amount included in the balance sheet for trade debtors. The following audit checks should therefore be made:

- Review the company's procedures for identifying bad and doubtful debts.
- Review aged listings of debtors balances ('aged debtors lists'). Bad debts and provisions for doubtful debts should only relate to overdue accounts. The auditor should enquire as to whether the overdue debts are collectable.
- Review any correspondence of the client company with customers, lawyers and collection agencies, that deals with unpaid debts or disputed debts.
- Review the calculation of any provisions against doubtful debts.
- Examine credit notes issued after the year-end, as evidence that some balances were over-stated at the year-end. (The customer and the client company may have been in dispute about an invoice at the end of the financial year, and the dispute may subsequently have been resolved by the issue of a credit note and a reduction in the amount debtor.)
- Review the replies from customers for the confirmation of balances exercise, for evidence of debts that may not be collectable.

Cut-off

The audit work after the physical stock count will also give evidence of the accuracy of sales cut-off. Sales cut-off was explained in an earlier chapter. It is concerned with ensuring that sales and debtors are fully and properly recorded **in the correct accounting period**. Sales that occur just before or after the year-end need to be allocated to the correct financial year.

Additional work on this area might include the following:

- The use of analytical procedures to confirm that stock levels, cost of sales and gross margins can be explained in terms of known business facts.
- Checking that sales invoices and credit notes dated shortly before and after the year end are recorded in the correct financial year.
- Review of the control account entries shortly before and after the year end for unusual items, which the client should then be asked to explain.

Example

The following is a summary of the year-end debtors balances at Mike's Manufacturing and the equivalent figures for the previous year. The materiality threshold for the audit has been set at £5,000.

Customer	**20X6**	**20X5**
	£	£
Jones	2,500	2,400
Smith	6,000	3,000
Brown	2,000	2,000
White	1,000	1,100
Crane	20,500	18,900
Other customers, all with balances under £1,000	16,600	7,400
	48,600	34,800

Brown went into liquidation during the year.

Required

Set out which of the above balances, as a minimum, the auditor should select for testing and explain why.

Answer

- Smith should be selected as this balance is above the materiality threshold. Also, the balance has doubled since the previous year.
- Brown should probably be selected. Although it is below the materiality threshold it would seem likely that the debt is bad.
- Crane should be selected as individually material.

- Although the "other customers" balances all fall well within the materiality threshold, they are material in total and so a sample of these should be verified. This would particularly be the case if the auditor was not expecting sales to smaller customers to have increased during the year. There could be a deliberate attempt to overstate a number of small balances (or invent fictitious customers and balances) in a deliberate attempt to boost assets and avoid audit detection.

1.9 The audit of prepayments

Prepaid expenses are often **estimated amounts** and so may not be open to precise and specific audit checking procedures. The problem of auditing accounting estimates was discussed in a previous chapter. In addition, for many business entities, prepayments are not material and so may not justify significant audit attention.

Audit procedures for checking prepayments may include the following:

- Obtain or prepare a list of prepayments with supporting calculations.
- Check the calculations if the list has been prepared by the client's staff.
- Apply analytical procedures (for example by comparing the balances for prepayments with the balances at the end of the previous financial year).
- Review the list of prepayments for any obvious errors or omissions, based on the auditor's knowledge of the business.

Substantive testing: bank and cash balances

- Features of the audit of bank and cash balances
- Bank balances: confirmation of balances
- Audit work on receipt of the banks' replies
- Cash balances: physical count

2 Substantive testing: bank and cash balances

2.1 Features of the audit of bank and cash balances

For the purpose of this chapter, bank balances are amounts held in a bank account, and cash balances are banknotes and coins (although coins are likely to be immaterial).

Assets held as bank balances and cash can be at risk of loss. There may be fraudulent activity, or the misappropriation of money by employees or others, particularly when many individuals have authority for dealing with receipts and payments.

However, bank balances and cash are also easily checked and verified. Bank balances can be confirmed directly in writing by the banks (third parties) and cash can be physically counted.

Bank balances and cash are also usually subject to rigorous internal controls, to prevent loss and theft. In the UK, it is regular practice for business entities to receive regular bank statements from their bank. A feature of internal control for bank balances is the reconciliation of the balance shown in a bank statement with the balance recorded in the entity's own accounting records (cash book).

The audit work on **cash** balances will be determined largely by materiality (how much cash does the entity hold and is it a material amount?) and the effectiveness of the client's internal controls for cash.

The main **financial statement assertions** that are relevant to the audit of bank and cash are:

- existence
- completeness, and
- ownership (rights and obligations).

Principal internal controls for bank balances and cash

The main control objectives are to make sure that money received is banked and fully accounted for, that payments are made only for approved expenses and that money is not lost because of fraud or misappropriation of funds.

The main internal controls relating to bank balances and cash will usually include the following measures:

- Listing all receipts of money, recording receipts promptly and making sure that all receipts are banked promptly
- A system of authorisation for all payments
- Regular bank reconciliations performed and reviewed
- Sound segregation of duties
- Proper physical custody controls over cash

2.2 Bank balances: confirmation of balances

Checking the accuracy of bank balances can be done effectively by means of **direct confirmation** to the auditor by the banks at which the entity's bank accounts are held. This is similar to written confirmation of balances from customers, in order to check trade debtors. The procedures described below follow PN13 *Bank reports for audit purposes.*

The bank confirmation letter

The auditor must decide which banks to contact for confirmation. Typically all banks that hold accounts for the client entity are contacted. However, the auditor may choose to omit some banks for reasons of immateriality.

The auditor can use either of two possible approaches to the confirmation of bank balances:

- Method 1. The auditor lists information about the bank balances from the client's accounting records and asks each bank to confirm that the balances are correct. (Note: Banks may operate several different accounts for the same customer.)
- Method 2. The auditor requests confirmation of the relevant bank balance(s) without providing any details to the bank. This method provides stronger audit evidence but it may be more time-consuming for the bank to provide the required confirmation.

The two methods are similar to the two methods of positive confirmation of balances from customers for trade debtors.

In the case of the external audit, permission must be given to the bank by the client to release information to the auditor. The reply should be sent by the bank direct to the auditor. (This is also the same as for the confirmation of balances from customers for trade debtors.)

Typical areas covered by the confirmation letter include the following:

- Confirmation of balances on all bank accounts at the balance sheet date.
- Details of any unpaid bank charges.
- Details of any liens (charges) over assets of the client entity.
- Details of any assets of the client entity held by the bank as security for lending.
- Details of any other client bank accounts that are known to the bank but not listed in the request to the bank for confirmation of balances.

2.3 Audit work on receipt of the banks' replies

The main audit work will focus on the confirmation letters from the bank (or the confirmation letter from the client's bank, if there is just one bank) and the client company's bank reconciliation statement. A statement should be provided by the bank for the balance sheet date.

- Obtain or prepare a bank reconciliation statement for each bank account.
- If the reconciliation is prepared by the company, check it for arithmetical accuracy.
- Check the bank balance confirmed in the bank's confirmation letter against the balance used in the bank reconciliation statement.
- Relate other information contained in the confirmation letter to other areas of the audit (for example, accrued bank charges must be provided for in the financial statements).
- Check items appearing in the bank reconciliation statement against any available supporting evidence (for example, unpresented cheques in the bank reconciliation statement should be shown as having been presented in a subsequent bank statement).
- Review the cash book and bank statements for unusual items, including unusual delays between cash book and bank statement entries. Investigate the reasons for any unusual item.
- Review the confirmation letter from the bank for any other information to be disclosed in the financial statements (for example charges on assets and security for loans).

2.4 Cash balances: physical count

The audit work performed on cash balances (as opposed to bank balances) will be largely dictated by materiality considerations. In this context, materiality should be considered not only in terms of the balance sheet amount, but also in terms of the value of total transactions passing through the cash account during the period.

In addition, the auditor needs to appreciate that certain businesses hold cash in a large number of locations (for example, in a company that operates a chain of hotels or supermarkets). In total, these balances may be material, whereas the amount of cash held in any single location may be insignificant.

The main audit work involved in verifying cash balances is a **physical count**.

Audit procedures include the following:

- The auditor should count cash at all locations **simultaneously** and in the presence of a company official. (Simultaneous counting is necessary, to prevent the client from moving cash that has been counted at one location to another location ready for the next count.)
- After the count the auditor should obtain a signed receipt for the amount of cash returned to the official, after the count.
- The auditor should check the cash balance obtained from the count against the client's cash records and cash balance in the draft financial statements.
- Where appropriate, the auditor should also investigate the treatment of any money advances to employees (for example, against wages or salary).

CHAPTER 14

Substantive testing: liabilities and equity

Contents

Substantive testing: trade creditors

- Introduction to the audit of liabilities
- The general approach to the testing of trade creditors
- General audit procedures for checking trade creditors
- Purchases cut-off
- Other audit procedures for trade creditors

1 Substantive testing: trade creditors

1.1 Introduction to the audit of liabilities

As discussed in previous chapters, **directional testing** is an approach to audit testing that an auditor may use to improve the efficiency of an audit. With directional testing, liabilities, income and equity are usually tested for **understatement** only. This is testing the **financial statement assertion of completeness**. The reason for this approach is that an auditor will consider it much more likely that an entity will understate its liabilities (in order to present a better financial position) than over-state its liabilities.

Because auditing liabilities involves testing for completeness, auditing liabilities is often more difficult than auditing assets (where the emphasis of audit testing is on over-statement and existence). The auditor is looking for something that is not recorded, rather then verifying something that has been recorded. This influences the audit approach and the type of audit work performed.

1.2 The general approach to the testing of trade creditors

Trade creditors are a material item in the balance sheet of many entities. Therefore this area is likely to receive a significant level of audit attention.

In some respects, the audit approach is similar to the approach used for the audit of trade debtors. However, a major difference lies in the fact that direct confirmation of balances with suppliers, although sometimes used, is **not** a typical audit testing procedure.

The reason why direct confirmation is not widely used is that the auditor normally has an alternative external source of written evidence. This evidence is provided in the form of supplier's statements.

- A suppliers' statement is a printed statement, received at regular intervals from a supplier (usually each month), showing details of transactions between the supplier and its customer (purchases, purchase returns and payments) since the previous statement, and the amount owing as at the date of the statement.
- These statements and the entity's own listing of trade creditors are the main records used by the auditor for testing trade creditors.

Audit work performed on purchases, cash payments and stock (including purchases cut-off) will also generate valuable audit evidence relating to trade creditors.

1.3 General audit procedures for checking trade creditors

The following procedures can be used for testing on trade creditors:

- Obtain or prepare a listing of balances on supplier accounts in the creditors ledger (a listing of trade creditors)
- If this listing is obtained from the client company, check it for arithmetical accuracy (perhaps by using audit software). In addition, check the creditors for accuracy and existence by taking a sample of the balances and checking them against the balance on the supplier's account in the creditors ledger.
- Similarly, take a sample of balances from supplier accounts in the creditors ledger and confirm that they are correctly included in the listing. This is a test for accuracy and completeness.
- Check that the total of the balances in the listing agrees with the balance for total trade creditors in the trade creditors control account in the main ledger.
- In selecting the sample of balances for testing, the auditor should consider the following points:
  - It is **not** important to select large balances, as the main audit emphasis is on completeness and understatement (not existence and over-statement).
  - For the same reason it is important to select a number of accounts showing nil balances and debit balances. (When there is a debit balance, the supplier owes the client entity, presumably because goods have been returned and a credit note has been issued by the supplier, or because an invoice was over-paid or paid twice.)
  - Include major suppliers in the sample. Identification of major suppliers should be based on the auditor's knowledge of the business. This knowledge may be derived from information gained at the stock count or from audit work on the purchases system.

  As with trade receivables, for an IT-based system , audit software can be used to assist in sample selection.
- For each supplier account balance in the sample, compare the balance from the creditors listing with the balance shown in the supplier's statement. (The first supplier's statement received after the balance sheet date should be used, because this will include the position as at the balance sheet date.)
- If there is a difference between the balance in the creditors listing and the balance shown in the supplier's statement, the auditor should ask the client company to prepare a reconciliation to explain the difference. The auditor should then check these reconciling items with the relevant supporting documentation.

1.4 Purchases cut-off

Purchases cut-off was explained in an earlier chapter. It is concerned with making sure that purchases transactions just before or after the year end are allocated to the correct financial year, so that purchases (for the profit and loss account) and stock and trade creditors (for the balance sheet) are correctly recorded.

- Work performed on cut-off (and recorded at the physical stock count) will provide evidence as to the accuracy of purchases cut-off.

- This work is based on preparing a list of the goods received notes that were prepared by the client entity immediately before and after the balance sheet date. The auditor should confirm that goods included in closing stock have also been recorded as a liability (trade creditor) and that purchased goods not recorded in closing stock have not generated such a liability.

1.5 Other audit procedures for trade creditors

In order to gain additional assurance about the completeness of trade creditors balances, the auditor should also carry out the following procedures:

- Review the list of account balances for any suppliers who are not in the listing of trade creditors, but who would be expected to be in the listing. These would include regular suppliers of frequently-purchased items.
- Compare the list of trade creditors balances with the listing that was prepared for the previous year's audit (at the same date in the previous year). Look for explanations as to why any major balances do not appear on the current year's listing when a major balance for the same supplier is in the listing in the previous year.
- Apply other analytical procedures and obtain explanations for any significant differences identified with this method of testing. For example, the auditor might compare the ratio of trade creditors to purchases in the year, and compare this with the same ratio in previous years. He might expect the ratio to remain fairly stable between one year and the next.

Substantive testing: accruals, provisions and contingencies

- Testing of accruals
- Provisions and contingencies: FRS 12
- Audit procedures for provisions and contingencies

2 Substantive testing: accruals, provisions and contingencies

The audit of accruals, provisions and contingencies can also be difficult areas for the auditor. Accruals are usually estimated amounts and will be subject to audit techniques which are similar to those applied to prepayments. Provisions and contingencies can be highly subjective areas where a considerable amount of judgement may be called for. Evidence may be needed from outside experts such as legal advisors.

2.1 Testing of accruals

Accruals balances are difficult to audit as the figures reported are often based on estimates. However, the amounts involved may not be material, in which case the auditor will not devote a significant amount of time and resources to this area.

As with all liabilities, the emphasis will be on **completeness**. The nature of the items involved means that analytical procedures and the auditor's knowledge of the business are useful in reaching a conclusion on this area.

Audit procedures include the following:

- Obtain or prepare a listing of accruals as at the balance sheet date.
- If the list is prepared by the client company, check the calculations and additions for arithmetical accuracy. Check the amounts in the listing against the balances in the relevant main ledger expense accounts and ensure that the amounts are the same.
- Where invoices have been received, or payments made, after the year end, confirm that the amount accrued appears reasonable in relation to this evidence. For example, suppose that a company makes an accrual for two months of electricity charges, and receives an invoice for three months' supply of electricity one month after the year-end. If the accrual for electricity is, say, £6,000 (£3,000 per month), the auditor should expect the total invoice to be for about £9,000.
- Compare the list of accruals with the list that was prepared at the same date in the previous financial year, and enquire about items not listed in the current year that were in the list in the previous year.
- Review the list of accruals for completeness, based on the auditor's knowledge of the business.
- Relate items on the list of accruals to other audit areas, such as the bank confirmation letter (which might provide details of unpaid/accrued bank charges).

Accrued wages and salaries may be more material than other items and may require a higher level of audit attention.

- Consider what items should be accrued for at the balance sheet date, such as unpaid wages, overtime, holiday pay, bonuses.
- Check the amounts for accrued wages and salaries by comparing them with personnel records and payroll records (records of time worked, records of wage rates and salaries, details of dates for the payment of wages and salaries, and so on).
- Confirm that any additional costs (such as employer's National Insurance Contributions) have been accounted for.
- Perform analytical procedures on accrued wages and salaries. For example, the auditor might measure the ratio of accrued payroll expenses to total payroll costs for the year, and compare this with the similar ratio in previous years. Significant differences should be investigated.

2.2 Provisions and contingencies: FRS 12

Accounting for provisions and contingencies can be a subjective area, which may require a high level of audit attention because the amounts involved could be material. Part of the work of the auditor will be to establish whether the provisions of FRS 12 have been complied with. You therefore need to be aware of the key points of FRS 12. This was covered in Paper F3 but the main provisions of FRS 12 are revised below.

Provisions

FRS 12 gives the following definitions:

- A **provision** is a type of liability. It is a liability of **uncertain timing** or **uncertain amount**.
- A **liability** is:
  - a present obligation
  - arising from past events
  - the settlement of which is expected to result in an outflow of economic benefits.

An 'ordinary' liability is for a **known amount**. For example, an amount payable under the terms of a finance lease agreement is a liability. The obligation arises from the lease agreement. The settlement of the obligation by means of the lease payments will result in a known outflow of cash on known dates.

A provision is a liability of an **uncertain amount** or **uncertain timing**, such as:

- amounts that an entity might have to pay under a guarantee, or
- amounts that an entity might have to pay as the result of a legal claim.

An entity may know that it will have to incur expenses or will have to make a payment under guarantees it has given to customers. It therefore has a liability – an obligation that already exists arising from past events that will result in an outflow of economic benefits in the future. However, it will not know for certain when claims might be made under the guarantees and how much the claims will cost. The entity should therefore make a provision for expenses or payments that it expects to make under the terms of its guarantees.

Recognising a provision

FRS 12 states the criteria for recognising a provision as a liability in the financial statements. A provision should only be recognised when:

- an entity has a present obligation as a result of a past event
- it is probable that an outflow of economic benefits will be required to settle the obligation, and
- a reliable estimate can be made of the amount of the obligation.

There must be an obligation already in existence. The obligation may be legal or constructive.

- A **legal obligation** is one arising from a contract, or some other aspect of the law.
- A **constructive obligation** is one arising from the entity's actions, whereby
  - through established past practice, published policies, or a specific current statement, the entity has indicated to other parties that it will accept certain responsibilities, and
  - as a result, the entity has created a valid expectation that it will discharge those responsibilities. For example, a clothing retailer may have a policy of taking back items of clothing that customers have purchased, and refunding the purchase price, simply because the purchaser has changed his or her mind after purchase. The retailer is not under a legal obligation to take back purchased items in this way, so there is no legal obligation. However, if this is the usual practice of a particular retailer, then a constructive obligation arises.

The event leading to the obligation must be **past**, and must have occurred before the balance sheet date when the provision is first recognised. No provision is made for costs that may be incurred in the future but where no obligation yet exists. For example, if an entity is planning a reorganisation but does not yet have an obligation (legal or constructive) to undertake the reorganisation, it cannot create a provision for reorganisation costs.

The outflow of benefits must be **probable**. 'Probable' is defined by FRS 12 as '**more likely than not**'. For example, an entity may have given a guarantee but may not expect to have to honour it. In such a situation, it cannot create a provision for the cost of expenses that it may have to incur under the terms of the guarantee. This is because a payment under the guarantee is not probable.

Measuring a provision

The amount recognised as a provision should be the best estimate of the expenditure required to settle the obligation at the balance sheet date.

Risks and uncertainties should be taken into account in reaching the best estimate. Events after the balance sheet date will provide useful evidence. However, entities should:

- **avoid** creating **excessive provisions** (which could be used as a way of manipulating profits between financial years), or
- **avoid underestimating** provisions.

Contingent liabilities

A contingent liability is **either of the following**:

A contingent liability is:

- a possible obligation
- arising from past events
- whose existence will be confirmed only by the occurrence or non-occurrence of one or more uncertain future events.

A contingent liability is:

- a present obligation
- arising from past events
- which is not recognised as an actual liability because
  - an outflow of economic benefits is not probable, or
  - the amount of the obligation cannot be estimated reliably.

A contingent liability arises when some, but not all, of the criteria for recognising a provision are met. For example, a contingent liability exists, but not a provision or an actual liability if:

- a reliable estimate cannot be made, or
- no legal obligation or constructive obligation exists: there is merely a **possible** obligation.

Contingent assets

A contingent asset is:

- a possible asset
- arising from past events
- whose existence will be confirmed only by the occurrence or non-occurrence of one or more uncertain future events.

An example of a contingent asset might be a possible gain arising from an outstanding legal action against a third party. The existence of the asset (the money receivable) will only be confirmed by the outcome of the legal dispute.

Recognising contingent liabilities or contingent assets

Unlike provisions, contingent liabilities and assets:

- **are not recognised** in the financial statements and
- are not recorded in the ledger accounts of an entity. (They are not included in the double entry ledger accounting system.)

In some circumstances, the existence of a contingent asset or a contingent liability is **disclosed** in the notes to the financial statements.

- Contingent liabilities are disclosed **unless** the possibility of any outflow in settlement is remote (the meaning of 'remote' is not defined in FRS 12).
- **Contingent assets** are **only disclosed where** an inflow in settlement is **probable**. 'Probable' is defined by FRS 12 as 'more likely than not'.

Disclosures about contingent liabilities and contingent assets

Where disclosure of a contingent liability or a contingent asset is appropriate, FRS 12 requires the following disclosures in notes to the financial statements:

- A brief description of the nature of the contingent liability/asset
- Where practicable:
  - an estimate of its financial effect
  - an indication of the uncertainties.
- For contingent liabilities, the possibility of any reimbursement.

2.3 Audit procedures for provisions and contingencies

The auditor needs to be satisfied that the client has correctly distinguished between provisions (recognised in the financial statements), contingent liabilities (not recognised in the financial statements but disclosed in a note) and items that should not even be disclosed.

Similarly, it may be necessary to assess whether an item is an actual asset (recognised in the financial statements), a contingent asset (not recognised in the financial statements but disclosed in a note) or not likely to happen and so not disclosed.

The audit or must also be satisfied about the measurement/valuation of the items in the financial statements or disclosed by way of a note.

Provisions

The audit work to test provisions should normally include the following measures.

- Obtain a listing of provisions that the client has included in the (draft) financial statements.
- For each item in the listing, confirm that the accounting provisions of FRS 12 have been complied with. Does the item meet the definition of provision?
- Review the changes in the provision for the period during the financial period.
- Review the measurement of the closing balance for each provision and discuss these with management if appropriate. Consider whether it might be appropriate to take expert advice on the existence or measurement of a provision.
- Review the list for possible omissions, based on the auditor's knowledge of the business and the industry in which it operates.
- Compare provisions for the current financial year with provisions in previous years, and investigate any major differences or omissions.
- Relate the testing of provisions to other areas of the audit work, such as correspondence with lawyers (which might reveal more information about matters to which the provisions relate).

Contingencies

The audit approach to checking contingencies may be as follows:

- Ascertain the approach taken by the client's management to identifying contingencies.
- Review the minutes of board meetings (where such matters are likely to be discussed).
- Review relevant sections of the business press and trade journals for areas in which possible industry-wide contingencies may arise.
- Review the client's correspondence with lawyers and invoices for legal services. These may help the auditor to identify contingencies that the client has not disclosed in the notes to the draft financial statements, or that provide additional information for the auditor about contingencies that have been disclosed.
- Consider direct confirmation from lawyers of matters handled on behalf of the entity under audit. Any letter should be sent by management with an instruction for the reply to be sent directly to the auditor. It is more likely that lawyers will respond if the letter lists specific areas where contingencies may exist, together with an assessment by management of the possible outcome. The lawyers should then be asked to comment on the information in the letter.
- Consider whether expert advice may be required from outside sources other than lawyers.

Substantive testing: long-term liabilities

- Aspects of reporting long-term liabilities
- Audit procedures for long-term liabilities

3 Substantive testing: long-term liabilities

3.1 Aspects of reporting long-term liabilities

Long-term liabilities are liabilities repayable after more than one year from the balance sheet date. They may include:

- debentures
- loan stock
- loan notes
- bank loans
- finance lease obligations.

It may be that loans are repayable at regular intervals throughout the term of the loan, in which case a part of the overall balance owing may be a current liability (repayable within the next 12 months) with the remaining part being a long-term liability. This is an important point for the auditor to consider, in terms of ensuring the proper disclosure of information in the financial statements (and the classification of liabilities as long-term or current).

The agreements under which these long-term liabilities are taken out may impose conditions on the company which, if broken, may give the lender the right to impose penalties or possibly withdraw the finance. This is another significant consideration for the auditor.

3.2 Audit procedures for long-term liabilities

Procedures in the audit of long-term liabilities may be as follows:

- Obtain or prepare a listing of long-term borrowings/long-term liabilities. The listing should include, for each item, details of the lender and the movement on the borrowing in the financial period. (Opening balance plus interest charges minus payments on the loan equals closing balance.)
- If the list is obtained from the client entity, check it for accuracy.
- Agree the opening balances on the listing with the amount for long-term liabilities in last year's balance sheet.
- Check that any new borrowings during the year have been authorised in accordance with the correct company procedures.
- Agree the details of each loan with the loan agreement/documentation.

- Check whether any restrictions contained in the lending agreements have been complied with. For example, check that the client entity has not been in breach of any covenant in a borrowing agreement.
- Confirm loan repayments in the listing with payments recorded in the cash book, entries in bank statements and also with any correspondence or receipts or statements from lenders.
- Check the interest calculations and confirm that the correct accounting entries for interest have been made, recognising any opening and closing accruals for interest expenses.
- Obtain direct confirmation from lenders of amounts outstanding.
- Confirm that any relevant statutory requirements have been complied with (such as whether charges on assets have been properly registered, if there is a legal obligation to register charges).
- Confirm the correct allocation of the total amounts outstanding between current liabilities (repayable within 12 months) and long-term.
- Review cash book entries for unusual cash receipts that may represent new loans taken out during the period. Where unusual cash book entries are found, obtain an explanation.

Audit of equity

- Audit procedures: share capital
- Audit procedures: reserves
- Audit of statutory books

4 Audit of equity

To some extent, the nature of the specific audit work performed on equity in the balance sheet will be dictated by the requirements of company law. The procedures described here cover general audit principles which are likely to be relevant in most circumstances.

The amount of audit work performed on this area is usually not significant. If the auditor is confident that assets and liabilities are correctly stated, the total of equity (capital and reserves = assets minus liabilities) must also be correct.

4.1 Audit procedures: share capital

The auditor may need to make the following checks on share capital:

- The auditor should check that the total authorised share capital in the draft financial statements is consistent with the company's constitution.
- The auditor should check the nominal value of shares issued during the year, by reading the supporting documentation, and should ensure terms of issue were properly complied with.
- If new shares were issued during the year, check that cash received for them has been properly recorded in the main ledger.
- Check that the amount reported as issued share capital agrees with the amount recorded in the register of members/shareholders.

4.2 Audit procedures: reserves

The auditor should make the following checks on reserves:

- Obtain an analysis of movements on all reserves during the period.
- Check the accuracy of these movements by checking supporting documentation.
- Ensure that any specific legal requirements relating to reserves have been complied with. (For example, check that the entity has not breached legal restrictions on use of the share premium account.)
- Confirm that dividends have been deducted only from those reserves that are legally distributable (usually the accumulated profits reserve).
- Check the authorisation for the amount of dividends paid.
- Check the dividend calculations and check that the total dividends paid are consistent with the amount of issued share capital at the relevant date.

4.3 Audit of statutory books

UK company law requires companies to maintain certain 'books' or records containing defined information, in addition to their normal accounting records. These '**statutory books**' include the following:

- Minutes of board meetings and minutes of general meetings of the company.
- Register of members/shareholders.
- Register of directors and their interests in the shares and loan capital of the company.
- Register of charges on the company's assets.
- Copies of directors' service contracts and details of directors' remuneration packages. (Audit work on this area can be included in payroll testing procedures. The auditor should confirm that relevant company law disclosure requirements are complied with.)

The auditor should confirm that the required statutory records are maintained by the client company and are up-to-date.

CHAPTER 15

Audit finalisation

Contents

Going concern review: ISA 570

- Going concern basis and FRS 18
- Going concern: duties of the directors
- Going concern: duties of the auditor

1 Going concern review: ISA 570

After carrying out substantive testing, the auditor is getting close to the end of the audit process. However, several steps remain to be performed before the auditor can reach a conclusion on the financial statements or the other information that is subject to audit. These steps are the subject matter of most of this chapter.

Most of the procedures described here relate to the work of the external auditor, but some may also be relevant to the work of internal auditors.

1.1 Going concern basis and FRS 18

As covered in Paper F3, it is normally assumed that financial statements can be prepared on a **going concern basis.** Under the going concern basis it is assumed that the entity will continue in operational existence for the foreseeable future. The 'foreseeable future' (according to FRS 18) is at least 12 months.

FRS 18 states that management should make an assessment about whether the entity is able to continue as a going concern. The financial statements should be prepared on a going concern basis unless management intend to cease trading in the foreseeable future or will have no realistic alternative but to cease trading.

- When management makes an assessment that there are material uncertainties about whether the entity will continue as a going concern, the financial statements may be prepared on a going concern basis. However, the uncertainties about going concern status must be disclosed in a note to the financial statements.
- If the financial statements are not prepared on a going concern basis, this fact must be disclosed, together with:
  - the basis that has been used instead to prepare the statements, and
  - the reason why the going concern basis has not been used.

1.2 Going concern: duties of the directors

In preparing the financial statements, the **directors must satisfy themselves** (in accordance with FRS 18) **that the going concern basis is appropriate**. In the UK, there is a requirement for large companies (listed companies) to disclose the fact that, in the opinion of the directors, the company **is** a going concern.

It is therefore the responsibility of management to make the going concern assessment.

1.3 Going concern: duties of the auditor

The work of the external auditor on the going concern status of an entity is covered by ISA 570 *Going concern*. Key points from ISA 570 are set out below.

ISA 570 states that: 'When planning and performing audit procedures and in evaluating the results…, the auditor should **consider the appropriateness of management's use of the going concern assumption** in the preparation of the financial statements.'

This is a subjective area where judgement will be required to assess the uncertainties surrounding the assumptions that were made by management in reaching their conclusion about the going concern status of the company.

The auditor should review the procedures that were carried out by management to assess the going concern status. This review should check the future period of time that was considered by management in reaching their conclusion. If they looked less than 12 months into the future, the auditor should ask management to make a re-assessment and look at least 12 months into the future.

The auditor should remain alert throughout the audit process for factors or events that may indicate that the going concern status could be questionable/doubtful. Factors that may cast doubt on the going concern status of the company include the following:

- Recurring operating losses.
- Heavy dependence on short-term finance for long-term assets.
- Working capital deficiencies (such as a large bank overdraft, or exceptionally low levels of stocks).
- High gearing (a high ratio of debt capital to equity).
- Loan interest payments are in arrears.
- Excessive or obsolete stock.
- A deterioration in the company's relationships with its banks (evidenced, perhaps, in written correspondence) .
- Increased use of lease and hire purchase finance, in place of purchasing assets.
- Use of out-of-date technology.
- A low level of current sales orders.
- The company relies very heavily on the success of one product.
- There are legal proceedings that may jeopardise the company's ability to continue in business.
- A loss of key management or staff.
- A loss of a key customer or supplier.
- A significant increase in the level of competition in the market.

If there are indications that the going concern basis may not be appropriate, the auditor should:

- review management's plans for future action
- seek written representations from management regarding these plans
- gather additional audit evidence to enable him to reach a judgement about the degree of uncertainty that should be attached to the going concern status of the company.

The procedures for obtaining this additional audit evidence may include the following:

- Making an examination of cash flow forecasts for the client entity, the extent of its borrowing facilities (unused as well as used), the bank's intentions regarding these facilities, the amount and pattern of supplier credit review, and management's plans for future action. For example, the auditor may learn from the client entity's bank that the bank may withdraw its bank overdraft facility: this could put the entity at risk of immediate insolvency and liquidation.
- Discussions with the directors regarding their future plans. These may be sufficient to satisfy the auditor about the appropriateness of the going concern basis.
- Consideration of events after the balance sheet date that may have an impact on the future activities of the company.

Subsequent events: ISA 560

- FRS 21 and ISA 560
- Events occurring up to the date of the audit report
- Facts discovered after the date of the audit report

2 Subsequent events: ISA 560

2.1 FRS 21 and ISA 560

It is not possible to prepare financial statements that present a true and fair view by considering only those events and transactions that take place before the date at which the balance sheet is prepared. Material events that occur after the balance sheet date should also be considered when preparing the financial statements for the year. Although FRS 21 was covered in your Paper F3 studies, it is such an important standard in relation to ISA 560 that its principles are revised below.

Purpose of FRS 21

FRS 21 *Events after the balance sheet date* has two main objectives:

- to specify when an entity should adjust its financial statements for events that occur after the balance sheet date, but before the financial statements are authorised for issue, and
- to specify the disclosures that should be given about events that have occurred after the balance sheet date but before the financial statements were authorised for issue.

Events after the balance sheet date are defined in FRS 21 as 'those events, favourable and unfavourable that occur between the balance sheet date and the date when the financial statements are authorised for issue.'

There are two types of post-balance sheet event:

- **Adjusting events**. These are events that provide evidence of **conditions that already existed at the balance sheet date**.
- **Non-adjusting events**. These are events that have occurred due to **conditions arising after the balance sheet date**.

Accounting for adjusting post-balance sheet events

FRS 21 states that if an entity obtains information about an adjusting post-balance sheet event, it should **adjust the financial statements to reflect this new information**.

FRS 21 gives the following examples of **adjusting events**:

- The settlement after the balance sheet date of a court case, confirming that the entity had a present obligation as at the balance sheet date as a consequence of the case.
- The receipt of information after the balance sheet date indicating that an asset was impaired at the balance sheet date.
- The determination after the balance sheet date of the purchase cost of an asset, where the asset had already been purchased at the balance sheet date, but the purchase price had not been finally agreed or decided.
- The discovery of fraud or errors showing that the financial statements are incorrect.

Disclosures for non-adjusting post-balance sheet events

Non-adjusting post-balance sheet events are treated differently. A non-adjusting event relates to conditions that did not exist at the balance sheet date; therefore the **financial statements should not be updated** to include the effects of the event.

However, FRS 21 states that if a non-adjusting event is **material**, a failure by the entity to provide a disclosure about it could influence the economic decisions taken by users of the financial statements. For **material non-adjusting events** FRS 21 therefore requires disclosure of:

- the nature of the event, and
- an estimate of its financial effect, or a statement that such an estimate cannot be made.

This information should be disclosed in a note to the financial statements.

FRS 21 gives the following examples of **non-adjusting events**:

- A fall in value of an asset after the balance sheet date, such as a large fall in the market value of some investments owned by the entity, between the balance sheet date and the date the financial statements are authorised for issue.
- The acquisition or disposal of a major subsidiary.
- The formal announcement of a plan to discontinue a major operation.
- Announcing or commencing the implementation of a major restructuring.
- The destruction of a major plant by a fire after the balance sheet date.

The role of the auditor: ISA 560

The work of the external auditor in this area is covered by ISA 560: **Subsequent events**. ISA 560 requires the auditor to consider the impact of subsequent events on:

- the financial statements, and
- his audit report.

This means that audit procedures must be planned and performed so as to consider all significant transactions occurring after the balance sheet date. This means that the audit work does not stop with events only up to the balance sheet date. There are two key dates after the balance sheet: the date of the audit report and the date that the financial statements are issued.

- **Before the issue of the audit report**, the auditor should **actively look for** significant subsequent events. This is sometimes referred to as an **active review.**
- **After the issue of the audit report** (and up to the time that the financial statements are issued), the auditor has to consider the impact of any significant subsequent events **that come to his attention**. However, he does not have to look for these events actively. This is sometimes referred to as a **passive review.**

2.2 Events occurring up to the date of the audit report

Between the balance sheet date and the date of the audit report, the auditor is required to perform audit procedures to **identify** all significant transactions that may require either an adjustment of the financial statements or disclosure in the financial statements.

Normal audit verification work

The auditor may find evidence of subsequent events in the course of normal audit verification work. For example:

- The audit of debtors will consider whether debtors at the balance sheet date are collectable. Cash receipts after the year-end may indicate a significant non-payment, suggesting the need to write off a debt as 'bad'.
- The audit of stock includes a review of the net realisable value of stock. Sales of stock after the year-end may indicate that some stock in the balance sheet is over-valued (because subsequent events have shown that its NRV was less than cost).
- A search for unrecorded liabilities may discover the existence of some unrecorded liabilities, from invoices received after the balance sheet date but relating to the period covered by the financial statements.
- A review of the entity's cash position at the balance sheet date may find that a cheque from a customer, recorded as part of the bank balances, was dishonoured after the balance sheet date.

Procedures aimed specifically at identifying subsequent events

The auditor should also actively look for 'subsequent events', up to the time that he prepares the audit report. He should:

- discuss with management their procedures for identifying subsequent events
- carry out a review of management accounts in the new financial period, looking for subsequent events that are relevant to the financial statements
- review the client's profit forecasts and cash flow projections (for the same purpose)
- investigate known risk areas
- review minutes of shareholders' meetings, meetings of the board of directors and senior management meetings

- look for relevant information from other sources (competitors, suppliers, customers)
- assess any changes in legislation
- obtain written representations in respect of subsequent events (covered in a later section).

2.3 Facts discovered after the date of the audit report

Even after the date on which the audit report is signed, the auditor retains some degree of responsibility for **events of which he becomes aware**, up to the time that the financial statements are issued. He is not required, during this period, to actively look for subsequent events. His level of responsibility is therefore much reduced compared with the period before the signing of the audit report.

Between the date of the audit report and the issue of the financial statements

If the auditor becomes aware of facts or events during this period, he should:

- assess their impact on the financial statements
- consider whether the financial statements need amending
- discuss the matter with management, and
- take appropriate action.

If the financial statements are amended, the auditor should perform an additional review of subsequent events up to the date he now completes his audit work, because this will now become the new date of the audit report.

If management do not amend the financial statements for the subsequent event, but the auditor feels that an amendment should be made, the auditor must discuss the matter with management and consider the form of the audit report that he should now issue.

Facts discovered after the financial statements have been issued

The auditor has no obligation to perform audit procedures or make enquiries regarding the financial statements after they have been issued.

If the auditor becomes aware of a situation that **existed at the date of the audit report**, and that may have resulted in him issuing a 'modified' report, he should:

- consider whether the financial statements should have been revised
- discuss the matter with management, and
- take appropriate action.

Note: 'Modified' audit reports are explained in a later chapter.

If the event leads to management issuing revised financial statements, the auditor should:

- update his review of subsequent events (as above)

- review the steps taken by management to ensure that the revision of the financial statements is notified to anyone who received the original financial statements and audit report
- issue a new audit report, containing an **emphasis of matter paragraph**. This should refer to a note in the revised financial statements that explains in more detail the reason for the re-issue of the financial statements.

As usual, in the real exam, you are likely to be asked to **apply** your knowledge to a given scenario.

e

Example

You are the auditor in charge of the audit of Hindsight which has a 30th June year end. The subsequent events review for the year ended 30th June 20X5 revealed that, on 1st August 20X5, a receiver was appointed at a major customer. At 30th June 20X5 that customer owed £200,000 and goods costing £300,000 made to that customer's specification were held in stock. Both these amounts are material.

Required

List the matters to which you would direct your attention in respect of the above in relation to the audit for the year ended 30th June 20X5.

a

Answer

- Check that the directors are willing to adjust the financial statements for this adjusting post balance sheet event.
- Establish whether any cash has been received from this customer since the year end.
- Review any correspondence from the receiver to establish to what extent the outstanding debt will be recovered.
- Consider whether the goods held in stock are now valued at the lower of cost and NRV, given that these goods were made to the customer's specification. This may depend on whether or not those goods can be sold to a different customer.
- In the light of the above, consider whether any write downs proposed by the directors to debtors and/or stock are reasonable.
- If they are not, or if the directors refuse to adjust the financial statements, consider the impact on the audit report.

Management representations: ISA 580

- Definition of management representations
- Representations by management as audit evidence
- Unadjusted audit differences
- Documentation of representations by management
- Contents of the letter of representation

3 Management representations: ISA 580

3.1 Definition of management representations

A **management representation** is a statement made by management to the auditor during the course of the audit work.

Before the audit report is issued, the auditor should obtain written confirmation from management of appropriate representations. These are usually set out in a single document.

These management representations may be an important source of audit evidence.

3.2 Representations by management as audit evidence

During the course of the audit, management will make many representations to the auditor. Some of these are unsolicited and some are given in response to specific enquiries from the auditor. Where these representations relate to **material matters**, the auditor should:

- seek evidence that corroborates the representations given by management
- evaluate whether the representations appear reasonable and consistent with other audit evidence, and
- consider whether the individuals who made these representations can be expected to be well-informed on those matters (and so whether the auditor can rely on them in any way).

Representations by management **cannot be a substitute for other audit evidence**. If a representation by management is contradicted by other audit evidence, the auditor should:

- investigate the circumstances, and
- where necessary, reconsider the reliability of other representations made by the same management.

Required representations from management

The auditor is also required by ISA 580 to obtain certain other specific written representations from management. These will be included in the document of representations obtained from management before the issue of the audit report. These representations are as follows:

- Management acknowledges its responsibility for the fair presentation of the financial statements in accordance with the applicable financial reporting framework.
- Management has approved the financial statements.
- Management acknowledges its responsibility for the design and implementation of internal controls to prevent fraud and error.
- Management believes that the effect of 'unadjusted audit differences' are immaterial to the financial statements, both individually and in total.

3.3 Unadjusted audit differences

A **summary of the unadjusted audit differences** should be included in the written representations, or attached to them as an appendix.

During the course of the audit work, the auditor may identify what he considers to be errors in the client's measurement of certain items in the financial statements, such as stock or debtors. When this happens, the auditor should try to persuade the client to amend its figures for these items. If the client refuses to do so these differences become unadjusted audit differences.

The actual audit differences relate to the sample of items used by the auditor in his audit work, such as a sample of debtors or a sample of stock items. The actual differences found in the samples should be 'extrapolated', to estimate the audit difference for the entire 'population', such as total debtors and total stocks.

The summary of audit differences will summarise and assess the actual and extrapolated audit differences. Although this will be included in the written representations from management, the auditor is required to form his own view about the differences.

He should compare this schedule from management to the materiality thresholds he has set, to decide:

- whether or not the difference is material, and so
- whether or not he can issue an unmodified audit report.

3.4 Documentation of representations by management

The auditor records verbal discussions with management in the audit working papers. However, verbal evidence from the client's management is not strong audit evidence. In order to improve the quality of this evidence, the auditor will ask for these discussions to be confirmed in writing, along with the other acknowledgments to be made by management (listed above). This can take the form of:

- a **letter of representation**: this is a formal letter setting out all the representations from management, including those listed above, or
- a letter from the auditor outlining his understanding of management's representations: this letter should then be acknowledged and confirmed by management, or
- relevant minutes of meetings of the client's board of directors, containing evidence in support of the management representations.

A letter of representation is the most common form.

3.5 Contents of the letter of representation

The letter of representation is usually:

- drafted by the auditor (since he knows the areas on which he requires written representations)
- addressed to the auditor
- signed on behalf of the client's board of directors by the board member with primary responsibility for the entity and the financial aspects of its operations
- dated on the day the financial statements are approved by the board.

The contents of the letter of representation will cover:

- a number of general areas, common to most audits, plus
- specific matters which will depend on the circumstances of the particular audit in question.

General matters

In addition to those acknowledgments listed above, the **general matters** may include the following representations:

- The directors acknowledge the basis on which the financial statements have been prepared. This is normally the going concern basis.
- The directors provide a statement confirming the completeness and accuracy of its records and minutes of meetings.
- The directors confirm their compliance with legal obligations.
- The directors give details of matters affecting their company where there are, or may be, outstanding legal claims.
- A statement regarding loans and other transactions by the company with any directors.
- The directors confirm that no undisclosed events have taken place since the balance sheet date that change the financial position of the entity.

Example

The following points have arisen during the audit for the year ended 30th June 20X6 of Compo, a nationwide dealer in used cars:

1. During the year, five of Compo's properties were revalued by an independent surveyor.
2. One property was sold during the year to the marketing director.
3. It was discovered that some cars were scrapped for cash. Not all of these transactions have supporting documentation.
4. The directors have refused to make provision against a bad debt.

Required

Explain whether or not each of the above would be referred to in the letter of representation for the year ended 30th June 20X6.

Answer

1. No – other evidence should be available (the independent surveyor's report).
2. Yes – as part of the statement of loans and other transactions with directors.
3. Yes – evidence is needed of the completeness of such cash sales (although other evidence will also be required, such as analytical procedures and review of cash received).
4. No – the impact on the audit report will need to be considered. (And if the directors have refused, and the auditor is sure the debt is bad, the directors are not going to provide evidence to support this view in the letter of representation.)

Overall review of the financial statements

- General review
- Specific review

4 Overall review of the financial statements

After the detailed audit work has been completed, the auditor will carry out an overall review of the financial statements. By this stage of the audit, the financial statements should be in their final draft form.

This review will normally be carried out by a senior member of the audit team, often the manager or partner.

4.1 General review

At a general level, the review will check that a clear conclusion has been reached and documented on each of the financial statement areas. Analytical procedures may be used as a final check that the information contained in the draft financial statements 'makes sense'.

4.2 Specific review

More specifically, the overall review will cover the following matters:

- Compliance by the client with the relevant accounting framework (UK legislation and relevant accounting standards).
- A review of the accounting policies adopted by the company, to assess whether they are acceptable (and comply with accounting standards and industry practice).
- A review of the financial statements for adequate disclosure of relevant information.
- An assessment of whether the information contained in the financial statements is consistent with known business facts.

CHAPTER 16

The external audit report

Contents

Purpose of the audit report

- Introduction
- The audit report and your examination
- The expectation gap

1 Purpose of the audit report

1.1 Introduction

The audit report is the end-product of the external audit process. It is the document in which the auditor expresses his professional judgement on whether the financial statements present a 'true and fair view'.

The contents of the audit report are regulated by UK legislation. In addition, the external auditor is governed by:

- ISA 700 *The auditor's report on financial statements*, and
- Bulletin 2006/6 *Auditor's reports on financial statements in the United Kingdom.*

If the auditor is not able to state unreservedly in the report that a true and fair view is presented by the financial statements, a 'modified' report is issued.

1.2 The audit report and your examination

The examiner has stated that you will not be required to produce an audit report in full in an examination answer. However, you may be expected to:

- describe the appropriate type of audit report to be issued in a specific situation
- supply appropriate wording for a modification to an audit report (for example, drafting the "opinion" paragraph)
- explain extracts from a given audit report (such as one with errors of wording in it).

1.3 The expectation gap

The audit report is the only direct means of communication between the auditor and the users of the financial statements (who are mainly, but not exclusively, the shareholders). In recent years, auditing has suffered from an 'expectation gap' as the role of the auditor in law does not match what the users of financial statements expect from an auditor.

The term 'expectation gap' refers to the fact that the public perception of the role and responsibilities of the external auditor is different from his statutory role and responsibilities. The expectations of the public are often set at a level higher than that at which the external auditor actually operates.

Some examples of the misunderstandings inherent in the public's expectations are as follows:

- The public believes that the audit opinion in the audit report amounts to a 'certificate' that the financial statements are correct and can be relied upon for all decision-making purposes, including decisions about takeovers.
- The public also believes that the auditor has a duty to prevent and detect fraud and that this is one reason for an audit.
- The public assumes that, in carrying out his audit work, the auditor tests 100% of the transactions undertaken during the accounting period.

One consequence of these misunderstandings has been an increasing tendency to undertake legal action against the auditors, sometimes on a 'frivolous' basis, in the belief that the auditor should have prevented misstatements in the financial statements or should have prevented fraud.

Responses to the problem of the expectation gap have varied between countries. In the UK, corporate governance codes have been changed to strengthen the role and responsibilities of directors for sound internal control and accounting systems.

In addition, the standard format of the audit report has been expanded in recent years in an attempt to clarify what is involved in an audit and the relative responsibilities of the directors and the auditors.

Critics argue that these moves are not likely to be effective as those groups in society who are promoting the expectation gap may not understand these attempts that have been made to remedy the problem.

The unmodified audit report: ISA 700

- Definition of an unmodified audit report
- Main elements in the report

2 The unmodified audit report: ISA 700

2.1 Definition of an unmodified audit report

An unmodified audit report is an audit report containing an unmodified audit opinion (or 'unqualified' opinion).

An unmodified opinion should be expressed when the auditor concludes that the financial statements give a true and fair view, in all material respects, in accordance with the identified financial reporting framework.

An unmodified audit report provides a high level of assurance that a professional, independent examination of the financial statements has not revealed any material misstatements in those financial statements.

2.2 Main elements in the report

The main elements of the auditor's report, as given in ISA 700, are as follows:

Title

The auditor's report should have an appropriate title. It is now usual for the term 'independent auditor' to be used in the title. This is to distinguish this type of auditor's report from other reports that might be issued by other auditors (who may not have to abide by the same ethical requirements and requirement for independence as the independent auditor - for example, internal auditors).

Addressee

The report should be appropriately addressed, as required by law and the circumstances of the engagement. In the UK the report is usually addressed to the shareholders of the entity whose financial statements are being audited.

Introductory paragraph

The introductory paragraph in the report should:

- identify the entity whose financial statements have been audited
- state that the financial statements have been audited
- identify the title of each of the financial statements that make up the complete set of financial statements (profit and loss account, balance sheet, and so on) or

refer to the page numbers that contain the financial statements that have been audited.

- refer to the summary of significant accounting policies and other explanatory notes
- specify the date and period covered by the financial statements.

Directors' responsibility for the financial statements

The report should state that the directors of the client company are responsible for the preparation and presentation of the financial statements in accordance with the applicable financial reporting framework. It might also state that this responsibility includes:

- designing, implementing and maintaining appropriate internal controls
- selecting and applying appropriate accounting policies
- making accounting estimates that are reasonable in the circumstances.

Alternatively these responsibilities could be set our elsewhere in a separate statement of directors' responsibilities.

Auditor's responsibility

The report should state that the auditor's responsibility is to express an opinion on the financial statements based on the audit.

Scope paragraph

This section of the report describes the **scope** of the audit by summarising the audit work that has been done. This gives the reader of the report assurance that the audit has been carried out in accordance with established standards and practices.

Note. 'Scope' refers to the auditor's ability to perform the audit procedures which he deemed necessary in the circumstances. Any restriction on the scope of the audit can lead to a 'modified' audit report (which is explained later).

Basis of audit opinion

- The report should describe an audit, by stating that:
  - the audit was conducted in accordance with ISAs
  - an audit involves performing procedures to obtain audit evidence about the amounts and disclosures in the financial statements
  - the procedures selected depend on the auditor's judgment, including his assessment of the risks of material misstatement of the financial statements.
  - an audit also includes evaluating the appropriateness of the accounting policies used, the reasonableness of accounting estimates made by management, and the presentation of the overall financial statements.

Auditor's opinion

An unmodified opinion (unqualified opinion) should be expressed when the auditor concludes that the financial statements **give a true and fair view**, in all material respects, in accordance with the applicable financial reporting framework.

In the UK, auditors are specifically required to report on three matters in their audit report:

- whether the financial statements give a true and fair view in accordance with UK Generally Accepted Accounting Practice
- whether the financial statements have been properly prepared in accordance with the Companies Act 2006, and
- whether the information given in the directors' report is consistent with the financial statements.

Where UK accounting standards are not used as the financial reporting framework, the reference to the financial reporting framework in the wording of the opinion should identify the jurisdiction of the financial reporting framework.

Other matters

Standards, laws or generally-accepted practice may require or allow the auditor to elaborate on matters that provide further explanation of the auditor's responsibilities in his audit or the audit report. Such matters may be covered in a separate paragraph, following the auditor's opinion.

Auditor's signature

ISA 700 states that the report should be signed:

- in the name of the audit firm, or
- in the personal name of the auditor, or
- both.

However, the Companies Act 2006 now states that audit reports must be signed by the "senior statutory auditor" in his/her own name (on behalf of the firm).

Date of the auditor's report

The report should be dated no earlier than the date on which the auditor has obtained sufficient appropriate evidence on which to base his opinion on the financial statements.

This will not be earlier than the date on which the financial statements are signed or approved by the directors of the client company.

The date of the report informs the reader that the auditor has considered the effect on the financial statements (and on his audit report) of subsequent events which occurred after the balance sheet date and up to that date.

Auditor's address

The report should give a specific location for the auditor. This will usually be the city where the office responsible for the audit is located.

Example

An example of an unmodified audit report is set out below.

INDEPENDENT AUDITOR'S REPORT TO THE SHAREHOLDERS OF XYZ LIMITED

We have audited the financial statements of XYZ Limited for the year ended 31st December 20X7 which comprise the Profit and Loss Account, the Balance Sheet, the Cash Flow Statement, the Statement of Total Recognised Gains and Losses and the related notes. These financial statements have been prepared under the accounting policies set out therein.

Respective responsibilities of directors and auditors

The directors' responsibilities for preparing the Annual Report and the financial statements in accordance with applicable law and United Kingdom Accounting Standards (United Kingdom Generally Accepted Accounting Practice) are set out in the Statement of Directors' Responsibilities.

Our responsibility is to audit the financial statements in accordance with relevant legal and regulatory requirements and International Standards on Auditing (UK and Ireland).

We report to you our opinion as to whether the financial statements give a true and fair view and are properly prepared in accordance with the Companies Act 2006. We also report to you whether in our opinion the information given in the Directors' Report is consistent with the financial statements.

In addition we report to you if, in our opinion, the company has not kept adequate accounting records, if we have not received all the information and explanations we require for our audit, or if information specified by law regarding directors' remuneration and other transactions is not disclosed.

We read other information contained in the Annual Report, and consider whether it is consistent with the audited financial statements. This other information comprises only the Directors' Report, the Chairman's Statement and the Operating and Financial Review. We consider the implications for our report if we become aware of any apparent misstatements or material inconsistencies with the financial statements. Our responsibilities do not extend to any other information.

Basis of audit opinion

We conducted our audit in accordance with International Standards on Auditing (UK and Ireland) issued by the Auditing Practices Board. An audit includes examination, on a test basis, of evidence relevant to the amounts and disclosures in the financial statements. It also includes an assessment of the significant estimates and judgments made by the directors in the preparation of the financial statements, and of whether the accounting policies are appropriate to the company's circumstances, consistently applied and adequately disclosed.

We planned and performed our audit so as to obtain all the information and explanations which we considered necessary in order to provide us with sufficient evidence to give reasonable assurance that the financial statements are free from material misstatement, whether caused by fraud or other irregularity or error. In forming our opinion we also evaluated the overall adequacy of the presentation of information in the financial statements.

Opinion

In our opinion:

- the financial statements give a true and fair view, in accordance with United Kingdom Generally Accepted Accounting Practice, of the state of the company's affairs as at 31st December 20X7 and of its profit for the year then ended;
- the financial statements have been properly prepared in accordance with the Companies Act 2006; and
- the information given in the Directors' Report is consistent with the financial statements.

Registered auditors *Address*
Date

The modified audit report

- The nature of a modified audit report
- The emphasis of matter paragraph
- Qualified opinions

3 The modified audit report

3.1 The nature of a modified audit report

A modified audit report will be issued where the auditor is not able to express an **unreserved** opinion that the financial statements present a true and fair view.

Before issuing a modified report, the auditor should discuss with management the reason for the modification. The reason should be explained and the auditor should ask the client entity's management to amend the financial statements.

- If management make the necessary adjustments, the auditor will not need to issue a modified report.
- If management refuse to make the amendments, a modified report may be the only course of action available to the auditor.

An audit report is said to be **modified** where either:

- a matter arises which **does not affect the opinion** given by the auditor, but which gives rise to an **'emphasis of matter paragraph'** in the audit report, or
- a matter arises which **does affect the opinion** issued on the financial statements. This will give rise to a **qualified opinion**.

3.2 The emphasis of matter paragraph

An emphasis of matter paragraph is used to draw the reader's attention to a matter affecting the financial statements which:

- does not affect the opinion given by the auditor, and
- is explained more fully in a note to the financial statements.

The 'emphasis of matter' should be presented in a separate paragraph in the audit report:

- preferably after the opinion paragraph,
- but before any section on other reporting responsibilities.

It should be made clear that the audit opinion is not affected by the emphasis of matter.

When an emphasis of matter paragraph should be used

An emphasis of matter paragraph **should be used** to highlight a **material matter** relating to a **going concern problem**. The following illustrative wording for this type of emphasis of matter paragraph is based on ISA 570.

Note that this is only appropriate where the issues relating to the going concern of the entity are not such that a qualified audit report should be given.

> Without qualifying our opinion, we draw attention to Note X to the financial statements which indicates that the company incurred a net loss of £... during the year ended December 31st, 20X7 and, as of that date, the company's current liabilities exceeded its total assets by £.... These conditions, along with other matters as set forth in Note X, indicate the existence of a material uncertainty which may cast significant doubt about the company's ability to continue as a going concern.

When the auditor should consider using an emphasis of matter paragraph

The auditor **should consider using** an emphasis of matter paragraph if there is significant uncertainty (other than a going concern problem) which:

- may affect the financial statements, and
- the outcome of which depends on future events.

A further example of this type of emphasis of matter paragraph is given in ISA 700.

> Without qualifying our opinion we draw attention to Note X to the financial statements. The company is the defendant in a lawsuit alleging infringement of certain patent rights and claiming royalties and punitive damages. The company has filed a counter action, and preliminary hearings and discovery proceedings on both actions are in progress. The ultimate outcome of the matter cannot presently be determined, and no provision for any liability that may result has been made in the financial statements.

3.3 Qualified opinions

All qualifications arise from either:

- a **limitation on scope** (where the auditor is unable to generate the amount of audit evidence which he ideally requires), or
- a **disagreement** (the auditor disagrees with the information in the financial statements, and the client entity's management has refused to alter it).

Qualification grid: summary of modified audit reports

The following qualification 'grid' provides a useful summary of the decisions the auditor has to make in drafting a qualified audit report.

Reason for qualification	The effect on the financial statements is **material**	The effect on the financial statements is **pervasive/fundamental** *(Note that instances of these qualifications are rare in practice)*
Limitation on scope The auditor is unable to carry out procedures because of a lack of evidence. (For example, accounting records may have been lost or destroyed, or there has been a lack of information and explanations from the directors of the client company). As a result of this lack of audit procedures the auditor will be **uncertain** as to the view shown in the financial statements.	**'Except for'** opinion Example (a) below	The auditor is unable to form an opinion and **does not know** whether the financial statements give a true and fair view. This gives rise to a **'disclaimer' of opinion**. Example (b) below
Disagreement The auditor **disagrees** with the accounting treatment or disclosure of a particular matter.	**'Except for'** opinion Example (c) below	The financial statements **do not** give a true and fair view. This gives rise to an **'adverse' opinion**. Example (d) below

An opinion in the **materiality** column will be relevant when the auditor encounters a material problem with one or more **specific items** in the financial statements (such as a problem with stock or sales turnover), but the remaining items and the financial statements as a whole provide a true and fair view.

An opinion in the 'pervasive and fundamental' column applies in different circumstances. A 'pervasive' or 'fundamental' qualification is one that relates to the **overall true and fair view** given by the financial statements.

- In the case of a disagreement, the effect is to make the financial statements seriously misleading.
- In the case of limitations on scope it renders the auditor unable to form an opinion.

The difference between a 'material' and a 'pervasive' qualification is a matter of judgement. There are no absolute cut-off points or dividing lines that separate one from the other.

In all cases where a qualified opinion is issued, the auditor should adequately describe and quantify, if possible, the reason for and effect of the disagreement or uncertainty.

Examples of opinions in modified audit reports

Illustrative examples of the four types of modified opinion (or 'qualified' opinions) are shown below. They are all in line with examples given in Bulletin 2006/6. Where paragraphs in the examples are incomplete, the wording of the report concludes in the same way as in the example of the unmodified report, shown above.

(a) This is an example of an 'except for' opinion, relating to a material limitation on scope:

> We have audited....
>
> We planned and performed......................in the financial statements.
>
> We have audited........................any other information.
>
> **Basis of audit opinion**
>
> We conducted our audit in accordance with International Standards on Auditing (UK and Ireland) issued by the Auditing Practices Board, except that the scope of our work was limited as explained below.
>
> An audit includes examination, on a test basis, of evidence relevant to the amounts and disclosures in the financial statements. It also includes an assessment of the significant estimates and judgments made by the directors in the preparation of the financial statements, and of whether the accounting policies are appropriate to the company's circumstances, consistently applied and adequately disclosed.
>
> We planned our audit so as to obtain all the information and explanations which we considered necessary in order to provide us with sufficient evidence to give reasonable assurance that the financial statements are free from material misstatement, whether caused by fraud or other irregularity or error. However, with respect to stock having a carrying amount of £X the evidence available to us was limited because we did not observe the counting of the physical stock as of 31st December 20X1, since that date was prior to our appointment as auditor of the company. Owing to the nature of the company's records, we were unable to obtain sufficient appropriate audit evidence regarding the stock quantities by using other audit procedures.
>
> In forming our opinion we also evaluated the overall adequacy of the presentation of information in the financial statements.
>
> **Qualified opinion arising from limitation in audit scope**
>
> Except for the financial effects of such adjustments, if any, as might have been determined to be necessary had we been able to satisfy ourselves as to physical stock quantities, in our opinion the financial statements:
>
> - give a true and fair view, in accordance with United Kingdom Generally Accepted Accounting Practice, of the state of the company's affairs as at 31st December 20X1 and of its profit [loss] for the year then ended; and
> - have been properly prepared in accordance with the Companies Act 2006.
>
> In respect solely of the limitation on our work relating to stocks:
>
> - we have not obtained all the information and explanations that we considered necessary for the purpose of our audit; and
> - we were unable to determine whether adequate accounting records had been maintained.
>
> In our opinion the information given in the Directors' Report is consistent with the financial statements.
>
> *Registered auditors* *Address*
> *Date*

(b) This is an example of a 'disclaimer' of opinion, relating to a pervasive limitation on scope:

We have audited….

Basis of audit opinion

We conducted our audit in accordance with International Standards on Auditing (UK and Ireland) issued by the Auditing Practices Board, except that the scope of our work was limited as explained below.

An audit includes examination, on a test basis, of evidence relevant to the amounts and disclosures in the financial statements. It also includes an assessment of the significant estimates and judgments made by the directors in the preparation of the financial statements, and of whether the accounting policies are appropriate to the company's circumstances, consistently applied and adequately disclosed.

We planned our audit so as to obtain all the information and explanations which we considered necessary in order to provide us with sufficient evidence to give reasonable assurance that the financial statements are free from material misstatement, whether caused by fraud or other irregularity or error. However, the evidence available to us was limited because we were unable to observe the counting of physical stock having a carrying amount of £X and send confirmation letters to trade debtors having a carrying amount of £Y due to limitations placed on the scope of our work by the directors of the company. As a result of this we have been unable to obtain sufficient appropriate audit evidence concerning both stock and trade debtors. Because of the significance of these items, we have been unable to form a view on the financial statements.

In forming our opinion we also evaluated the overall adequacy of the presentation of information in the financial statements.

Opinion: disclaimer on view given by the financial statements

Because of the possible effect of the limitation in evidence available to us, we are unable to form an opinion as to whether the financial statements:

- give a true and fair view, in accordance with United Kingdom Generally Accepted Accounting Practice, of the state of the company's affairs as at ... and of its profit [loss] for the year then ended; and
- have been properly prepared in accordance with the Companies Act 2006.

In respect solely of the limitation of our work referred to above:

- we have not obtained all the information and explanations that we considered necessary for the purpose of our audit; and
- we were unable to determine whether adequate accounting records have been maintained.

Notwithstanding our disclaimer on the view given by the financial statements, in our opinion the information given in the Directors' Report is consistent with the financial statements.

Registered auditors *Address*
Date

(c) This is an example of an 'except for' opinion relating to a material disagreement:

> We have audited..........in the financial statements.
>
> **Qualified opinion arising from disagreement about accounting treatment**
>
> Included in the debtors shown on the balance sheet is an amount of £Y due from a company which has ceased trading. XYZ plc has no security for this debt. In our opinion the company is unlikely to receive any payment and full provision of £Y should have been made. Accordingly, debtors should be reduced by £Y, deferred taxes should be reduced by £X and profit for the year and retained earnings should be reduced by £Z.
>
> Except for the financial effect of not making the provision referred to in the preceding paragraph, in our opinion the financial statements:
>
> - give a true and fair view, in accordance with United Kingdom Generally Accepted Accounting Practice, of the state of the company's affairs as at ... and of its profit [loss] for the year then ended; and
> - have been properly prepared in accordance with the Companies Act 2006.
>
> In our opinion the information given in the Directors' Report is consistent with the financial statements.
>
> *Registered auditors* *Address*
> *Date*

(d) This is an example of an 'adverse' opinion relating to a pervasive disagreement:

> We have audited..................in the financial statements.
>
> **Adverse opinion on the financial statements**
> As more fully explained in note x to the financial statements no provision has been made for losses expected to arise on certain long-term contracts currently in progress, as the directors consider that such losses should be off-set against amounts recoverable on other long-term contracts. In our opinion, provision should be made for foreseeable losses on individual contracts as required by [specify accounting standards] .... If losses had been so recognised the effect would have been to reduce the carrying amount of contract work in progress by £X, deferred taxes payable by £Y, and the profit for the year and retained earnings at 31st December 20X1 by £Z.
>
> In view of the effect of the failure to provide for the losses referred to above, in our opinion the financial statements do not give a true and fair view, in accordance with United Kingdom Generally Accepted Accounting Practice, of the state of the company's affairs as at 31st December 20X1 and of its profit [loss] for the year then ended.
>
> In all other respects, in our opinion the financial statements have been properly prepared in accordance with the Companies Act 2006.
>
> Notwithstanding our adverse opinion on the financial statements, in our opinion the information given in the Directors' Report is consistent with the financial statements.
>
> *Registered auditors* *Address*
> *Date*

Example

The audit junior of ErrataCo has drafted the audit report for the year ended 31st December 20X4. The following are extracts from that report:

> **AUDITOR'S REPORT**
>
> We have audited the accompanying financial statements of ErrataCo.
>
> Management have failed to provide against a material debt in the financial statements.
>
> Without qualifying our opinion, we draw attention to the above fact.
>
> In our opinion, the financial statements give a true and fair view ....

Required

Set out the errors in the above report and explain why they are errors. Note: You are not required to refer to the paragraphs not reproduced above.

Answer

- The report is headed up "Auditor's Report". It should be headed up "Independent Auditor's Report" to distinguish it from reports by other auditors which might not be independent.
- The report does not set out which financial statements have been audited. It should refer to the year end and the specific statements audited (for example income statement, balance sheet, cash flow statement and notes to the financial statements) to ensure there is no misunderstanding about exactly what has been audited (for example, not the directors' report).
- The amount of the error should be quantified (e.g. the receivable is stated at £400,000 and should have been included at £nil).
- The report contains an emphasis of matter and then an unqualified opinion. The report should have been qualified on the basis of a material disagreement (i.e. with the valuation of the debtor) and an "except for" opinion given.

The impact of going concern on the audit report: ISA 570

- Where the going concern assumption is appropriate but a material uncertainty exists
- Where the going concern assumption is inappropriate

4 The impact of going concern on the audit report: ISA 570

As discussed in a previous chapter, if indications are found which suggest that the going concern basis might not be appropriate for preparing the financial statements, the auditor should consider the appropriate form of the audit report.

The form of the report will depend on the auditor's judgement. There are two possible views he could take:

- the going concern assumption is appropriate but a material uncertainty exists, or
- the going concern assumption is inappropriate.

4.1 Where the going concern assumption is appropriate but a material uncertainty exists

Where the auditor considers that the going concern assumption is **appropriate, but a material uncertainty exists,** he must consider whether the financial statements adequately disclose:

- the principal events that give rise to the uncertainty, and
- the existence of the material uncertainty itself.

If there **is adequate disclosure**, then the auditor should express an unqualified opinion. However, he should use an **emphasis of matter paragraph** to highlight the uncertainty. (This paragraph was described earlier.)

If there **is not adequate disclosure** then the auditor should express a qualified opinion. This will be on the grounds of disagreement with the client company's management over disclosure, and will lead to:

- an 'except for' qualification, or
- an adverse qualification.

4.2 Where the going concern assumption is inappropriate

Where the going concern assumption is **inappropriate**, the auditor should express:

- an adverse opinion if the financial statements have been prepared on a going concern basis
- an unqualified opinion if the financial statements have been prepared on an alternative acceptable basis (for example, a break-up basis) and there is adequate disclosure of this basis. An emphasis of matter paragraph may be required in the audit report.

Other information issued with the audited financial statements: ISA 720

- Purpose of ISA 720
- Material inconsistencies
- Material misstatements of fact
- Responsibility in relation to the directors' report

5 Other information issued with the audited financial statements: ISA 720

5.1 Purpose of ISA 720

Although the auditor reports only on the financial statements themselves, the financial statements are issued with other, unaudited, information. The nature of this additional unaudited information may vary according to statutory requirements and individual companies. However, it may include items such as a directors' report, a chairman's report, financial highlights or employment data.

In order that the credibility of the financial statements is not undermined by any of this additional information, ISA 720 *Other information in documents containing audited financial statements* imposes certain duties on the auditor.

5.2 Material inconsistencies

ISA 720 requires the auditor to read the other (unaudited) information in order **to identify material inconsistencies** with the audited financial statements.

A **material inconsistency** exists when the other information contradicts information contained in the audited financial statements.

Where a **material inconsistency** is identified, the auditor should decide what should be amended, and whether it is the audited financial statements, or the other unaudited information, that needs to be amended.

- If the auditor judges that the **financial statements need to be amended**, and the directors refuse to do so, then the auditor should express a qualified opinion in his audit report.
- If the auditor believes that the **other information needs to be amended**, and the directors refuse to do so, then the auditor should consider using an emphasis of matter paragraph in his audit report. Alternatively, he may take some other action, probably after taking legal advice.

5.3 Material misstatements of fact

A **material misstatement of fact** exists when unaudited information is incorrectly stated or presented, but the information is **not related to** matters appearing in the audited financial statements. (The misstatement of fact therefore does not contradict the financial statements.)

If the auditor **becomes aware** of a material misstatement of fact, he should:

- discuss the matter with management, and
- consider whether the other information needs to be amended.

If the auditor considers that the other information needs to be amended, and the directors refuse to do so, the auditor should consider other action, and may take legal advice about the matter.

5.4 Responsibility in relation to the directors' report

For most of the 'other information' in the annual report, the auditor has the general responsibility described above to read the information and deal with any inconsistencies or misstatements that are identified.

However, the Companies Act gives the auditor a specific responsibility in relation to the directors' report: the auditor must read the directors' report and must specifically state in the audit report whether or not the information given in the directors' report is consistent with the financial statements.

CHAPTER 17

Other audit and assurance situations and reports

Contents

Tutorial note

This final chapter deals with a number of syllabus topics each of which has its own particular characteristics.

Not-for-profit organisations

- Auditing of not-for-profit organisations (NFPOs)
- NFPOs: the audit approach

1 Not-for-profit organisations

1.1 Auditing of not-for-profit organisations (NFPOs)

In any audit or review, it is important to understand the entity and its environment. A key aspect of an audit or review may be the objective that the entity is trying to achieve.

- In commercial organisations, the objective is to make a profit for the shareholders.
- In the case of not-for-profit organisations (NFPOs), the objective is very different. It is usually the provision of a service to society as a whole or to a group in society. Examples are charities, clubs and societies and publicly-owned organisations.
- The service provided by an NFPO will have to be provided within the constraints of the resources it has at its disposal. In other words, an NFPO will seek to achieve its objective as much as possible with the money and other resources available.

Example

A charity organisation is an example of an NFPO.

- It has certain defined beneficiaries, since it was established for the purpose of providing benefits to them.
- It raises funds from the public.
- It seeks to spend those funds as effectively as possible to help its beneficiaries.

NFPOs may be required to have an audit performed under law, or may choose to have an audit performed on a voluntary basis in order to add credibility to their financial statements.

The difference in the objectives of an NFPO, compared with the objectives of a commercial company, will influence the approach to the audit.

In addition, there may be specific auditing and reporting requirements set out in regulations for certain types of NFPOs. This may also influence the audit work performed and the form and content of the opinion issued.

If the NFPO requests an audit to be performed on a voluntary basis, or requires a review to be carried out, the scope of the work and the nature of any report issued will be agreed in advance between the auditor and the NFPO.

1.2 NFPOs: the audit approach

The auditor should recognise the specific features of the NFPO. However, it is important to realise that the auditor is still performing an audit, and the overall **structure** of the audit of an NFPO will be similar to the audit of a commercial organisation. However, the detail of the audit will probably differ.

The main points to bear in mind with the audit of an NFPO are summarised below. These are general principles. They should be modified as appropriate to reflect the circumstances of each particular NFPO.

Audit area	Comments
Planning	Consider: ▪ the objectives and scope of the audit work ▪ any specific regulations that apply ▪ the environment in which the organisation operates ▪ the form and content of the final financial statements and the audit opinion ▪ key audit areas, including risk.
Risk	Carry out an audit risk analysis under the usual headings of inherent risk, control risk and detection risk: ▪ inherent risk (reflecting the nature of the entity's activities and the environment) ▪ control risk (internal controls, and the risk that these may be inadequate: controls over cash collection and cash payments may be a key area for an NFPO such as a charity, because large amounts of cash may be collected from the public by volunteers) ▪ detection risk (the risk that the auditor will fail to identify any material error or misstatement in performing the audit).
Internal control	Key areas of internal control in a NFPO might include: ▪ segregation of duties (although this may be difficult in a small NFPO with only a few employees) ▪ authorisation of spending ▪ cash controls ▪ controls over income (donations, cash collections, membership fees, grants) ▪ the use of funds only for authorised purposes.

Table continues

Audit area	Comments
Audit evidence	▪ A substantive testing approach (rather than a systems based approach) is likely to be necessary in a small NFPO, because of weaknesses in its internal control system. ▪ Key areas may include: – the completeness of recording transactions, assets and liabilities – the possibility of misuse of funds. ▪ Analytical procedures may be used to 'make sense' of the reported figures. ▪ There should be a review of the final financial statements, including a review of the appropriateness of the accounting policies.
Reporting	▪ If a report on an NFPO is required by law, the standard external audit report covered in a previous chapter can be used. ▪ If the audit is performed on a voluntary basis, the report needs to reflect the agreed objective of the audit. However, it is good practice for the report to follow the general structure laid down by ISA 700: – addressee – scope of the report – responsibilities of auditors versus the responsibilities of management – the audit work done – the audit opinion – date, name and address of auditor.

The external auditor's report to management: ISA 260

- Introduction
- Reports to management on control weaknesses
- Communication with management at the end of the audit
- Communication of other relevant matters to those charged with governance

2 The external auditor's report to management: ISA 260

2.1 Introduction

In the UK the audit report for a company is addressed to the shareholders, as owners of the company. ISA 260 *Communication of audit matters with those charged with governance* requires that in addition, the external auditors should report to management as a 'by-product' of the audit process.

There are three main aspects to this communication process:

- During the audit work the auditor should report to management on control weaknesses that have been identified.
- At the end of the external audit process, the auditor should communicate with management on the audit in general.
- In addition, the external auditor should also communicate other relevant matters to 'those charged with governance'. (This usually means the directors of the company.)

Each of these is dealt with in more detail below.

2.2 Reports to management on control weaknesses

The auditor should make management aware of significant weaknesses in the design or operation of the control systems in place. Typically, this information is communicated by means of a letter or report sent by the auditor to management. It is prepared and sent after the results of the tests of control are known – usually after the **interim audit**.

The report may later be updated after the **final audit**, if further weaknesses have been found, or if weaknesses that were reported to management previously have not yet been dealt with by management.

The letter or report should make clear the following points:

- The report covers only those weaknesses that have been discovered as a result of the audit work that has been undertaken. It is a by-product of a statutory audit, and is not the result of a full review of systems and controls. As a consequence, other weaknesses may exist that are not mentioned in the report.

- The weaknesses have already been brought to the attention of appropriate members of the finance department.
- The report is issued for use by management only (or possibly for the use of other persons identified in the report).

The report should identify the following information for each weakness reported:

- The nature of the weakness in the present system, in terms of both design and operation. (In other words, is there a control weakness 'on paper'? If there is no control weakness 'on paper', are the controls applied effectively in practice?)
- The implication of this weakness in controls.
- Recommendations for improvement.

The auditor should ask management to provide a response and action plan for each weakness identified in the report. He should also mention that the contents of the report will be followed up in future audits.

This **management letter** or **letter of weakness** is provided as an extra service to the client by the external auditor. If management address the points in the letter, the controls in place will be improved. This may enable future audits to focus on the more efficient systems-based approach. This in turn may reduce the cost of the audit to the client.

An earlier chapter looked at the identification of specific control "risks" and asked for suggestion of controls to mitigate these risks. This topic could also be tested in the exam in the context of the preparation of a management letter.

Example

You are the auditor of AdviceCo. During your audit of the purchases cycle you have identified the following weaknesses:

1. Purchase ledger clerks amend standing data held on the standing data masterfile when they are instructed to do so by the buying manager.
2. The financial director signs cheques made out to suppliers without sight of any supporting documentation.

Required

In respect of the above weaknesses set out the consequences of each weakness and the recommendations you would suggest as they might appear in the management letter.

a

Answer

Weakness 1

Consequence

Inappropriate amendments could be made leading to a loss to AdviceCo. For example, incorrect standing data could lead to incorrect discounts being claimed or supplies being purchased from non-authorised suppliers.

Recommendation

All amendments to standing data should be instigated on standard documentation, counter-signed by the buying director. This documentation should be retained and subsequently reviewed by a responsible official (such as the financial controller) to ensure that the correct amendments have been made and that the amendments were properly authorised.

Weakness 2

Consequence

A supplier could be overpaid or paid twice or a cheque could be paid to an entity which has not supplied the organisation (if an employee wishes to commit fraud).

Recommendation

Cheque signatories should inspect supporting documentation such as original purchase invoices made out to AdviceCo. This check should be evidenced by signature on the invoices being paid.

2.3 Communication with management at the end of the audit

The communication with management at the end of the audit may be provided either in writing or orally. It often takes place as a discussion between the auditor and an appropriate level of management, perhaps with the audit committee in the case of a larger company. The process should be completed before the audit report is finalised.

The communication may cover such matters as:

- significant audit adjustments that were identified during the audit
- difficulties encountered during the audit
- disagreements or difficulties the auditor had in his dealings with management
- concerns relating to accounting policies or practices
- significant business risks identified
- recommendations for improvement.

2.4 Communication of other relevant matters to those charged with governance

ISA 260 requires that auditors should communicate matters relevant to corporate governance arising from the audit work. This can be either verbally or in writing to those charged with the governance of an entity. In the case of a company, this is the board of directors or audit committee (which is a sub-committee of the board of directors).

The matters communicated will be similar to those listed above, for items to communicate at the end of the audit. Specifically, they may include:

- the possible effect of significant risk areas (such as legal actions) on the financial statements
- material uncertainties over the going concern status of the entity
- significant disagreements with management
- possible modifications to the audit report
- questions regarding the integrity of management.

The audit of small businesses

3 The audit of small businesses

3.1 Introduction

Detailed guidance in this area is provided by Practice Note 13 *The audit of small businesses.*

Standard audit practice requires the auditor to gain an understanding of the business and its environment in developing an audit strategy. Applying this principle to the audit of small businesses will allow the auditor to focus attention on the main features of the client, which will affect the audit approach.

As discussed in a previous chapter, the key point here is likely to be internal control.

- Segregation of duties is likely to be weak as a result of restricted numbers of staff being employed.
- Owners or senior management are likely to dominate all major aspects of the business activities. This is useful as a form of supervisory control, but there is often little in the way of control over management themselves.
- In an expanding business, senior management may be more involved in developing the business, leaving little time for implementing supervisory or other controls.
- Record keeping may be informal or inadequate.

3.2 Audit approach to small entities

The list below summarises the main additional points for the auditor to consider when dealing with a small business:

- **Acceptance of the audit appointment**: The auditor should be aware of the possible risks to independence resulting from close involvement with management and pressure on the audit fee.
- **Engagement letter:** This formalises the relationship between the auditor and the client. If necessary, it separates the accounts preparation function from the auditing function.
- **Planning and recording:** This process will be similar to any audit engagement, but is likely to be simpler.
- **Accounting systems:** The systems may not be adequate for audit purposes and the auditor may not be able to rely on the controls in place. As a result, control risk is likely to be high.

- **Substantive procedures**: These are likely to form the basis of the audit work, if controls are weak. However, it is difficult to reach a conclusion on *completeness* of accounting records based only on substantive procedures.
- **Audit evidence**: High quality evidence may be more difficult to find than in a larger entity.
- **Management representations:** become more important in smaller businesses. However, the auditor must look for evidence to *support* the representations.
- **Audit report**: There may be insufficient evidence as to the completeness and accuracy of the records, which may lead to a qualified opinion.
- **Review of financial statements:** As for any audit but it may be that smaller businesses may be exempt from certain reporting requirements (for example, from the application of certain requirements of International Financial Reporting Standards).

Q&A

Practice questions

Contents

1 Audit and review

(a) Explain the difference between an audit and a review.

(b) Explain why an audit is necessary.

(c) Briefly explain the meaning of the following terms:

  (i) A true and fair view

  (ii) Materiality

2 Corporate governance

(a) Explain what is meant by corporate governance.

(b) Explain how the following fit into the workings of corporate governance:

  (i) Management

  (ii) The external auditor

  (iii) The internal auditor

  (iv) The audit committee

3 Zubrovka

The directors of Zubrovka, a newly-formed company, have written to you with a view to securing your services as auditor. Within their letter you note the following comments:

'Your duties and rights as auditor will be determined by the board of our company. In the main, these duties are in line with the requirements of company law, but in the event of conflict or exclusion we will indemnify you against any legal action brought as a consequence of the position adopted. The board also retains the right to dismiss you at any time without necessarily disclosing the reasons for their action.'

Required

(a) Describe your understanding of your duties as auditor of Zubrovka.

(b) As auditor, describe your relationship as the auditor to the directors of Zubrovka.

(c) Outline your rights under the Companies Act 2006 as auditor of a limited company.

(d) Consider whether or not the directors have the authority to dismiss you.

(e) Set out the steps you would take prior to accepting the appointment as auditor to the company.

4 Babushka

John Ford is the managing director of Babushka, a private company. Babushka is currently audited by Old and Co. John has informed you that the directors of Babushka wish to appoint your firm, New and Co as auditors in place of Old and Co, but they consider that Old and Co will not be willing to resign.

Required

(a) Assuming that Old and Co are not willing to resign, set out the statutory and other procedures which will have to be followed by Babushka, your firm and which may be adopted by Old and Co in connection with this proposed appointment. You should assume that New and Co have adequate resources to take on the audit of Babushka, and that there are no issues surrounding independence or client integrity.

(b) Assuming that Old and Co are willing to resign part way through their term of office, set out the procedures to be followed by Old and Co and Babushka in order to effect the resignation.

5 Keane

It has been suggested that the most important matter affecting the credibility of the auditor is that of 'independence'.

Required

(a) Discuss, giving examples, matters other than independence, which might be relevant in relation to the credibility of the auditor and steps that the accounting profession has taken or might take in relation to them.

(b) Comment on the following situations in the context of the independence of the auditor, showing clearly the threats involved and the safeguards required by the ACCA Code and the APB's Ethical Standards.

(i) The audit manager in charge of the audit assignment of Keane holds 1,000 £1 ordinary shares in the company (total shares in issue – 100,000). The audit partner holds no shares.

(ii) An audit partner of a firm of Certified Accountants is a personal friend of the chief accountant of Scholes. The chief accountant is not a director of the company and the partner is not responsible for the audit of Scholes.

(iii) The audit fee receivable from Giggs, a listed company, is £100,000. The total fee income of the audit firm is £700,000.

(iv) The audit senior in charge of the audit of Fletcher, a bank, has a personal loan from the Fletcher Bank of £2,000 on which he is currently paying a market rate of interest.

(v) An audit partner is responsible for two audit assignments: Ronaldo and Neville. Ronaldo has recently tendered for a contract with Neville for a supply of material quantities of goods over a number of years. Neville has asked the audit partner to advise on the matter.

6 Dilemma and Co

(a) State how legislation and the ACCA Code each seek to ensure the independence and objectivity of auditors.

(b) The following three situations have arisen in the audit firm of Dilemma and Co:

(i) One of the partners, Mr Smith, and his wife have been invited by the managing director of Fancy Ceramics, an audit client, to celebrate the company's 20th anniversary with management over a long weekend in France. Mr Smith has been the engagement partner since incorporation of the company.

(ii) The firm has been approached and asked to accept appointment as auditors of Gorgeous Potteries. One of the firm's audit managers is company secretary of the company, although he takes no part in the management of the company. His parents are the directors and shareholders of Gorgeous Potteries.

(iii) The directors of Green Goods are unhappy with the level of fees charged by the firm. They are still refusing to agree an outstanding bill for taxation and advisory work, and are demanding a reduction in the audit fee this year to match a quote they have received from another firm.

Required

Comment on the situations described above, recognising any threats to independence or objectivity, and suggesting what safeguards the firm should put in place to deal with such threats.

7 Engagement letters

(a) Explain the purpose of an engagement letter and when it may be appropriate to send a new letter to an existing client.

(b) Set out the main components of an engagement letter.

8 Usefulness of internal audit

Explain the usefulness of the internal audit function to the management of a business. Illustrate your answer with practical examples.

9 Venture Videos

You are the internal auditor of Venture Videos, which runs a chain of video rental stores.

The company guarantees that if a video is not available for rental, the customer will get free rental when that video comes back into stock. It is not possible for customers to pre-book videos.

The company purchases a number of copies of each video, taking the above policy into account, but has no way of monitoring whether their procurement strategy is effective. Procurement decisions are made and actioned locally and no central budgets are produced.

You have been asked by the directors to review the above procurement and other strategies.

Required

Identify and explain the potential business risks arising from the above procurement and other strategies. Suggest controls and strategies that management could instigate to mitigate those business risks.

10 Planning

ISA 300 *Planning an audit of financial statements* requires the auditor to plan his audit work so that the audit will be performed in an effective manner.

Required

(a) Explain why the need for planning exists and what benefits are to be derived from adopting such an approach.

(b) Set out the steps you would take prior to the commencement of an audit of a limited company which has been a client for a number of years.

(c) Planning is equally relevant to the work of the internal auditor. Explain how the internal auditor's planning differs to that of the external auditor.

11 Beautiful Jewels

Beautiful Jewels designs, manufactures and retails expensive jewellery. Stock is held at the design warehouse and at three shops. Stock is also sometimes sent to customers for approval prior to a sale being made. Your firm has been re-appointed as auditors for the year ended 31st December 20X4.

Beautiful Jewels has had a difficult year. A recession has caused a fall in sales and the future is uncertain. A fourth shop was closed during the year and the premises are still up for sale. The financial director was dismissed half way through the year and is pursuing a claim for unfair dismissal. A replacement has not yet been found.

The managing director is due to retire next year and is likely to require loans he has made to the business to be repaid. Negotiations with the bank in respect of loans to cover these repayments have started.

Required

(a) State what you understand by audit risk and why it is important to the auditor.

(b) Identify the risks arising from the above that will need to be taken into account when planning the audit of Beautiful Jewels. Explain why these risks need to be taken into account.

12 Blunkett Manufacturing

You are planning the audit of the sales system and year end trade debtors of Blunkett Manufacturing.

The company has turnover of approximately £15 million and all of its sales are made on credit. The year end value of trade debtors is approximately £3 million, and there are about 1,000 customers on the sales ledger.

You have been asked by the partner in charge of the audit to consider whether it would be appropriate to use statistical or judgemental sampling in your audit work. You have also been asked to consider the advantages and disadvantages of using these techniques.

Required

(a) Describe and illustrate, by the use of suitable examples, the way in which statistics and judgement can be used in audit sampling, in relation to:

- (i) the audit of the sales system
- (ii) writing directly to trade debtors, asking them to confirm the balance owed
- (iii) the verification of year end trade debtors.

(b) Based on your answer to (a) above, discuss the advantages and disadvantages of the use of statistical or judgemental sampling.

13 Woolacombe Souvenirs

The directors of your client, Woolacombe Souvenirs, have telephoned to tell you that one of their junior employees has been caught stealing petty cash and has admitted to several previous thefts. The total amount of lost cash has been estimated by the directors to be £300. The thefts took place in the year in respect of which you have just completed the audit. The materiality level on the audit was set at £100,000.

The directors are demanding to know why this was not picked up during the audit work, and when the audit report will be reissued as the audit report and accounts have now been signed.

Required

(a) Set out the points you would include in a response to the directors of Woolacombe Souvenirs.

(b) Explain why the auditor, when planning and performing his audit, should consider whether his client has complied with laws and regulations. Set out the actions which may be appropriate if the auditor discovers material areas of non-compliance.

14 Financial statement assertions

ISA 500 *Audit evidence* requires the auditor to obtain sufficient, appropriate evidence to be able to draw reasonable conclusions on which to base the audit opinion. That evidence should be relevant to the so-called 'financial statement assertions'.

Required

(a) Set out the main financial statement assertions and provide an example of each one by reference to the audit of sales or trade debtors.

(b) Set out the five main audit testing procedures and give an example of how each might be used in the audit of plant and machinery.

15 John

Your office has recently taken on a new student, John. You have been asked to explain to John what information is recorded in the audit process and where.

Required

Set out a brief explanation for John.

16 Internal audit questionnaire

As external auditor, you are planning to rely on the work of the internal audit department at your client.

Required

Prepare questions for inclusion in a questionnaire to be sent to the head of the internal audit function, which, when completed, will allow you to assess how much reliance, if any, you can place on the work of the internal audit function.

17 Sopot

You are auditing the purchases system of Sopot. In this system:

(1) purchase orders are raised by the purchasing manager and signed by the managing director

(2) goods are received by the goods receiving department, which prepares a goods received note

(3) purchase invoices are posted to the purchase ledger by the book-keeper. The purchase ledger is maintained on a small microcomputer

(4) cheques paying suppliers are signed by the managing director.

A junior member of the audit staff has asked you a number of questions on the subject of internal control.

Required

(a) Define the term 'internal control' and set out the five elements which make up an internal control system.

(b) Describe the reasons why it is important to the auditor that there should be a good system of internal controls in operation.

(c) List the stages you would go through in carrying out the audit of the purchases system and briefly describe how these involve consideration and testing of the system of internal control.

(d) Describe the effect on your audit work, and the action you would take:

  (i) if you found a weakness in one of the controls in the purchases system

  (ii) if you concluded that weaknesses in the system of internal control in the purchases system were so serious that you would not be able to rely on internal controls in your audit work on purchases.

18 Control activities

ISA 315 defines control activities as 'the policies and procedures that help ensure that management directives are carried out'. These activities are detailed procedures designed to prevent, or to detect and correct, errors that may arise in processing information.

Required

(a) Set out six examples of types of controls and illustrate each one in the context of the purchases or trade creditors system.

(b) Explain why, even where tests of controls prove satisfactory, substantive procedures can never be completely eliminated.

19 Ascertaining and recording accounting systems

Discuss the usefulness of the different methods available to an auditor for ascertaining and recording an entity's accounting and internal control system.

20 Grander Products

Grander Products has the following wages and salaries system for its 40 pieceworkers who are paid weekly in cash.

Each employee fills in a record of work completed which is signed by one of two supervisors before being passed to the accounts department. The payroll clerk takes these details, and prepares the payroll, referring to the personnel records kept by the company secretary. The payroll clerk then requests a cheque for the weekly cash wages and prepares the pay packets which are distributed by the supervisors.

Required

Draft questions to be included in an internal control questionnaire for weekly wages paid in cash.

21 Pivo

Mr Pivo, a client of your firm, is the managing director of Pivo, which buys do-it-yourself tools from large manufacturers and sells them to small retailers.

As the firm has been expanding, Mr Pivo has recently purchased a microcomputer. He has asked your advice about the controls which should be exercised over the computer when processing accounting data. Initially, Mr Pivo is proposing to use the computer for producing sales invoices and maintaining the sales ledger.

The sales system data files will comprise:

- standing data files containing customer names, addresses and credit limits and a price file containing the part numbers, descriptions and selling prices of the company's products
- transaction files containing the outstanding transactions for each customer's account, the values of individual invoices, credit notes, cash, discount and adjustments posted to the sales ledger in the month and the ageing and the total balance on each customer's account.

The system will operate as follows:

(1) The customer details, and the part numbers and quantities of the goods dispatched are input into the computer, which calculates the invoice value by accessing the standing data file. When the operator confirms that the invoice details have been input correctly, the computer prints the invoice and posts it to the sales ledger.

(2) Cash received and discounts are input into the system from the cash book, and they are matched to the invoices which are being paid.

(3) Credit notes and adjustments can be input directly into the sales ledger.

(4) At the end of the month the computer prints:

  (i) a summary of the invoices, credit notes, adjustments, cash and discounts posted to the sales ledger in the month

  (ii) an aged list of debtors

  (iii) customer statements, which show the outstanding transactions at the end of the month.

(5) The computer has the facility to print out during the month the summaries described in part (4) above, and the details of any customer account.

Required

(a) List and describe the procedures which should be carried out in setting up the files containing:

  (i) the customer names, addresses and credit limits

  (ii) the price list of the products the company sells

  (iii) sales ledger balances which are to be transferred from the manual system to the new computer system.

(b) List and describe the controls which should be exercised over:

(i) the input of transaction data, to ensure the risk of errors is minimised and that there is no unauthorised input of transactions

(ii) the amendment of standing data files containing customer names, addresses and credit limits

(iii) the amendment of the prices of the products the company sells.

(c) List and describe the procedures which should be carried out to ensure the accuracy of the transaction file data, which contains balances on customers' accounts and the outstanding transactions making up those balances.

22 Sales cycle controls

When considering the internal controls in a sales cycle the auditor will need to consider the following stages:

- The processing of orders
- The despatch and return of goods

Required

(a) Specify the internal control objectives for each of the above stages in a sales cycle where all sales are made on a credit basis, and explain their importance.

(b) List the internal control procedures you would expect to see in place in a simple manual system in order to achieve those objectives.

23 Countrywide Sales

The transport department of Countrywide Sales operates a fleet of 100 motor vehicles. Some vehicles are purchased for cash and some are leased.

Required

(a) List the internal control procedures you would expect to see in place over capital and revenue expenditure on the vehicle fleet.

(b) Set out the tests of control that the auditor might perform.

24 Faroff Supplies

Faroff Supplies employs 100 salesmen, each of whom covers a different area and is supplied with a car. At the end of each week each salesman submits an expense claim on a pre-printed form with supporting vouchers attached. Expenditure is on fuel together with invoices for hotel accommodation, meals and entertaining.

Each claim is scrutinised by the assistant accountant. He raises any queries with the salesman concerned and makes out cheques for signature by two directors.

The amount of salesmen's expenses paid out annually is material to the financial statements.

Required

(a) Discuss the shortcomings of this system and suggest ways in which it could be improved.

(b) List the tests of control that the auditor might perform on this system.

25 Caraway Manufacturing

Caraway Manufacturing is a long-established manufacturing company. The audit manager has been provided with the following extracts from the draft financial statements for 20X6 prior to the final audit planning meeting with the financial controller.

Draft balance sheet (extracts)

	Draft 20X6	Actual 20X5
	£000	*£000*
Property, plant and equipment at net book value	32,560	31,850
Debtors		
Trade	3,600	2,150
Other	250	200
Stocks		
Raw materials	1,200	870
Work-in-progress	350	450
Finished goods	1,860	1,610
Current liabilities		
Trade	2,060	1,470
Other	500	450

Draft profit and loss account (extracts)

	Draft 20X6	Actual 20X5
	£000	*£000*
Turnover	43,150	40,750
Cost of sales	(29,180)	(29,040)
Gross profit	13,970	11,710
Depreciation and loss on sales of property, plant and equipment	(3,450)	(2,010)
Other expenses	(2,340)	(2,280)
Profit before tax	8,180	7,420

The manager has reviewed these extracts and has identified three financial statement headings which he believes require further investigation. These are property, plant and equipment, trade debtors and stock. He has also calculated the following accounting ratios:

	Draft 20X6	Actual 20X5
Trade debtors collection period	30 days	19 days
Stock turnover	8.6 times	9.9 times
Gross profit percentage	32%	29%

Required

(a) Explain why the manager has selected these three headings for further investigation.

(b) Set out the further information that the manager should request from the financial controller at the final audit planning meeting in order to clarify the situation with regards to these financial statement headings.

26 Opening balances

Set out:

(a) the auditor's responsibilities in respect of the opening balances in the financial statements which he is auditing

(b) the audit work that might be used to reach a conclusion on the opening balances.

27 Compton Components

The audit manager of Compton Components has decided that audit software can be used effectively in the audit of sales and trade debtors. He has discussed this with the firm's computer audit department and with the finance director of Compton Components and this approach has been agreed as a feasible one. Furthermore, the finance director has asked his internal audit department to investigate the possibility of installing embedded software to help the external auditors in their work.

Required

(a) Describe, giving examples, how audit software in general could assist the audit firm in their audit of sales and debtors.

(b) Discuss the extent to which the external auditor could rely on the results of the internal auditor's use of embedded software.

28 Ray Products

Ray Products is a manufacturing company. As external auditor you have been provided with the following schedule of the company's property, plant and equipment at 30th June 20X7. This reflects a revaluation carried out by a firm of chartered surveyors in April 20X7.

	Freehold land and buildings	Plant and machinery
	£000	£000
Cost at 1st July 20X6	1,000	753
Additions	-	129
Revaluation	120	-
Disposals	-	(85)
Cost/valuation at 30th June 20X7	1,120	797

Accumulated depreciation at 1st July 20X6	50	231
Charge for the year	22	130
Disposals	-	(46)
Accumulated depreciation at 30th June 20X7	72	315
Carrying value at 30th June 20X7	1,048	482
Carrying value at 30th June 20X6	950	522

Required

List the audit tests you would carry out on the above figures.

29 Invisible Industries

Invisible Industries specialises in the development of drugs for the pharmaceutical industry.

Required

State how you would verify the following items appearing in the balance sheet of Invisible Industries at 31st December 20X6.

(a)	Patents	£350,000
(b)	Research and development	£1,200,000
(c)	Goodwill on the acquisition of a sole trader competitor	£50,000

30 Plastico Products

Plastico Products manufactures plastic products and has an extensive product range which is revised frequently. Your firm has audited Plastico Products for many years.

The company maintains computerised stock records and carries out quarterly stock counts. The stock records are adjusted for any discrepancies between the records and the physical count.

The managing director is concerned that the quarterly stock counts are disruptive and time-consuming. He has proposed the introduction of continuous checking throughout the year with no full year end stock count.

Required

(a) Describe how you might use audit software to assist you in your testing of the current stock system.

(b) List the concerns you, as auditor, would have when deciding whether you support the managing director's proposal.

31 Count instructions

The following is a set of instructions for the year end physical stock count at a manufacturer. Production is to continue on the day of the year end count.

(1) Counting is to be carried out by staff from the warehouse and the accounts department. Counters are to report at 8am on 30th June to the warehouse manager.

(2) The warehouse manager will issue sequentially numbered stock sheets which will include pre-printed descriptions of the stock lines and the quantities supplied by the stock controller.

(3) The count area is to be divided into sections and each will be allocated a section by the warehouse manager. Items are to be marked once counted.

(4) The production manager will estimate the materials required for use in production on the day and ensure that they are taken out of the warehouse and moved to the production department.

(5) Goods to be despatched on the day are to be taken out of the warehouse before counting commences and labelled accordingly. Any items not despatched at the end of the day will be included in stock. The number of the last despatch note will be recorded by the warehouse manager.

(6) Any emergency requisitions of raw materials are to be reported to the warehouse manager.

(7) Damaged stock is to be noted as such on the stock sheets.

(8) Any discrepancies between physical and book stock will be referred to the warehouse manager.

(9) All stock sheets are to be signed by the counter and returned to the warehouse manager at the end of the count. The warehouse manager will check the numerical sequence of the stock sheets.

Required

Identify the strengths and the weaknesses of the above instructions, explaining clearly their significance.

32 DebtCo

The sales turnover of DebtCo for the year ended 30th June 20X5 was £7.5 million, its draft profit before tax was £200,000 and its net assets £1.8 million. At that date the sales ledger contained 140 live accounts totalling trade debtors of £1.6 million. The accounts can be broken down as follows:

Value range	Number of balances
£000	
100 -150	2
50 - 100	6
10 - 50	40
1 - 10	60
0 - 1	29
Credit balances (all less than £1,000)	3
	140

The auditor is to use direct confirmation to confirm debtors balances.

Required

(a) List the factors which should be taken into account when selecting a sample of debtors for confirmation and how those factors should be applied to Debtco's debtors.

(b) Set out the procedures to be performed:

 (i) when planning and performing the confirmation

 (ii) when following up the results.

33 Cash and bank

(a) Describe four matters which would be included in a bank confirmation letter and explain why they are important to the auditor.

(b) State the evidence you would seek in respect of the following.

 (i) Cash at bank and bank loan

 (ii) Cash (comprised of floats, unbanked cash and travellers' cheques).

34 Purchase ledger balances

In your audit procedures to date you have found a large number of errors in your client's purchase ledger. You have decided to write to a number of trade creditors to obtain direct confirmation of the balances due.

Required

(a) The confirmation letter to the suppliers could either state the balance or ask the supplier to give the balance himself. Set out the arguments for each of these two approaches.

(b) List other substantive audit procedures which you could use to verify the amount of trade creditors.

(c) List the audit tests you would carry out to discover the existence of unrecorded liabilities.

35 Audit of accounting estimates

(a) Explain why the audit of accounting estimates is a difficult area for the auditor.

(b) List the audit evidence you would seek in respect of a provision for damages in respect of an action brought by a customer for breach of contract.

36 Izzard Electronics

You are the external auditor of Izzard Electronics.

A management representation letter has been prepared in which the directors have been asked to confirm that all sales income has been included in the financial statements and that when there is weak evidence of expenditure, the expenditure has been for the benefit of the company and not for the personal benefit of any employee or director.

Required

(a) Discuss the reliability of audit evidence provided by directors in the management representation letter and whether you should rely wholly on the representations of the directors or whether you should obtain other evidence.

(b) Describe the action you would take and the conclusions you would reach if the directors refused to sign a management representation letter. Your answer should specifically consider the statements in the letter concerning completeness of sales income and validity of expenditure.

37 Subsequent events

Identify four areas of the financial statements to which a review of subsequent events might be relevant. For each area state what kind of information available after the balance sheet date might be relevant, and why.

38 Eden Electronics

During the course of your audit of Eden Electronics for the year ended 30th April, you establish that the company did not carry out a year end physical stock count at one of its retail branches and there are no alternative procedures that can be applied to confirm the quantities. The directors have estimated the branch stock value.

At the conclusion of your audit you decide that the problem is material, but not pervasive, to the view given by the financial statements.

Required

(a) Explain the types of audit reports other than 'clean' audit reports, giving an example of situations which may give rise to each type.

(b) Set out the main elements of the audit report for the situation set out above.

39 Posh Perfumes

Posh Perfumes has been in existence, importing perfume, for a number of years. The managing director had built up the business using contacts he already had in the industry. The company imports only one brand of perfume which is manufactured exclusively by one company. The perfume is distributed via 'shops within shops' at 20 branches of a well-known store. Under this agreement, Posh Perfumes pays a percentage of its takings to the store, with a minimum annual payment of £10,000 per store.

The audit is nearing completion but you have just heard that the French manufacturer is facing serious financial difficulties and that supplies have ceased.

Required

(a) Set out the further information the auditor would require before reaching his audit opinion.

(b) Set out the possible forms of opinion that the auditor may issue.

40 Creed Computers

Creed Computers sells personal computers (PCs) to independent shops. You are the external auditor of Creed Computers. Your interim audit revealed the following issues:

(1) The half year physical stock count revealed that some PCs supposed to be in stock were missing and that other machines which had been returned by customers were in stock but had not been recorded as having been returned. A few of the missing PCs have been traced to directors who borrowed them for use at home.

(2) Two customers had been allowed to exceed their credit limits and new customers in the last year had not been allocated credit limits.

Required

Draft the section of your report to management dealing with the above weaknesses. Set out the weaknesses, their implications and your recommendations for improvement.

Paper F8 (UK)
Audit and assurance

Q&A

Answers

Contents

1 Audit and review

(a) Difference between an audit and a review

Both an audit and a review are types of assurance engagements. In an assurance engagement, an assurance firm is engaged by one party to give an opinion on a piece of information which has been prepared by another party. The opinion is an expression of assurance, or comfort, about the information which has been reviewed.

- **An audit**

  In a statutory audit, rather than the shareholders merely accepting the information provided by the financial statements as being sufficiently accurate and reliable, the statutory audit provides assurance as to the quality of that information. That assurance adds credibility to the information provided by the financial statements, making the information more reliable and therefore more useful to the user.

  An audit is the work carried out by an auditor in order to reach his opinion on those financial statements. That opinion is usually expressed in terms of whether (or not) the financial statements show 'a true and fair view' (see below).

  An audit provides a *high, but not absolute,* level of assurance that the information being audited is free of material (see below) misstatement. This is often referred to as *reasonable* assurance.

- **A review**

  A review provides a *moderate* level of assurance that the information under review is free of material misstatement. The resultant opinion is usually expressed in the form of *negative assurance* i.e. 'nothing has come to our attention to suggest that the information is misstated'.

  Because the level of assurance given by a review is lower than that provided by an audit, a review usually involves less work on the part of the reviewer than the auditor would carry out.

(b) Why an audit is necessary

An audit is necessary because, in incorporated entities, the shareholders own the company, but the directors manage that company on the shareholders' behalf. The directors have a *stewardship* role.

Although in small companies the shareholders may be the same people as the directors, in large companies, the two groups are likely to be very different.

In order to show their *accountability* to the shareholders it is therefore a general principle of company law that the directors are required to prepare financial statements, which are presented to the shareholders. An independent audit report, addressed to the shareholders, is published with those financial statements. Thus the audit report adds *credibility* to the financial statements produced by management.

(c) Meanings

(i) A true and fair view

The auditor reports on whether (or not) the financial statements give 'a true and fair view' of the period end position and the performance of the company for the period. He *does not* certify or guarantee that those financial statements are correct.

The use of such a phrase indicates the use of judgement which is exercised both by the directors in preparing the financial statements, and by the auditor in reaching his opinion. The phrase 'true and fair' indicates that overall the financial statements can be relied upon and have been properly prepared in accordance with an appropriate financial reporting framework (for example, UK Financial Reporting Standards).

Although the phrase has no legal definition, 'true' implies free from error, 'fair' implies that there is no undue bias in the financial statements and the way in which they have been presented.

(ii) Materiality

Materiality is defined by International Standards on Auditing as follows:

'Information is material if its omission or misstatement could influence the economic decisions of users taken on the basis of the financial statements.'

The auditor will not aim to examine every number in the financial statements. He will concentrate his efforts on the more significant items in the financial statements, either because of their (high) value, because they are at a greater risk of misstatement or because of their nature (i.e. they are of particular interest to the user).

In this way the auditor should pick up any errors which would be significant to the shareholders. This might be because of the *size* of the error (e.g. a £500,000 misstatement in a company with turnover of £1 million) or because of the *nature* of the error (e.g. areas such as directors' salaries are usually expected by the user of the financial statements to be disclosed with 100% accuracy).

2 Corporate governance

(a) Meaning of corporate governance

Corporate governance is the system by which a company is directed and controlled. For a company to be properly directed and controlled there must be a clear view of the entity's objectives and risks and how those risks will be managed.

(b) Parts played in corporate governance

(i) Management

It is management's responsibility to put in place a suitable system of internal controls to manage the risks of the company. These controls will include:

- controls to safeguard the assets of the company
- the maintenance of adequate books and records
- the preparation and delivery of annual financial statements.

(ii) The external auditor

The external auditor is part of the corporate governance system. He:

- provides an independent check on the integrity of the financial information prepared by the directors for the use of the shareholders
- may have a responsibility for forming an opinion on the extent to which the directors have complied with the specific corporate governance regulations imposed on them either voluntarily or by law.

In order to do this the external auditor will examine the company's systems and controls but he is *not responsible* for those systems or controls.

(iii) The internal auditor

The internal audit function is used by management as a means of *monitoring* the controls management has set up. The internal audit function is seen as an essential element of sound corporate governance, because one of the key functions of internal audit is to review and report to the directors on the effectiveness of the organisation's accounting and control systems. This will help the organisation to achieve its corporate goals.

(iv) The use of audit committees

The existence of an audit committee is one way in which the independence of the external auditor can be maintained, as the audit committee can act as a 'buffer' between the external auditor and the executive directors, who may, on occasions, place undue pressure on the auditor. This should strengthen the independence of the external auditor by providing a point of liaison for him and lead to better communication between the external auditor and the board of directors.

The existence of an audit committee should also assist the executive directors in meeting their responsibilities.

3 Zubrovka

(a) Duties of auditor

The duties of the auditor of Zubrovka are defined by statute. An audit is an independent, professional examination of, and expression of an opinion on, the financial statements of the company.

The opinion is given as to whether a true and fair view is presented of the company's affairs as at the end of its financial year (balance sheet), and of the company's profit or loss for its financial year (profit and loss account), whether the financial statements have been properly prepared in accordance with company law, and whether the directors' report is consistent with the financial statements.

The auditor is also required by exception to report if:

- adequate accounting records have not been kept
- the financial statements are not in agreement with the underlying accounting records, or
- he did not receive all the information he required during the audit.

In addition to statutory requirements, the auditor must also ensure that his audit is performed according to approved auditing standards (e.g. International Standards on Auditing(UK and Ireland)).

The directors may extend the scope of the audit beyond the statutory requirements if the auditor is agreeable but they cannot limit the scope of the audit or indemnify the auditor against any legal action arising from the non-performance of duties.

(b) Relationship between the auditor and the directors

As Zubrovka is a newly formed-company, the directors may appoint the first auditor to hold office until the conclusion of the first annual general meeting. However, the auditor has no relationship with the directors other than as the practical means by which the company enters into a contract with the auditor.

The directors are responsible for the preparation of financial statements, and the auditor for the formation and expression of an opinion on those statements to the members of Zubrovka. The auditor does this for a fee. Although, in theory, this fee is set by whoever appoints the auditor (usually the shareholders), in practice this responsibility is delegated to the directors.

(c) Rights of the auditor

- To receive notice, to attend and be heard at all meetings of shareholders.
- Access at all times to all books and accounting records.
- To be informed of any proposal to dismiss him and to take certain actions in that event.
- To obtain all necessary information and explanations required for the conduct of his audit.

(d) Authority of the directors to dismiss the auditor

The directors do not have the authority to dismiss the auditor – only shareholders have that authority. An auditor is removed from office by a simple majority of shareholder votes, cast at a shareholders' meeting.

(e) Steps prior to acceptance of the appointment

It would be impossible for the auditor to accept the appointment as currently specified by the directors. The scope of an audit is limited by statute only, not at the request of directors.

If the firm still wishes to take up the appointment it should discuss the matter with the directors and eliminate their misunderstanding of the audit requirement. Then a letter of engagement should follow indicating clearly the auditor's duties and rights.

4 Babushka

(a) Statutory and other procedures to dismiss Old and Co and appoint New and Co

Before New and Co can accept nomination as auditor of Babushka

- The directors of Babushka should write to Old and Co informing them of the company's intention to nominate New and Co as its next auditors.
- With Babushka's permission, New and Co should write to Old and Co asking if there is any professional reason why New and Co should not accept nomination.
- Old and Co will then write back to Babushka asking for permission to respond.
- Babushka should give that permission.
- Provided that Old and Co give no professional reasons why New and Co should not accept appointment, New and Co should write to Babushka formally accepting nomination.

Before and at the general meeting at which Old and Co will be removed from office and New and Co appointed as auditors

- Old and Co should be given notice of the meeting by Babushka.
- Old and Co have the right to attend the meeting and make statements to the members of Babushka.
- Alternatively, Old and Co may require written statements to be circulated to the members in advance of the meeting.
- At the meeting, the shareholders should vote on the appointment of New and Co as auditors. A simple majority will secure the appointment.
- There is no vote to dismiss Old and Co. They are simply not re-appointed.

Following the general meeting

- New and Co should send a letter of engagement to Babushka.
- Documentation should be filed by Babushka with the appropriate regulatory authority.

(b) Procedures if Old and Co are willing to resign

- Old and Co should tender their resignation to Babushka in writing.
- Babushka should file this with the Registrar of Companies.
- Old and Co should prepare a 'statement of the circumstances' of the resignation, if they believe there are circumstances of relevance to the shareholders or creditors of the company. If no such circumstances exist, Old and Co should make a statement to this effect. This statement should be sent:
  - by Old and Co to the regulatory authority
  - by Babushka to all persons entitled to receive a copy of the company's financial statements (principally the shareholders) and to the Registrar of Companies.
- Old and Co may require the directors of Babushka to call a meeting of the shareholders in order to discuss the circumstances of the resignation.

5 Keane

(a) Other matters affecting the auditor's credibility

The auditor must be **professionally competent**. This means that the auditor must be properly trained in the first place and must then maintain his skill at such a level that the client receives a competent service based on current developments in practice, legislation and techniques. He must, amongst other things, be a good accountant, understand clearly audit objectives, be able to interpret systems, be a good communicator, use general and specific techniques (for instance, statistical sampling), and have a good understanding of the impact of modern technology on information and information systems.

The auditor must **possess integrity**. To be a member of a professional body carries significant responsibility as each member is representative of the profession and any departure from the generally accepted professional standards of integrity and care will only bring the whole profession into disrepute.

(b) Situations

(i) Keane

Holding a financial interest (such as shares) in client companies may create a self-interest threat to independence.

The audit partner in this case has no shares in the audit client and would therefore seem to be in an objective position. However, the audit manager holds 1% of the ordinary shares of Keane. Although this holding is not material in relation to the total shares in issue, it may be very material in relation to the total personal wealth of the audit manager.

Both the ACCA Code and ES2 state that audit team members should not hold *any* direct financial interest in client companies. Therefore the only possible safeguards are to:

- require the manager to dispose of his shares, or
- remove the manager from the audit team.

(ii) Scholes

Personal relationships may create self-interest, familiarity or intimidation threats to independence. The significance of these threats will depend on the individual's responsibilities on the assurance engagement, the closeness of the relationship, and the role of the other party at the assurance client.

With this in mind, where an immediate family member of a member of the audit team is in a position to influence the financial statements at the client, the ACCA Code and ES2 require that the individual should be removed from the audit team. The chief accountant of Scholes is not an immediate family member of the partner and the partner is not involved with the audit so neither the Code nor ES2, per se, have been broken.

However, the firm is required by the Code to consider any other personal relationships which might have a bearing on independence and consider what safeguards need to be put in place. If the chief accountant has a very close relationship with the partner and exerts strong influence over him, and the partner in turn is in a position to exert a strong influence over the audit partner (if, perhaps, he is the senior partner) then the firm should seriously consider whether it should act as auditor for Scholes.

(iii) Giggs

If too large a proportion of the audit firm's fee income is derived from one client, the dependence on that client and concern about the possibility of losing that client may create a self-interest threat to independence.

Both the ACCA Code and ES4 state that the public may perceive that independence is impaired where the fees for audit and other recurring work paid by one client, or a group of connected clients, exceeds 15% of the income of the audit practice (10% for listed and other public interest clients). A review of independence is recommended when fees reach 10% (5% for listed clients).

In the case of Giggs, the audit fee represents slightly more than 14% of total fee income. Since Giggs is a listed client, this work would not ordinarily be acceptable unless the auditor could show that, in spite of the level of fees from Giggs, his independence was not affected.

(iv) Fletcher

If the assurance client is a bank or similar institution both the ACCA Code and ES2 state that there is no threat to independence where a loan is made on normal terms to the assurance firm or a member of the assurance team. These conditions are met in this case therefore there is no threat to independence.

(v) Ronaldo and Neville

This is a clear case where a conflict of interest might well occur. According to the ACCA Code, whether the firm should advise Neville depends on whether a "reasonable and informed third party" would consider the conflict of interest as likely to affect the judgment of the member or the firm. However, where the acceptance of the engagement would materially prejudice the interests of either Neville *or* Ronaldo, the appointment should not be accepted.

This would seem to be a case where it would be undesirable for the audit firm to advise Neville at all. The firm should explain carefully the professional reasons for not accepting the appointment and suggest that advice on the contracts be obtained from another professional firm.

6 Dilemma and Co

(a) Ensuring independence and objectivity

Legislation

UK legislation states that a person is ineligible to accept appointment as auditor of a company if he is not independent due to being:

- an officer or employee of the company

- a partner or employee of such a person
- a partnership in which a person above is a partner.

Auditors must be a member of an appropriate regulatory body, such as the ACCA. Such bodies will also regulate the independence of their members.

Legislation also provides statutory protection to auditors if threatened with removal, to ensure that their objectivity is not swayed by such threats. On removal, auditors have the right to:

- attend the meeting at which they would have been re-appointed and make statements to the members, or
- require written statements to be circulated to members in advance of the meeting.

The ACCA Code

The ACCA Code identifies a number of circumstances where independence may be (or be seen to be) under threat. The main threats are:

- undue dependence on an audit client due to high levels of fees
- family and personal relationships
- the provision of other (non-audit) services
- loans and overdue fees
- the acceptance of gifts or and hospitality
- financial interests in shares or other investments.

It is up to individual audit firms to apply this guidance and to consider the use of safeguards to negate or reduce these threats.

(b) Three situations

(i) Fancy Ceramics

In this situation there are two apparent threats to objectivity. The first is that being invited to the long weekend with his wife may constitute a significant gift to Mr Smith if the client offers to pay for it. This may create both self-interest and familiarity threats. The ACCA Code and ES4 specify that hospitality should only be accepted if the value of it is clearly insignificant.

The second is that Mr Smith has been partner for 20 years on this engagement. This may create a familiarity threat such that Mr Smith may trust the client's representations too much or be too sympathetic to problems it faces.

In order to mitigate the risks, the firm could insist that it or Mr Smith pays for the trip or Mr Smith should not go. More importantly, Mr Smith should be rotated off the audit and a different partner appointed as the engagement partner. Mr Smith could possibly become the client relationship partner provided that he is not in a position to exert influence over the new engagement partner.

(ii) Gorgeous Potteries

Family and personal relationships may create self-interest, familiarity or intimidation threats to independence. The significance of these threats will depend on the individual's responsibilities on the assurance engagement, the closeness of the relationship, and the role of the other party at the assurance client.

With this in mind, where an *immediate* family member of a member of the audit team is in a position to influence the financial statements at the client, both the ACCA Code and ES2 require that the individual should be removed from the audit team. Although the audit manager is said to take no part in the management of the company, he may be in a position to influence the financial statements through his relationship with his parents.

Although the audit manager's parents are not "immediate" family but "close" family, as defined by the Code/the ESs and therefore there is no strict prohibition on the manager taking part in the audit of Gorgeous Potteries, it does seem likely that there may be threats to the manager's objectivity and independence as he could be intimidated by his parents or have some self-interest in their investment.

The firm should therefore ensure that this manager is not involved in the audit and is not in a position to influence any members of the audit team. If this cannot be shown to be the case, then the firm should not accept appointment as auditors.

(iii) Green Goods

The firm faces self-interest threats to independence from both the outstanding fees and the threat of losing the client. If it is worried about not receiving the fees or may lose the client, then it will want to keep the client happy and could relax its objectivity and independence to do so. The ACCA Code therefore recommends that overdue assurance fees are paid before next year's report is issued. ES4 states that if fees remain overdue, the audit engagement partner, together with the ethics partner, should consider whether the firm can continue as auditors or whether it should resign.

If the client's demands are met, the firm may also open itself to intimidation in other areas such as the audit, and also the standard of audit work could fall if the fee is reduced to save costs.

The firm should ensure that its negotiations over fees are kept separate from all other considerations, especially the audit. It must not threaten objectivity to keep the audit.

If the relationship with the client has collapsed, the firm should consider resignation.

7 Engagement letters

(a) Purpose of an engagement letter

The engagement letter forms the contract between the company and the auditor. Its main purpose is to confirm:

- the auditor's acceptance of the appointment
- the scope of the audit work

- the basis of the audit opinion
- any other, non-audit services to be provided (although this may be in a separate engagement letter)
- the extent of the auditor's responsibilities in respect of the financial statements.

When a new letter should be sent to an existing client

ISA 210 *Terms of audit engagements* suggests that the following factors may indicate that the issue of a revised engagement letter is appropriate:

- Revised or additional terms of engagement.
- Indications that management may not understand the nature of the audit.
- A change in senior management.
- A major change in the nature or size of the client's business.
- Any relevant changes in legal or professional requirements.

(b) Main components of an engagement letter

ISA 210 states that the form and content of an audit engagement letter will vary depending on the circumstances of each client. However, a letter would generally include reference to the following:

- The objective of the audit.
- Management's responsibility for the financial statements.
- The scope of the audit, including reference to appropriate legislation and professional standards.
- The form of the audit report and any other formal communication from the auditor to management.
- The fact that because of:
  - the test nature of auditing
  - the inherent limitations of an audit, and
  - the inherent limitations of internal controls

  there is a risk that even some material misstatements could remain undetected.
- The auditors' (statutory) right of unrestricted access to books, records and explanations.

In addition to the above, the auditor may feel that it is appropriate to include additional points, such as:

- the basis on which fees are charged
- planning information, such as an outline timetable for the audit work
- a request for management to formally acknowledge their acceptance of the contents of the letter
- arrangements for the involvement of client staff, including the internal auditors, in the audit process.

8 Usefulness of internal audit

An internal audit function is an essential element of a sound corporate governance system. It may also liaise with the audit committee, who may themselves require special reports from the internal auditors.

The role of internal audit is set by management and the type of work they do will depend on what management requires of them. However, their work is likely to encompass the following, all of which are useful to management:

(a) **Review of accounting and internal control systems**

This involves an assessment of the adequacy of the entity's systems and controls in managing the risks of the business and could encompass IT audits. Where there are deficiencies, the internal auditor will recommend cost-effective improvements to management. For example, if the company does not properly check goods received for quality and quantity, the entity is at risk of accepting substandard goods or the wrong quantity of goods. The internal auditor would require procedures to be put in place to prevent losses incurred by such a lack of controls.

(b) **Examination of financial and operating information**

Such 'financial audits' form another part of the traditional role of the internal auditor – reviewing accounting and other records to substantiate figures in the financial statements or management accounts. For example, the internal auditor might trace items on stock sheets to the stock figure in the financial statements.

(c) **Other audits**

The internal auditor might carry out specific other types of audits such as 'value for money' or 'best value' audits.

(d) **Special investigations**

Internal auditors will perform any necessary investigation into unusual matters. An example of this might be a fraud investigation.

(e) **Operational internal audit assignments**

These involve the internal auditor considering particular areas of the entity's business such as marketing or human resources. For example, work could be carried out to ensure that there are appropriate recruitment and selection procedures in place.

In addition, the internal audit function will also liaise with the external auditors and may provide valuable evidence to the external audit team. This may result in a more efficient (and hence cheaper) external audit.

9 Venture Videos

Potential business risk	Suggested controls and strategies
▪ Procurement decisions are made locally. This could lead to too few copies being purchased, leading to lost revenue, or too many copies, incurring unnecessary cost.	▪ Head office should consider cinema viewing ratings to improve predictions of the likely level of rentals.
▪ Procurement decisions are made locally. Bulk discounts for purchase may therefore not be obtained.	▪ Centralised purchasing of all videos should be carried out by head office to ensure that the maximum discounts are obtained.
▪ A guarantee is offered in respect of non-availability. This could lead to over-purchasing locally, as local managers purchase excessively to try and avoid the guarantee coming into force (assuming they are not penalised for over-purchasing).	▪ Consideration should be given to abandoning this guarantee system, although a cost/benefit analysis would need to be undertaken. ▪ Centralised purchasing of all videos should be carried out by head office to ensure that the optimum number of videos is purchased. ▪ A policy of a guarantee whereby the video is made available within, say, two days, could be implemented. This could be made more feasible by introducing a system of transfers between stores.
▪ There is no pre-booking system in operation so stores cannot predict demand. This makes it more likely that the current guarantee will come into force.	▪ A (possibly discounted) pre-booking system could be introduced.
▪ No central budgets are produced.	▪ A central budget should be introduced, establishing criteria by which the performance of individual stores is measured.

10 Planning

(a) The need for and benefits of planning

As well as allowing the audit to be performed in an effective manner, the planning process allows the auditor to establish an overall strategy for the audit:

- defining the scope and reporting objectives of the audit,
- considering matters such as materiality thresholds and high risk areas
- setting out the nature, extent and timing of the resources needed to perform the audit.

The more detailed audit plan then sets out the nature, timing and extent of audit procedures to be performed by audit team members.

This documented plan allows the auditor to control the audit by ensuring that it is performed in accordance with the plan and that the work is of an acceptable standard. It will also provide a basis for drawing up audit programmes, which will be used to instruct the members of the audit team. Less senior members of the team will be supervised by those with more experience, and all work will be reviewed.

The benefits of such an approach are that the work will be performed in an orderly and efficient manner and that the audit opinion will be formed on a sound basis.

(b) Steps to be taken prior to the commencement of the audit of a long-standing client

The audit should be planned by a senior member of staff who is familiar with the company and the industry in which it operates. The purpose of the overall audit strategy and plan will be to outline the audit approach; hence the procedures should include the following:

- Review the previous year's audit files for matters which will be relevant in the current year.
- Consider the effect of any changes in legislation or accounting practices.
- Meet with the client to discuss any significant changes in the client's accounting system.
- Consider the effect of any systems changes on the audit approach and time needed for the audit.
- Obtain and review copies of management accounts.
- Discuss with the client the timing of both interim and year end visits.
- Decide on the audit approach and draft a memorandum outlining it to be approved by the audit partner.
- Decide on the number and grade of staff required for the audit and ensure that appropriate people will be available at the agreed time.
- Prepare detailed time and cost budgets.
- Inform the client in writing of the dates as agreed for audit visits and of the names of the staff involved.
- Brief the audit team on the client and their individual responsibilities.

(c) How the internal auditor's planning differs to that of the external auditor

The benefits of planning and the importance of developing a sound up-to-date knowledge of the business also apply to the internal audit planning process. However, the timescale within which internal auditors may operate will tend to be different from that in which external auditors operate.

The external audit operates essentially on an annual cycle, geared to the entity's financial reporting date.

Internal audit work is not linked precisely to the financial reporting date. As a result of this, internal audit departments have more flexibility in the timing of their work and have scope for operating in a longer time frame.

This may result in internal audit work plans being drawn up at three 'levels', strategic, periodic, and operational, with each one reflecting a different time scale.

A strategic level plan may cover a period of up to five years. During this period, the internal auditors will aim to test all the major systems and controls operating on all aspects of the business activities.

A periodic level plan will normally relate to the financial reporting period and will express key aspects of the strategic plan in terms of particular goals and targets for that period.

An operational level plan will set out day-to-day audit objectives and procedures for each particular audit assignment to be performed.

11 Beautiful Jewels

(a) Meaning and importance of audit risk

'Audit risk' is the risk that an auditor forms an inappropriate audit opinion on the financial statements. It has three components: inherent risk, control risk and detection risk. The following equation represents the relationship:

Audit risk = Inherent risk × Control risk × Detection risk

If inherent risk is high, there is greater potential for material misstatement in the financial statements. This risk of misstatement is reduced if control risk is low, i.e. the accounting and internal control systems of the enterprise are effective in detecting and correcting errors arising.

Detection risk is under the control of the auditor and is dependent on the assessment of inherent and control risk. In the audit risk model detection risk is the balancing figure to satisfy the ultimate risk accepted.

If detection risk needs to be kept low (e.g. because inherent and control risk are high), this would mean increased audit testing to ensure that the financial statements are not materially misstated.

The level of risk also affects the nature and timing of audit work. For example, when risk is increased, more reliable evidence should be sought, e.g. more independent/third party evidence.

(b) Risks arising and why they need to be taken into account

Risk	Why to be taken into account
Stock is moved about between the design warehouse and the shops and occasionally is sent out to customers for approval.	Because of the portable and valuable nature of the stock, strong controls will be needed to ensure it is not stolen – both in general and to control these movements. Where customers hold goods on approval it may be difficult to determine when revenue should be recognised.
Some items of stock will be individually material.	Stocktaking and valuation procedures will need to be carefully assessed.
The entity operates from multiple locations.	Cut-off will need to be carefully controlled.
The entity is likely to keep permanent stock records.	This may reduce the amount of work the auditor needs to carry out at the year end stock count.
Significant stock may be held by customers.	Confirmation from customers as to stock held at the year end will be needed. In the case of individually material items a visit to the customer by the auditor may be considered appropriate.
Stock is of a specialised nature.	Evidence from an independent expert may be required (e.g. to certify that gemstones are real and not fake).
Because of the decline in sales, the closure of one shop and the imminent retirement of the managing director, the ability of the entity to continue in business must be in doubt.	The going concern basis may not be appropriate. The auditor will need to consider any future orders/projected sales, the progress of the negotiations with the bank and plans to replace key staff.
The premises from the closed shop are still held for sale.	The accounting treatment and disclosure of these premises in the year end financial statements will need to be checked.
The financial director has been dismissed and not replaced.	The accounting systems and internal controls may not be operating reliably due to the loss of a key member of staff.
The financial director is suing for unfair dismissal.	A provision may be needed in the financial statements if the claim is likely to succeed.

12 Blunkett Manufacturing

(a) Use of statistical and judgemental sampling

(i) In the audit of the sales system

When carrying out the audit of the sales system the auditor is aiming to assure himself that the transactions within the system are being accurately and completely processed, and also that the system will act as a sound base for the preparation of the financial statements.

There are areas of the sales system when the throughput of transactions is great, e.g.

- the opening of new customer accounts
- the despatch of goods
- the raising and processing of sales invoices

- the processing of remittances
- the maintenance of day books and ledgers, including additions, postings and analysis.

For areas such as these within the sales system, statistical techniques can be used to select items for testing.

The use of statistical techniques, based on the mathematical theories of probability, will provide the auditor with the assurance that the total population has the same characteristics as the sample selected for testing.

The number of items to be tested will depend on the confidence required by the auditor and also the error rate which he is prepared to accept.

To determine which particular transactions are included within the sample, the auditor may use any one of a number of selection techniques including interval sampling, random sampling (using random number tables), cluster sampling or block sampling.

There will also be areas within the sales system where the volume of transactions is not great, such as:

- month-end reconciliations
- month-end, or period-end, postings to the nominal ledger
- the write-off of bad debts.

In these circumstances the use of statistical techniques will not be appropriate because valid conclusions cannot be drawn when population sizes are small.

In such cases, judgmental sampling would be more appropriate. However, the auditor should carefully consider which and how many items should be tested. For example, if the auditor is aware that the sales ledger manager/controller was on holiday in the month of August, he may decide that testing transactions in that month should be considered.

(ii) In the direct confirmation of trade debtors (circularisation)

Before deciding on whether to use statistics or judgement for the selection of debtors in a circularisation, the auditor must establish the purpose of the circularisation.

If the circularisation is part of the auditor's systems work, to establish that the system is working as prescribed, he should use statistical techniques.

The auditor must first establish the confidence level he requires, (i.e. how certain he wants to be that the results of the sample are truly representative of the population). Then, based on an acceptable error rate, a sample size can be established.

It may be appropriate for the auditor to divide the sales ledger balances into two populations – the first being all of the debit balances, and the second being all of the credit balances. The credit balances should be subject to separate and more extensive tests because they have a higher probability of being inaccurate.

If the circularisation is to be used as a means of verifying year end trade receivables, the auditor will attempt to prove as large a proportion of debts as possible using the most cost-effective means.

The auditor should consider dividing the balances into tiers or strata with each stratum being the subject of separate examination. The high value stratum of debtors can then be the subject of more extensive testing.

(iii) In the verification of year end trade debtors

The audit of year end trade debtors will involve verifying the total value of debtors and also ensuring the reasonableness of the doubtful debts provision.

The auditor will check the trade debtors figure in the financial statements to the summary of sales ledger balances, and for this test the question of statistics or judgement is irrelevant.

However, individual ledger balances should then be checked to sales ledger accounts, and provided that individual balances are homogeneous in terms of value, statistics may be used. Sales ledger balances rarely are homogeneous and so judgement should play an important role especially when considering high value debts and credit balances.

The auditor's past experience and his own personal judgement will play an important role when verifying the reasonableness of the doubtful debts provision.

The auditor will be looking carefully at old and doubtful debts, ensuring that they have been provided for in the doubtful debts provision.

If the provision relates to specific debts, these will be examined. If the provision is general, the auditor may consider comparisons with previous years and determine how accurate provisions have been in the past.

(b) Advantages and disadvantages of the use of statistical and judgemental sampling

Many of the strengths and weaknesses of both statistics and judgement have already been discussed. However the following points are also relevant:

- Statistics avoids the use of personal bias – nevertheless many people believe that the auditor's own personal intuition should not be overlooked.
- Statistics will allow the auditor to draw valid conclusions about the population as a whole, which may ultimately be defensible in a court of law, whereas, with judgement, the auditor may find it hard to justify his conclusions with any authority.
- Judgement is an easier method to understand and calculate, whereas the use of statistics requires certain amount of skilled and specialist knowledge.
- The use of statistics requires more time in selecting items and performing calculations.

- Statistics require certain decisions, such as confidence levels and anticipated error rates, which diminish the value of the mathematical calculations to follow.
- Statistics can only be effectively used when population sizes are large, and so become ineffective when these sizes are small.
- Statistics do not take account of prior years' experience, which forms a valuable source of knowledge to the auditor.

The use of statistics or judgement in relation to the audit of the sales system and year end trade debtors will depend on the circumstances of each assignment.

However, as a rule of thumb, when carrying out a systems audit the auditor will want to ensure that the system as a whole is working in theory and practice as prescribed. The use of judgement may direct the auditor to areas that 'do not look right', which may be inappropriate, because the auditor primarily wants to draw conclusions about the population as a whole, not to problem areas that will compromise his overall view.

For year end verification work, judgement may be more appropriate because the preparers of financial statements will invariably use a degree of judgement themselves. However, because statistics are based on mathematical formulae, the auditor will probably have a better defence in a court of law than if his conclusions are all based on judgement.

13 Woolacombe Souvenirs

(a) Discovery of fraud

The following points should be made in response to the directors:

Why the fraud was not picked up/auditors' responsibilities:

- The objective of a statutory audit is to express an opinion on the truth and fairness of the view shown by the financial statements.
- It is not the auditors' function to prevent fraud and error.
- However, the auditors' work should be designed to pick up *material* misstatements.
- Material misstatements are those that if not picked up would have a significant impact on the financial statements such that their subsequent disclosure would affect the opinion of a reader of the financial statements.
- As part of our audit procedures we set a materiality level. In the case of Woolacombe Souvenirs this was set at £100,000.
- Hence the theft of £300, although of obvious concern to the directors, would not be considered material to the overall view shown by the financial statements.
- As this fraud was not material, although it may have been picked up, our tests were not designed to ensure that it would be discovered.
- To ensure that material errors or fraud are identified, we must have an adequate understanding of your business, and its operating methods, and the legal and regulatory framework applicable to the industry in which you operate.

- In order to have a reasonable expectation of detecting fraud or error, we ensure that when undertaking an audit we:
  - use personnel with appropriate knowledge and experience for the size and complexity of the company
  - assess the risk of fraud and error given the control environment
  - understand the business, particularly the substance of the company's transactions
  - ensure that where reliance is placed on the control system, that the system is evaluated and any weaknesses investigated
  - discuss any events involving dishonest or fraudulent conduct and any breakdown or weaknesses in the internal control system with management and obtain written representations where appropriate
  - remain alert to possible instances of fraud and error during the course of our work indicated by unusual transactions
  - where possible, obtain evidence from external sources.
- Unless there is evidence to the contrary, we are entitled to accept representations as truthful and records and documents as genuine. However, we do plan and perform the audit with an attitude of professional scepticism, such that we remain aware of the possibility of the existence of fraud or error.

Adjustment required

- Our work programme was designed to ensure that material fraud and errors were identified.
- In this case, the amount is immaterial and hence outside the scope of our responsibilities.
- There is therefore no need to adjust the accounts that have just been finalised or reissue the audit report.

(b) Consideration of laws and regulations

Non-compliance with appropriate laws and regulations may have a material impact on the information under audit. For example, breaches of legislation could:

- lead to fines, which need to be accrued for in the financial statements, or
- in extreme circumstances, could lead to the company being closed down.

Therefore ISA 250 *Consideration of laws and regulations in an audit of financial statements* requires that the auditor should, when planning and performing an audit, recognise these possibilities.

This can be seen as part of the general requirement that the auditor must understand the environment – here the legal environment – within which the entity operates. This might include such matters as employee rights legislation, health and safely law, consumer protection legislation or the current tough laws now in place in the UK relating to money laundering activities.

If the auditor identifies material areas of non-compliance the following actions may be appropriate.

- The auditor should confirm his understanding of non-compliance.
- The law may require appropriate authorities to be notified.
- The non-compliance should be discussed with management. If a particular level of management is seen to be involved in the non-compliance, the matter should be discussed with management at a higher level. If executive management as a whole may be involved, non-executive directors should be informed.

14 Financial statement assertions

(a) The financial statement assertions and the audit of sales/trade debtors

Financial statement assertion	Example from the audit of sales/trade debtors
Completeness: there are no unrecorded assets, liabilities, transactions or other undisclosed items.	All sales are recorded. This might be tested by checking that all goods despatched result in a sale (and a trade debtor) being recorded. Despatch notes could be traced through to sales and trade debtors.
Occurrence: transactions and events recorded in the financial statements took place during the accounting period and relate to the entity.	All recorded sales took place. This might be tested by checking back from sales as recorded to despatch notes.
Measurement: a transaction or event is recorded at the proper amount.	Sales are recorded at the correct amounts. This could be tested by checking the controls over invoice pricing by tracing despatch notes via official price lists to sales invoices.
Presentation and disclosure: an item is disclosed, described and classified according to the appropriate accounting framework (for example, UK Financial Reporting Standards).	Trade debtors, net of any doubtful debt provisions, are disclosed within current assets on the balance sheet.
Carrying value: assets and liabilities are properly valued.	Trade debtors are stated at their recoverable amounts (i.e. bad debts are written off and doubtful debt provisions are made). This would usually be tested via the direct confirmation of trade debtors and alternative procedures such as the receipt of cash after the year end.
Rights and obligations: assets and liabilities represent rights (assets) and obligations (liabilities) of the entity at the reporting date.	Debts (i.e. trade debtors) are not overstated/belong to the entity. Again, this would usually be tested via the direct confirmation of trade debtors.
Existence: an asset or liability exists at the reporting date.	

(b) The five main audit testing procedures and the audit of plant and machinery

Procedure	Example from the audit of plant and machinery
Inspection (looking at)	Physical inspection of plant (relevant to existence).
Observation (watching a procedure)	Observing maintenance procedures (relevant to carrying value).
Computation	Recalculating the depreciation charge for the year (relevant to carrying value).
Enquiry	Enquiring about useful lives/profits or losses on disposal (relevant to carrying value).
Analytical procedures	Calculate depreciation as a percentage of total asset value and compare to previous years.

15 John

What information is recorded

The auditor is required to plan his work so as to perform the audit in an effective manner. In particular, he should document matters which are:

- important in supporting the audit opinion, and
- provide evidence that the audit was carried out in accordance with auditing standards.

Such information and evidence is documented via **audit working papers** which may be in the form of paper, electronic or other media.

These working papers must record:

- the planning and performance of the audit
- the supervision and review of the audit work
- the evidence resulting from audit work performed
- the nature, timing and extent of the work planned and performed
- the conclusion drawn
- any reasoning on significant matters which require the exercise of judgement.

Where that information is recorded

On recurring audits, some working papers may be classified as **permanent files**. These are updated with new information of continuing importance, such as:

- copies of legal documents
- summaries of the client's history
- summaries of the accounting systems and procedures.

These files are distinct from **current audit files** which contain information relating primarily to the audit of a single period, such as:

- that period's financial statements and audit report
- a summary of final adjustments
- the audit plan
- audit working papers.

16 Internal audit questionnaire

Organisational status

- Are you entirely responsible for the appointment, remuneration and promotion of internal audit staff? If not, who is?
- Do you, as head of the department, report directly to the board of directors as a whole?
- Are there any limitations placed on the scope and nature of the work which your department carries out?
- Are you allowed free access to records, assets and personnel?
- Do you have access to senior management and the freedom to report and discuss matters with them?
- Are you free to communicate with us as external auditors?
- Do you have any responsibility for day-to-day operations?

Scope of work

- What are the principal areas of the work of your department?
- Do you identify, evaluate and test internal controls?
- What methods are used to ascertain and evaluate internal controls?
- Do you report weaknesses found to management?
- Does management involve your department in the implementation of systems changes?

Technical competence

- What resources, particularly financial, is your department provided with?
- What recruitment procedures are followed?
- Please provide details for all your staff members of:
  - professional qualifications
  - any specialist skills
  - training courses undertaken
  - number of years experience.
- What arrangements are in place to ensure that staff remain technically up-to-date?

Due professional care

- How is each assignment planned?
- What control procedures are adopted?
- Are standard working papers and audit programmes used?
- What review procedures are carried out?
- Is there an internal audit manual which we may review?
- Are staff allocated to work according to their training, experience and proficiency?
- Are staff briefed prior to commencement of an assignment?
- Does management review the reports issued following an assignment?
- Can we review those reports?
- Is a meeting held to discuss these reports?
- What follow up procedures are in place to ensure that recommendations are adopted by management?

17 Sopot

(a) Definition of internal control and the elements of an internal control system

ISA 315 *Obtaining an understanding of the entity and its environment and assessing the risks of material misstatement* defines internal control as follows:

'The process designed and implemented by those charged with the governance of the organisation and others to provide reasonable assurance about the achievement of objectives with regard to:

- the reliability of financial reporting
- the effectiveness and efficiency of operations
- compliance with appropriate laws and regulations.'

ISA 315 identifies five elements which together make up the internal control system.

- The control environment
- The entity's risk assessment process
- The information system
- Control activities
- Monitoring of controls

(b) Importance to the auditor of there being a good system of internal controls in operation

Modern auditing is, wherever possible, based on a 'systems' approach. The auditor *relies* on the accounting systems and the related controls to ensure that transactions are properly recorded. The audit emphasis is therefore, as much as possible, on the systems processing the transactions rather than on the transactions themselves.

Before the auditor can rely on the systems in place, he must establish what those systems are and carry out an evaluation of their effectiveness. The degree of effectiveness of an internal control system will depend on two main factors:

- the design of the system (is it able to prevent, or detect and correct, material misstatements)
- the implementation of the system (has it been operated correctly by staff)

ISA 315 requires the auditor to:

- gain an understanding of each of these elements as part of his evaluation of the control systems operating within an entity
- document the relevant features of the control systems together with his evaluation of their effectiveness.

Once this understanding has been gained, the auditor will confirm that his understanding is correct by performing walk-through tests on each major transaction type.

If the auditor's preliminary assessment is that internal controls are strong he will test those controls. If his tests prove that his initial assessment was correct then the auditor may rely on those internal controls and perform fewer substantive tests. This should reduce the time and cost of the audit.

(c) Stages in carrying out the audit of the purchases system

(i) Recording the system

This may be either by narrative, flowchart, questionnaire or some combination of the three. This involves recording who is responsible for authorising purchases and who processes the goods and accounting documents. Flowcharts will be useful in identifying key controls and segregation of duties.

(ii) Confirming the system

This will be done by performing walk-through tests to ensure that the system, as recorded, is the way it works in practice. This will involve tracing a number of transactions through the system from initiation to conclusion.

(iii) Evaluating the system

Use may be made of internal control evaluation questionnaires to identify the key controls and weaknesses in the system.

(iv) Testing the controls

These tests will provide evidence that the system of internal control is operating as laid down and that transactions are being properly recorded and processed in the accounts.

(v) Reduced substantive testing

Assuming that the tests of controls backed up an initial assessment of controls as strong, fewer tests of detail on the purchase transactions themselves will be needed.

(d) Effect on audit work and action

(i) A weakness in the system of internal control

The reasons for the weakness should be determined to ascertain if it is an isolated departure or is representative of other errors and therefore indicates the possible existence of errors in the accounting records.

If further tests suggest that the control was not operating properly throughout the period, no reliance can be placed on that control. However, it is also necessary to consider the existence of compensating controls.

If the weakness is serious and there are no compensating controls, it will be necessary to move directly to substantive testing. The weakness should also be reported to management.

(ii) Serious weaknesses in the system of internal control

If the weaknesses are so serious that the auditor cannot rely on the system of internal control, he should increase the amount of substantive testing on the purchases system. The weaknesses should be reported to management and, if they may result in serious errors, it may be necessary to qualify the audit report.

18 Control activities

(a)

Control type	Examples from the purchases system
Authorisation	All orders are authorised before being placed. This may involve a tiered system whereby orders under, say, £100 need authorisation by a department head, and orders over £100 need authorisation by a board member.
Physical	Access is restricted by the use of hierarchical passwords to master files of standing information.
Information processing (arithmetic)	Invoices received from suppliers are checked ▪ to the price on orders placed, and ▪ for arithmetic accuracy.
Information processing (accounting)	A monthly reconciliation is carried out between the purchase ledger control account and the list of purchase ledger balances.
Performance review/management	Management review monthly purchases against budget and investigate any significant variances.
Segregation of duties	Different personnel are responsible for ordering, receipt of goods and recording of invoices.

(b) Why substantive procedures can never be completely eliminated

No system of internal controls can guarantee the elimination of errors for the following reasons:

- Human error may result in incomplete or inaccurate processing which may not be detected by control systems.
- It may not be cost effective to establish certain types of controls within an organisation.

- Controls may be in place but they may be ignored or overridden by employees or management.
- Collusion (two or more employees working together) may mean that segregation of duties is ineffective.

19 Ascertaining and recording accounting systems

(a) Ascertainment

Inspection

The auditor can ascertain the working of an entity's system through a review of the records and documents which the entity itself maintains. This might be through systems manuals, or flowcharts, possibly prepared by internal audit.

This first-hand knowledge will provide a good starting point but the auditor will still need to confirm that the system operates in the manner specified. This might be done via walk-through tests. The auditor might also increase the reliability of what is, after all, internally generated (and therefore relatively weak) evidence by assessing the competence and integrity of the internal audit function or other preparers of the records.

Observation

Again, this will provide first-hand evidence of the way in which the system operates. However, observation is a notoriously weak procedure as it only provides assurance that the procedures are performed in a specified manner at the time of the observation, and not that it operates in that manner at all times.

Enquiry

The auditor can further improve his understanding of the system through discussion with management and key operational staff. However, he will need to seek further direct evidence of the workings of the system as this internal information may not be fully reliable.

(b) Recording

Narrative notes

These can provide a very detailed and complete record of the system, showing the flow of documents, the departments involved, the personnel and any areas of controls within the system.

However, notes can be very time-consuming to prepare and unless a clear, precise approach is adopted it can be very difficult to see clearly the overall picture and establish the system's weaknesses.

Flowcharts

These give a pictorial representation of the system and highlight the flow of documents, together with the operations and controls, in a way that is easily and quickly understood. A disciplined approach is required but the method is less complex and ambiguous than notes and provides a clearer picture. Controls which could be relied upon are also immediately apparent.

The drawbacks to flowcharts are that they, too, are time-consuming to prepare and wasteful if applied to simple systems (where narrative notes would suffice). In addition, a comprehensive examination of the system is required so as to ensure that the flowchart is not incomplete.

Questionnaires

Many auditors use questionnaires such as internal control questionnaires to help them ascertain and record a system. Questionnaires provide a quick and useful method of building up a picture of the system. They can also help to minimise audit costs as they are standardised and fairly simple to use.

A further advantage is that they can help the auditor to identify internal controls on which he may wish to rely. If the preliminary evaluation indicates strong controls, the auditor can design and carry out tests of controls. If weaknesses are noted the auditor can move directly to substantive testing and can report the weaknesses to management.

20 Grander Products

Can wages be paid other than to bona fide employees?

- Are personnel records maintained independently of the accounts department?
- Is written authorisation required for employees added to or deleted from the payroll?
- Are payrolls and payroll summaries approved and initialled by a responsible official?
- Are payrolls checked periodically against the independent personnel records?
- Are surprise checks made on the wages payout by a senior employee?
- Are there procedures in place to ensure that wage packets can only be handed out to the proper recipient?
- Is written authority required before an employee can claim wages on another's employee's behalf?
- Are unclaimed wages re-banked promptly?

Can employees be paid for work not done or at an incorrect rate of pay?

- Is written authorisation required for all changes in rates of pay?
- Does the personnel department notify the payroll department of all such changes?
- Are piecework records supervised by a responsible official?
- Are piecework records approved by a responsible official before being processed?
- Are piecework records checked before processing for:
  - evidence of appropriate approval
  - casts and calculations?
- Are proper controls exercised over adjustment for lateness, sickness and other absences?
- Is there adequate segregation of duties between the person responsible for the preparation of the payroll and the payment of the wages?

- Are payrolls checked:
  - with piecework records
  - for correct rates of pay
  - for casts and calculations?
- Are wages regularly compared with budgets and significant variances investigated?

Can errors occur in payroll deductions?

- Is there proper authorisation for all payroll deductions other than statutory deductions?
- Does the system provide adequate safeguards for dealing with statutory deductions such as taxation deducted at source?
- Are returns to the tax authorities agreed to the payroll?
- Is adequate control exercised over the processing of payrolls into the accounting records?

21 Pivo

(a) Procedures for setting up

(i) Customer files

- The computer system should be checked, and the method of storing customer files on the system ascertained. This will enable the key field for the customer file to be determined.
- A manual list of customers should be produced, showing for each customer, the address, credit limit and key field. The key field could be the customer name, or a reference number, or a combination of both of these.
- The list of customers should be approved as being correct, possibly by Mr Pivo before it is input to the computer.
- Hash totals (e.g. the total of all credit limits and key fields (if numeric)) may be calculated to check the completeness and accuracy of input.
- Customer details should be input to the computer. The data on the computer should be saved regularly during this process, and a printout obtained.
- The printout should be agreed back to the manual listing of customers, preferably by a person who is not responsible for the input of data. Any errors found should be marked and amendments made to the computer files.
- When all the customer details have been entered, the computer can generate the hash totals of credit limits and account references. These should be agreed back to the manual totals. If there are differences then the reason for the difference should be ascertained by checking the computer files to the manual listing in detail.

- Full back up copies of the complete customer file should be taken, and one copy always kept in a secure location, away from the computer.

(ii) Price list

The input of price list details is very similar to that of customer details.

- A manual list of products and prices is prepared.
- A key field is determined and hash totals calculated.
- A list of products is approved by Mr Pivo.
- Products are input to the computer with frequent back-ups and printouts produced of the items input.
- Printouts agreed to the manual list, and hash totals agreed to manually calculated hash totals.
- Independent person agrees accuracy of transfer of product details.

(iii) Sales ledger balances

The date of the transfer of balances must be decided in advance.

- On this date a manual list of the sales ledger balances should be taken, and reconciled to the sales ledger control account.
- Any differences in the above reconciliation should be investigated and the final listing produced.
- If only the balances are to be input to the computer system, then the list can be input, and the total generated by the computer of all balances agreed to the manual list. Any differences should be investigated and the totals finally agreed.
- Pivo may wish to input details of the invoices making up the individual sales ledger balances. In this case each balance will have a sublisting of invoices. Input will be the total as above, and then the supporting invoices for each ledger account. A print out of all balances and totals should be agreed to the manual listing and any errors corrected.
- During the input of balances, frequent back-ups should be taken to ensure that data is not lost.
- After the input, security copies of the data should be taken. At least one copy should always be kept in a secure location away from the computer.
- Manual update of the sales ledger may continue until the computer system is shown to be reliable. Processing will then only continue on the computer system.

(b) Controls over

(i) Input of transaction data

Transaction data being input will include:

- despatch notes
- credit notes
- cash received
- discount allowed.

It is likely that the input system is batch based, because of the good controls that can be built around this on a small microcomputer.

- A batch book will be used to record the batches of documents being input to the system.
- A batch will be created by getting a number of like documents, and generating batch and hash totals for them. Totals of cash received can be a batch total for money coming into the company, although batches of despatch notes will only give the hash totals of despatch note number and goods reference etc (the computer calculates the sales value).
- The batch will be given a unique reference number from the batch book, where a record of the batch will also be maintained.
- This reference number will assist in stopping unauthorised input as if unauthorised input occurs, the batch book's next batch number will not agree to the computer. Basic passwords should also be used to protect the system.
- The transaction documents should be input to the computer. After input, the batch and hash totals should be agreed to those manually calculated prior to input. Any differences should be investigated and reconciled.
- The person inputting the batch should sign the batch book as evidence that input was complete and accurate.
- After input has been reconciled, back-up copies of the master and transaction files should be taken.

(ii) Amendments to standing data (customer files)

- Only authorised personnel (perhaps Mr Pivo only) should be allowed to change the standing data.
- Special passwords should be used to protect the standing data files, and only authorised users given these passwords. The passwords themselves could be changed regularly.
- New customers should pass an initial credit vetting and be authorised as a customer by a responsible official, who will also determine their credit limit. Any other changes, such as increased credit limits, should be authorised in the same way.
- Customer details should be entered into the computer master file, and a printout immediately obtained of the amendment made.
- The new record should be checked for accuracy and initialled by an authorised official as being correct. A record of the amendment should be entered in the control book, which should log all changes to the master file.
- A printout of the entire master file details should be obtained periodically and be reviewed by Mr Pivo for any unauthorised changes that may have taken place.
- Old accounts that are no longer used should be deleted from the ledger.

(iii) Amendments to the prices of products

Controls here will be similar to (ii) above.

- Passwords should be used to prevent unauthorised access to the prices master file.
- Changes should only be made by a responsible official.
- A printout of all changes made should be obtained and agreed by this official as being correct.
- A log book should be kept showing all changes made.
- The complete list of stock prices should be printed out and checked by Mr Pivo regularly to ensure that they are correct.
- Products which are no longer held should be deleted from the computer.

(c) Procedures to ensure accuracy of transaction file data

The following assumes that a sales ledger control account is kept:

- The list of sales ledger balances should be obtained and agreed to the control account (the control account should be maintained by a person who is not responsible for the computerised sales ledger).
- The total of cash and discounts on the control account should be agreed to the cash book.
- Copies should be kept of all invoices produced by the computer. These copies should be reviewed by a responsible official to ensure that the invoices are reasonable, and that the numeric sequence is complete. Any abnormally large or small invoices should be investigated as should any breaks in the numeric sequence.
- Low volume transactions, such as bad debt write-offs and credit notes, should be authorised by Mr Pivo. Similarly, any abnormally large discounts should be investigated.
- The aged debtors listing produced at each month end should be reviewed by Mr Pivo. Any old balances should be investigated, not only to ascertain when payment can be expected and to stop sales turning to bad debts, but also to identify possible incorrect postings in the ledger.

22 Sales cycle controls

(a) Control objective	Explanation of importance	(b) Control procedures
Processing of orders		
To ensure that orders are only accepted from creditworthy customers.	To reduce the risk that bad debts occur.	▪ Establish credit limits for all customers. ▪ Credit limits should be authorised by the sales director. ▪ Prior to acceptance of an order, compare the balance on the customer's sales ledger account to their credit limit
To ensure that orders are only accepted at an appropriate price.	To avoid subsequent disputes over price/discount and to avoid accepting orders on which a loss would be made.	▪ Check order price to current price list prior to acceptance of the order. ▪ Check discounts to approved discount list. ▪ Any variations should be authorised by the sales director.
To ensure that orders are only accepted if goods of appropriate quality are in stock.	To reduce the risk of goods being returned due to their poor quality and the loss of customer goodwill due to the acceptance of an order which could not be properly fulfilled.	▪ Check availability of goods (to stores or stock records).
Despatch of goods		
To ensure that goods are despatched promptly.	To reduce the risk of a loss of customer goodwill due to the late despatch of an order. It will also (for perishable goods) minimise the deterioration of stock and avoid net realisable value problems.	▪ Prepare pre-numbered sales orders from approved customer orders. ▪ Regularly review outstanding sales orders and despatch goods as soon as available.
To ensure that goods are only despatched after authorisation.	To reduce the risk of bad debts and avoid despatch notes being raised for goods not currently in stock.	▪ Prepare pre-numbered despatch notes for approved sales orders. ▪ Only despatch goods for which a pre-numbered despatch note has been prepared.
To ensure that customers acknowledge the receipt of goods.	To avoid subsequent disputes over delivery. Without proof of delivery this could lead to financial loss.	▪ Despatch notes should be two part. The customer should sign as proof of delivery. One copy should be retained and returned.
Return of goods		
To ensure that returned goods are only accepted for genuine reasons.	To avoid customers being given refunds for invalid reasons.	▪ Review reason for return of goods and assess validity. ▪ Credit notes should be authorised by a responsible official. ▪ A pre-numbered goods returned note should be raised recording quantity and reason for return.
To ensure that only saleable goods are returned to stock.	If faulty goods are not separately identified, the faulty goods could be despatched to another customer or stock value could be overstated.	▪ Physically inspect returned goods, noting any damage on the goods returned note. ▪ Store faulty goods separately, clearly identified as such.

23 Countrywide Sales

(a) Internal control procedures over fleet capital and revenue expenditure

- The approval of a fleet capital and revenue expenditure budget by the board of directors.
- Regular monitoring of actual costs against budget.
- Authorisation procedures for purchase/leasing covering:
  - personnel allowed to authorise acquisitions/leases
  - ordering procedures through requisition and authorised order forms
  - registration and insurance of vehicles.
- Quality control procedures on delivery of vehicles.
- Procedures for authorisation and signature of cheques, standing orders and invoices.
- Authorisation of all revenue expenditure, including repairs (with a policy in respect of when to repair or replace), servicing and fuel.
- Procedures to ensure that all possible insurance claims are made and recovered.
- Choice made between cash purchase and leasing in accordance with company policy.
- All leasing contracts scrutinised by the company's legal department prior to signature.
- A fleet register maintained, showing for each vehicle: date of purchase, estimated useful life and depreciation rate.
- Physical maintenance of the fleet, with a policy in respect of the frequency of servicing.
- Authorisation procedures for disposals.

(b) Tests of control

Capital expenditure

- Check that new vehicles ordered were within expenditure limits, authorised, and orders were made on official order forms.
- Check that cash payments/leasing deposits/payments were authorised.
- Check that disposals were authorised and that there was control over sale proceeds and the recording of disposals.
- Check that the fleet register is maintained by reviewing for the recording of additions, disposals, depreciation rates etc.
- Check for evidence that new vehicles are inspected on delivery.
- Check that vehicles are registered, insured and regularly serviced.
- Check leasing files for evidence that leasing contracts are checked prior to authorisation.

Revenue expenditure

Tests should check for authorisation of expenditure over repairs, servicing, insurance and fuel consumption. Tests might include the gathering of evidence in respect of the following:

- Authorisation signatures in relation to work to be done.
- The allocation of repairs and servicing to the entity's own facilities or to approved, outside garages.
- Security arrangements over drawing fuel from the entity's own pumps or control over fuel from outside sources.
- Notification of accidents, investigation of circumstances and the recovery of all possible insurance claims.

24 Faroff Supplies

(a) **Shortcomings**

- There is no apparent check to ensure that expenditure is for genuine business purposes or that the money has actually been spent.
- There is no apparent review to prevent fraudulent collusion between the assistant accountant and salesmen.
- There is no apparent check by the directors on expense forms when cheques are being signed.
- There are no formal authorisation procedures in place (no evidence of signature).

Suggested improvements

- Each salesman should complete a weekly log showing visits made and mileage covered.
- These should be checked and signed by the sales director and submitted to the assistant accountant with the expense claims.
- Periodically, a member of the accounts staff should check that claimed mileage is consistent with the mileage shown on the cars.
- The assistant accountant should ensure that fuel claims appear reasonable in relation to mileage covered.
- The assistant accountant should ensure that accommodation and meals expenditure appears reasonable in relation to clients visited and that invoices attached are in fact receipts (i.e. the invoices have been paid).
- Entertainment expenses should be pre-authorised in principle by the sales director.
- The assistant accountant should check that entertainment expenses are reasonable and were pre-authorised by the sales director.
- The assistant accountant should sign each claim as authorised.
- Complete and authorised documentation should be presented to the directors with the cheques for signature. Once each cheque has been signed the directors should mark each claim as paid.

(b) Tests of control

- Select a sample of payments and agree them to supporting claims.
- Verify that each claim:
  - is properly supported by vouchers
  - has been authorised (signed) by the assistant accountant
  - was marked as paid by the directors.
- Review the supporting weekly log for evidence of authorisation by the sales director.
- Check that any entertainment expenses on the claims were pre-authorised by the sales director and relate to clients visited that week.
- Examine the returned cheques for the sample chosen and verify that they were:
  - made out to the salesman concerned
  - properly signed.

25 Caraway Manufacturing

(a) Explanation

Property, plant and equipment

Property, plant and equipment is material at 87% of net assets. Substantial amounts of property, plant and equipment would be expected in a manufacturing company.

However, property, plant and equipment has increased by 2% this year yet depreciation/loss on sale has increased by 72%.

Although this is usually a low risk area (except for the judgement needed to assess useful lives) the balance here may be overstated. Additions and disposals during the year need further investigation to ensure that they have been properly accounted for.

Trade debtors

Trade debtors have increased by 67% although turnover has increased by only 6%. This may indicate a recoverability problem – which is backed up by the increase in the collection period from 19 days to 30 days.

Although judgement is needed to decide on the extent of provisions for doubtful debts it would seem that credit control is slipping and that provisions may need to be increased.

More extensive testing than last year may be needed on the recoverability of debts and on the accuracy of cut-off.

Stock

Stock has increased overall by 16% due to increases in raw materials and finished goods of 38% and 16% respectively. This is in spite of a 22% reduction in work-in-progress. Stock turnover has fallen from 9.9 times to 8.6 times. All of these facts may indicate that stocks are building up with insufficient orders being available, or could indicate the existence of obsolete/slow-moving stocks.

Also, there has been no real increase in cost of sales, despite the 6% increase in turnover. This might indicate an error in cut-off or an over-valuation of closing stock.

Stock is typically a high risk area, particularly in a manufacturing entity with its three stages of stocks. Valuation will need to take into account the stage of completion and net realisable values.

(b) Further information

Property, plant and equipment

- An explanation for the increases in net book value and depreciation/loss on disposals.
- Confirmation of the accounting policy for depreciation to ensure it is consistent with the previous year.
- The company's policy for reviewing useful lives to ensure they are reasonable (especially where assets have been sold at a loss).
- A detailed analysis of movements on property, plant and equipment during the year, including details of additions and disposals and depreciation charges.
- Whether any assets are recorded at a valuation as opposed to cost.
- The split of the expense between depreciation and loss on sales.
- Any own work capitalised.

Trade debtors

- An explanation for the increase in the trade debtors collection period.
- Details of any significant new customers during the year and information on their credit ratings.
- An analysis of bad debts written off and the provision for doubtful debts.
- An aged debtors analysis.
- Details of post year end cash receipts.

Stock

- Explanations for the movements in raw materials, work in progress and finished goods and for the overall increase in stock.
- Details of any adjustment required to physical stock records as a result of the year end count.
- Details of post year end sales and next year's order book.
- An analysis of the provision for obsolete stock.
- Details of the increase in sales turnover and whether it has come from a different sales mix, price increases or volume increases.
- Confirmation that stock has been valued at the lower of cost and net realisable value.

26 Opening balances

(a) Responsibilities

ISA 510 provides that where the auditor is performing the audit for the first time, and another auditor audited the financial statements for the previous period, the auditor should obtain sufficient audit evidence to be able to conclude that:

- the opening balances do not include misstatements that materially affect the current period's financial statements
- opening balances have been brought forward correctly into the current period
- accounting policies have been consistently applied in the two periods.

If the auditor *did* audit the previous period's financial statements then both ISA 510 and ISA 710 *Comparatives* are relevant. Procedures in this case will be limited to ensuring that comparative figures have been correctly reported, and appropriately classified.

This involves the auditor evaluating whether:

- accounting policies have been consistently applied in the two periods
- comparative figures agree with the previous period.

(b) Audit work

If the auditor did audit the previous year's financial statements then the audit work will be uncomplicated as the auditor will have the results of audit work carried out in the previous period. He will be able to check that accounting policies are unchanged and check the comparative figures to last year's audit file.

If the auditor did *not* issue an unqualified audit report and the problem remains unresolved then he will need to modify this year's audit report.

Where the audit is a new one audit work may include the following:

- A review of the audit report (if any) on the prior period financial statements. This may involve a review of the audit files of the previous auditor (if any, and if permission is obtained). If the report did not give a true and fair view opinion, further investigation will be required.
- A review of the accounting policies adopted.
- A detailed review of those opening balances as a misstatement in them may have a material impact on current period figures.
- Use of current period information to substantiate opening balance sheet figures. For example, cash received from customers this period gives evidence of the existence of the debt at the opening balance sheet date.

27 Compton Components

(a) Use of audit software in the audit of sales and debtors

Tests of controls

Audit software could be used in the reperformance of computer controls such as sequence checks on pre-numbered documents.

Master file data

Audit software could be used to detect the violation of system rules or the presence of unreasonable items on the master file. Examples of such techniques might include the following:

- Identify (by comparison with sales ledger balances) all those customers who have exceeded their credit limits.
- Print a report of those customers with no entry in their credit limit field.
- Print a report of all customers whose trade discount exceeds, say, 30%.

Substantive procedures

Audit software can scrutinise large volumes of data very quickly and extract information for the auditor to check/investigate. Examples might include the following:

- Reperformance of the client's work (e.g. an aged analysis of debtors)
- Checking the casts on transactions making up a balance.
- Calculating key ratios, e.g. trade debtors collection period.
- Selecting a stratified sample for the direct confirmation of debtors and printing confirmation requests.
- Identifying unmatched transactions (e.g. round sum payments on account).
- Listing all credit notes issued after the year end in excess of a certain amount.
- Listing all accounts with a credit balance in excess of a certain amount.

(b) Extent of external auditor's reliance on the internal auditor's use of embedded software

The external auditor may not place uninformed reliance on the work of internal auditors. Before placing any reliance on internal audit the external auditor must assess the internal auditor's organisational status, the scope of his work, his due professional care and technical competence.

In addition, the following factors would affect reliance on the embedded software as an audit tool:

- Involvement of the external auditor's computer audit department in the design, development, implementation and monitoring of the software.
- The security of the software. The external auditor could keep a copy for periodic comparison with the operational program.
- The security of the data extracted for review.
- The specific tasks carried out by the software and their relevance to the external audit.
- The subsequent procedures carried out by the internal auditors on the data obtained.

28 Ray Products

Presentation and disclosure

- Discuss with management the company's policy for capitalising expenditure.
- Review any change in the ratio of repairs and maintenance expenditure to additions to plant and machinery. As an alternative, review variances between budgeted and actual expenditure or review the repairs and maintenance account and vouch unusual/large items.
- Check, by reference to this capitalisation policy, that additions sampled (see below) have been correctly classified.

Rights to benefits

- Review the minutes of directors' meetings for evidence that the property is still owned by Ray Products.
- Inspect the title deeds of the property or write to whoever holds the deeds (e.g. the bank).
- Select a sample of additions to plant and machinery and confirm their purchase was authorised.

Carrying value and measurement

- Inspect the valuation document prepared by the chartered surveyor.
- Confirm that all properties have been revalued.
- Review the assumptions and bases of valuations.
- For the sample of additions agree cost to purchase invoices.
- When inspecting assets (see below) ensure there are no obvious signs of obsolescence/damage.
- Prove the depreciation charge in total for plant and machinery after taking into account any fully depreciated assets.
- Test check the calculation of depreciation on individual items of plant.
- Check the calculation of the depreciation charge on buildings, ensuring that land is not depreciated.

Existence

- Physically inspect a sample from the opening balances and additions (see above).
- Verify disposals in the year to supporting documentation (e.g. invoices and correspondence). Confirm that the item has been removed from the asset register. Check the calculation of the profit/loss on disposal.
- Check that all freehold buildings are referred to in the insurance documents.
- Compare manufacturing output for the current and prior year to the cost of plant and machinery.

Completeness

- Agree opening balances to last year's working papers/audited financial statements.
- Confirm that all movements identified in the testing of transactions are reflected in the financial statements.
- Check that all assets physically inspected are included in the asset register.
- Agree totals of asset register with totals in the nominal ledger accounts.
- Use income and expenditure accounts (e.g. rents, rates, insurance, repairs and maintenance) to trace the existence of assets.
- To confirm there are no unrecorded disposals, ascertain whether additions to plant and machinery initiate disposals and read related correspondence.

29 Invisible Industries

(a) Patents

- A register should be maintained giving a description of each patent, its cost, amortisation and net book value. Test a sample of the patents from the register against patent documents.
- Ensure patent documents are stored in a secure place.
- Vouch additions in the year (or a sample) to purchase documentation, including authorisation in the board minutes, or evidence of approval by a senior company official. If the patent originates from the company itself, vouch to filing documentation.
- Agree costs of the company's own patents to the documentation supporting the direct costs of application. All other related costs should be treated as research and development.
- Ensure that patents are written off over their useful lives, and that the rates used are reasonable.
- Check (a sample of) the amortisation calculations.
- Consider whether the useful lives being used are reasonable.
- Consider whether there are any business circumstances which might necessitate the need for an impairment write off.
- Ensure any impairment has been correctly dealt with.

(b) Research and development

- Examine supporting documentation (invoices, timesheets etc) to ensure that any amounts capitalised are development costs, and comply with the strict criteria laid down in SSAP 13 i.e.
  - clearly defined project
  - identifiable expenditure
  - technically feasible
  - commercially viable
  - expected to be profitable
  - resources exist to complete the project.

- To verify these costs, consider:
  - project evaluation reports
  - whether an independent assessor should be consulted if the information is of a highly technical nature.
- Ensure that any fixed assets used for the purposes of research and development have been capitalised and depreciated as required by FRS 15.

(c) Goodwill on the acquisition of a sole trader

- Confirm the consideration paid for the business acquired.
- Review the reasonableness of the valuation placed on the net assets acquired.
- Review for the possibility of an impairment loss having arisen.
- Ensure any impairment has been correctly dealt with.

30 Plastico Products

(a) Use of audit software

- Use computerised sequence checks on stock record numbers and stock sheets. An exception report can highlight missing items in the sequence.
- Select items from stock records to be physically vouched. This could be done statistically within defined strata.
- Select stock balances held at third parties for external confirmation and print standard confirmation letters.
- Reperform casts and extensions of stock sheets.
- Interrogate cost or purchase records to check that costs on valued stock sheets are correct.
- Compare reports between cost and net realisable value with report produced to show adjustments required by stock type and in total.
- Reorganise client's stock records by stock volume, turnover and age to facilitate additional testing of material or potentially obsolete stock.
- If purchases and sales systems are computerised, a program could match purchases and sales during the cut-off period with the stock file. Further investigation would be required where, for example, an item in the stock file could not be matched with a purchase.
- Calculation and comparison of stock turnover ratios and ratio of stock to current assets.
- Analysis of gross profit by stock type.

(b) Concerns re continuous counting

- If continuous counting proves unsuccessful/unreliable a full year end count may still be necessary.
- The size and nature of current discrepancies found under the quarterly system need to be investigated as similar problems may arise with continuous counting.

- The discrepancies could indicate inadequate recording of returns, theft or timing differences. Until these problems are resolved a full year end count will probably still be necessary.
- Since computerised records are already maintained, book quantities are already available for checking against when continuous counts are made. However, it may be that, because employees know these records will be corrected at the end of every quarter, the records are not kept as accurately as they should be. Additional resources may be required to keep them up-to-date for continuous counting purposes. (However, the increased control over stock exercised by continuous counting may prevent/detect theft.)
- If the auditor relies on the current system (i.e. performs tests of control on it) he is more likely to rely on (and therefore recommend) the proposed system.
- The full year end count currently provides an opportunity to assess the condition of stocks. The computerised system may need to be amended to provide additional information which may help in identifying potentially obsolete stock (e.g. no sales in the last X months).

31 Count instructions

Strengths	Significance
▪ The instructions are written.	▪ Written instructions are more likely to be followed as they can be referred to during the count.
▪ The instructions are expressed in simple and unambiguous terms.	▪ This will make it more likely that the instructions are followed, particularly as some counters may not be familiar with the stock (accounts staff?).
▪ Stock sheets are to be sequentially numbered.	▪ Prenumbering helps to ensure the completeness of the count by providing the means to identify whether any sheets have gone astray.
▪ Materials expected to be required for production are to be separately identified/set aside.	▪ There should be no movements of raw materials, thereby keeping disruption to a minimum and ensuring a clean cut-off between raw materials and work-in-progress (WIP).
▪ Goods to be despatched on the last day of the year are to be separately identified/set aside.	▪ As a result, there should be no movements out of finished goods stock. This should ensure a clean cut-off between stock and sales.
▪ Damaged stocks are to be separately identified on the stock sheets.	▪ As a result, provisions can be made to write down damaged stocks to their net realisable value.
▪ The person responsible is identified.	▪ Someone must be designated to be responsible for ensuring that everything has been counted in an orderly fashion and for clearing queries.

Weaknesses	Significance
▪ The warehouse manager is not independent of stock functions and should not therefore have overall responsibility for the count.	▪ There is a lack of segregation of duties if the person responsible for the custody of assets is also responsible for their recording.
▪ The pre-printed descriptions include the quantities supplied by the stock controller.	▪ The expected counts should not be included as this can be used later to provide a check on the accuracy (or otherwise) of the counts and identify discrepancies requiring a recount. The inclusion of 'expected' quantities might also encourage staff to just record the expected quantity.
▪ The responsibilities of warehouse staff do not appear to be restricted/subject to supervision.	▪ Warehouse staff have access to physical stock and should not therefore be determining the physical counts. They should only participate in the count subject to appropriate safeguards (e.g. checkers – see below).
▪ Procedures for WIP in the production department are not included.	▪ Additional considerations must be applied to WIP (e.g. stage of completion and establishing cut-off).
▪ There are no instructions to deal with raw materials received from suppliers.	▪ Instructions must cover all aspects of stock movements to ensure an accurate cut-off between creditors/purchases and stock.
▪ Instructions do not specify how discrepancies are to be identified.	▪ To identify physical stocks not on the books there must be procedures to check the completeness of the physical count (by inspection of ticketing).
▪ Counters involved are not specifically identified.	▪ Who is in charge of which area and what teams are to count the stock in it should be specified to ensure that there are sufficient staff assigned.
▪ How items are to be marked (and where) is not specified.	▪ Counted items must be clearly identifiable to ensure the completeness of the count, prevent double-counting and facilitate subsequent checking (see below).
▪ There is to be no check on the counts.	▪ Some, if not all, counts should be independently counted by a checker to confirm the accuracy of the first count.

Overall evaluation

The instructions are currently inadequate. A new set of instructions should be drafted to deal, in particular, with:

- the roles of warehouse personnel
- how stocks are to be identified, quantities recorded and counts checked
- the additional stock movements which could occur (e.g. raw material supplies from suppliers).

32 Debtco

(a) Factors in selecting sample

The objective of the test

The objective is likely to be to test for overstatement. Therefore the sample should be weighted towards the higher value items.

High risk items

In selecting the sample, certain types of account should be considered for inclusion. These include:

- overdue accounts
- credit balances

- accounts on which round sum payments are received
- nil balances

as they may indicate errors or possible bad debts.

Individually significant items

The eight largest balances should be confirmed as any balance over £50,000, represents 25% of profit before tax and is therefore individually material.

Items to be confirmed

Balances or specific invoices can be confirmed. Balances would be preferable in the first instance as the percentage of the sales ledger confirmed will be greater.

Method of sample selection

Random, systematic or judgement sampling could be used. Systematic sampling would be preferable, as there is no bias. It could also be weighted towards higher value items.

Method of confirmation

This should be positive as opposed to negative. However, there is a choice to be made between whether the balance is supplied or not. The latter may provide stronger evidence but the former may lead to more replies.

(b) Procedures

Planning

- Discuss with management any customer balances which they consider should not be confirmed (e.g. credit balances).
- Plan the sample size to take account of such factors as materiality.
- Agree the client's reconciliation of the total of the individual balances (on the sales ledger) to the balance per the sales ledger control account (in the nominal ledger).
- Arrange when the requests are to be sent.

Performing

- Review all request letters to verify that they are on client's headed notepaper and signed by an appropriate client official.
- If the balance is provided, ask for any difference to be reconciled to an enclosed statement.
- Enclose a reply paid envelope (addressed to the audit firm) in each request letter.
- Mail the letters from the audit firm's office.

Following up the results

- Record all replies on a control schedule.
- Non-replies may be followed up with a second letter or (with the client's approval) fax or telephone.
- If direct confirmation is not obtained, examine customer orders, despatch records, invoices and after-date payments (for evidence of existence and amount due).

- Disputed balances or invoices should be investigated by the client (in the first instance).
- For invoices on a customer's statement but not included in the customer's records, agree invoice details to despatch records (to confirm existence at the confirmation date).
- For cash claimed to be in transit by the customer (not on the statement) agree the amount and date on which it was received to cash book receipts and bank records.
- For returns, agree amounts to after-date credit notes and, if material, confirm that the client has included them in a year end accrual.
- Summarise and evaluate the results. Review the nature and effect of any errors.

33 Cash and bank

(a) Four matters which would be included in a bank confirmation letter

Account balances

Any balances held by the bank (current, deposit or loan balances) will be confirmed by them. This will provide the auditor with reliable third party evidence in respect of amounts held or owed at the year end.

Assets held as security

The letter would detail any charges held by the bank over the client's assets. This information is needed by the auditor so that he can check that adequate disclosure has been made in the financial statements.

Other assets held

This would include particulars of assets such as title deeds and share certificates. This information provides evidence substantiating the ownership and existence of other assets such as property and investments.

Outstanding interest and charges

This information substantiates the accruals figure at the year end.

(b) Evidence

(i) Cash at bank and bank loan

- Reperform the year end bank reconciliation(s) and review earlier monthly reconciliations.
- Agree a sample of reconciling items (e.g. unpresented cheques, outstanding lodgements) to supporting documentation and to post year end bank statements.
- For outstanding lodgements check that paying-in slips are dated by the bank as pre year end.
- Ensure cut-off is correct by reviewing transactions either side of the year end.
- Obtain a bank confirmation letter.

- Check that any accounts opened or closed during the year were authorised.
- Note any rights of set-off.
- Confirm details of security given for the loan and ensure disclosure of such security is adequate.
- Check interest rates, terms of loan etc to the loan agreement.
- Check that loan repayments due within the next year are disclosed in current liabilities.

(ii) Cash

- Review system for ensuring security of travellers' cheques and cash.
- Count floats, cash and travellers' cheques at year end.
- Verify that unbanked cash was banked after the year end.

34 Purchase ledger balances

(a) Arguments for each approach

Suppliers are more likely to reply if the balance is given as there is less work involved for them. However, there may be a temptation just to agree the balance without checking it for timing differences or errors.

If the balance is given, the supplier may reconcile any difference. This is not possible if no balance is stated. In addition, the existence of any difference will alert the supplier to a potential need to take action.

If the balance is not given, suppliers may gain the impression that the client's records are so inadequate that the client does not know what the balance should be.

(b) Other audit procedures to verify the amount of trade creditors

- Examine supplier statement reconciliations. Balances should have been agreed/reconciled by the client and the detail on the statement agreed with the client's records.
- Test the reconciliation of the list of purchase ledger balances to the balance on the purchase ledger control account.
- Match after date payments to year end balances.
- Review cut-off procedures and test by reference to last delivery notes/goods received records prior to the year end and first ones after the year end.
- Compare trade creditors balances this year end to last year end and investigate any differences.

(c) Audit tests re the existence of unrecorded liabilities

- Enquire as to whether the directors are aware of any actual or contingent liabilities other than those recorded in the financial statements.
- Review minutes of directors' meetings.

- Examine:
  - after date cash book (for post year end payments of unrecorded year end liabilities)
  - purchase invoices received post year end (to check that if they relate to pre year end purchases, that those purchases have been accrued for)
  - sales returns made post year end (to see if a returns provision is needed).
- Compare liabilities last year end to this year end to see if similar categories of liabilities have been omitted this year.
- Request the directors to confirm the completeness of liabilities in the letter of representation.

35 Audit of accounting estimates

(a) Difficulty of auditing accounting estimates

Accounting estimates are just that – estimates. They are not capable of precise measurement and management will have used their judgment in arriving at those estimates. The auditor must therefore use his judgment in assessing whether those estimates are reasonable.

Because most of such estimates are made by management, independent audit evidence may be limited. Much of the evidence in respect of the estimates will depend on the reliability of management themselves.

Because of the subjectivity attached to estimates they are a means by which the financial statements could be manipulated. This is therefore a high risk area of the audit.

(b) Audit evidence re provision for damages

- Examine contract with the customer to establish the nature of the contract.
- Review correspondence with the customer and legal advisors to assess the likely outcome.
- Review events after the balance sheet date to establish if the claim was subsequently agreed or settled.
- Consider the possibility of other, similar breaches for which a provision is necessary.
- Obtain management representations, confirmed in writing, that all contingencies have been disclosed.

36 Izzard Electronics

(a) Management representation letter – reliability and need for other evidence

Normally, the management representation letter is drafted by the auditor, but it is written on the client's headed notepaper and signed by the directors. Alternatively, the letter may be written by the directors, but contain matters requested by the auditors.

As audit evidence, it is written evidence (which is better than oral evidence) but it is evidence from within the company and thus it is not as independent a source of evidence as most other evidence obtained by the auditor (e.g. third party evidence and evidence obtained directly by the auditor).

Arguably, evidence from the directors may be *less* reliable than evidence from the company's employees, as there may be more pressures and motivation for the directors to mislead the auditor (e.g. because of external pressures on them to produce good results). However, statements from the directors may be *more* reliable than those from employees, as they will have a better understanding of the situation and, in their position as directors, should be aware of the importance of the statements they make to the auditor. Under company law, a company director commits an offence if he knowingly or recklessly makes a misleading, false or deceptive statement to the auditor. The directors should be aware of such provisions and this should make them cautious of what they say to auditors, particularly when it is later put down in writing.

In some relatively immaterial areas, the auditor may accept the directors' statements without seeking further evidence. However, in most situations the auditor should attempt to find alternative evidence to support (or refute) the directors' representations. Thus, in determining whether all sales income has been recorded in the financial statements, the auditor should obtain other evidence and would probably be negligent if the directors' representations were relied on entirely.

In addition, the auditor must consider whether the directors' representations are consistent with the other information he has obtained. If this evidence is consistent, then the directors' representations will reinforce the evidence obtained by the auditor. However, if the other evidence obtained by the auditor is not consistent with the directors' representations, the auditor should be extremely careful before accepting what the directors say. The auditor should seek further evidence to either refute or confirm the directors' statements. If there is a material difference between the other evidence and the directors' representations, the auditor will probably have to qualify his audit report.

(b) If the directors refuse to sign the management representation letter

The auditor should ask the directors why they are refusing to sign the letter. The auditor should explain the following:

- It is a normal procedure for the auditor to draft the management representation letter and ask the directors to sign it.
- The audit opinion will be based mainly on audit work which does not involve representations from directors. However, directors' representations are helpful in providing further evidence that the financial statements are free from material error.
- Company law requires the directors to sign the financial statements. This provides evidence that the directors believe the financial statements are free from material error. Thus, this is similar to the directors signing the management representation letter.

If the directors are still unwilling to sign the letter, the auditor should ascertain which paragraphs they are unhappy about. The wording of these paragraphs should be discussed to see if alternative wording can be agreed. However, it would probably be unacceptable to remove the paragraphs where the directors confirm completeness of income or the validity of expenditure.

If the directors continue to refuse to sign the letter, the auditor should be put on his guard that the directors may be hiding something. Both of these areas create strong suspicion of potential fraud. Cash sales could be misappropriated and the directors could be putting personal expenses through as business expenditure.

The auditor should therefore carry out additional audit procedures in the areas over which the directors are refusing to sign.

If these additional procedures fail to provide adequate evidence then:

- the audit report should be qualified on the grounds of a scope limitation, and
- the auditor should consider the reliability of other representations obtained from the directors during the course of the audit.

37 Subsequent events

Stock of finished goods

- **Post year end sales** can be reviewed to check sales prices and therefore the net realisable value of stocks. A lack of post year end sales may indicate that a provision for obsolescence is needed.
- **Correspondence with customers** may provide evidence of product faults or other problems which may indicate that a provision for returns or legal claims is needed.
- **Credit notes issued after the year end** may provide evidence of product faults which may indicate that a provision for returns or obsolescence is needed.

Trade debtors

- **Post year end cash receipts** provide evidence as to the recoverability of year end balances.
- **Correspondence with customers** may provide evidence of disputes which may affect the recoverability of individual year end balances.

Trade creditors

- **Post year end payments to suppliers** may provide evidence of unrecorded year end liabilities.
- **Correspondence with suppliers** may provide evidence of unrecorded year end liabilities.

Bank overdraft

- **Post year end receipts and payments** may provide evidence of the likelihood of the company staying within its overdraft facility (as, if it does not, and the facility is withdrawn or secured on key assets, then the going concern of the company may be in doubt).
- **Correspondence with the bank** may indicate whether support is ongoing or likely/about to be withdrawn.

38 Eden Electronics

(a) **Types of qualified opinions**

ISA 700 **The auditor's report on financial statements** states that qualified opinions are issued in the following circumstances:

(i) **There is a limitation on the scope of the auditor's examination**

If the possible effect of a limitation on scope is 'material and pervasive', the auditor is unable to express an opinion on the financial statements. He will thus express a **disclaimer of opinion**.

An example might be where a company's accounting records have been completely destroyed by fire and therefore the financial statements may include a significant amount of information which has been estimated. In such circumstances, the auditor will be unable to form an opinion as to whether the financial statements show a true and fair view, and a disclaimer of opinion must be given.

If the auditor concludes that the possible effect of the disclaimer is material but not 'pervasive', he will give an **'except for' opinion**.

An example might be where a material amount of a company's sales are cash sales over which there was no system of control on which the auditor could rely and there were no other satisfactory audit procedures which are able to confirm that cash sales are correctly recorded.

(ii) **The auditor disagrees with the view given by the financial statements**

If the matter is pervasive to the view given by the financial statements, an **adverse opinion** will be given.

An example might be where a company has not provided for large losses expected to arise on contracts being worked on. In such circumstances the auditor may give an adverse opinion because he concludes that the significance of the matter is pervasive to the view given by the financial statements.

If the matter is material, but not pervasive, then an opinion will be given **'except for'** an adverse opinion on that particular matter.

An example might be where a company has not provided against a debt outstanding at the year end when the customer has subsequently gone into liquidation. In such circumstances, the auditor will give an 'except for' opinion disagreeing with the non-provision against the doubtful debt.

(b) Eden Electronics

The situation of Eden Electronics would lead to a limitation in scope 'except for' qualification. The main elements of the audit report would therefore consist of the following:

(i) Title – indicating that it is the report of an *independent* auditor.

(ii) Addressee – report to the shareholders.

(iii) Introductory paragraph identifying the entity and its financial statements that have been audited.

(iv) Management's responsibility section – describing management's responsibilities for internal controls, accounting policies and accounting estimates.

(v) Auditor's responsibility section – describing the process of audit and stating that except for this issue the audit was conducted in accordance with ISAs.

(vi) Opinion paragraph stating that in the auditor's opinion the financial statements give a true and fair view except for any adjustments that might have been necessary if the auditor had been able to obtain sufficient evidence concerning stock.

(vii) The report would be signed (as registered auditors), the address given, and dated.

39 Posh Perfumes

(a) Further information

- Whether the supplier difficulties are temporary or permanent.
- Whether the supplier is taking action to overcome its problems (and whether Posh Perfumes is considering offering financial support to the supplier).
- Legal advice taken with regards to the possibility of negotiating a break clause in the agreement with the store.
- Any costs/penalties arising from the above.
- Legal advice taken with regards to the possibility of altering the agreement to cover an alternative acceptable product or sub-leasing to a competitor to mitigate costs.
- The nature and extent of Posh Perfumes' other activities and its ability to expand trade in those areas.
- What the current level of stock is and whether it is sufficient to tide over the company until supplies are resumed or an alternative product is found.
- Willingness of Posh Perfumes' bankers to extend/grant any overdraft facility.

(b) Possible forms of opinion

Where the going concern assumption is appropriate but a material uncertainty exists the auditor must consider whether the financial statements adequately disclose:

- the principal events that give rise to the uncertainty, and
- the existence of the material uncertainty itself.

If there is adequate disclosure then the auditor should express an unqualified opinion but should use an emphasis of matter paragraph to highlight the uncertainty.

If there is not adequate disclosure then the auditor should express a qualified opinion. This will be on the grounds of disagreement over disclosure and will lead to an 'except for' or adverse qualification.

Where the going concern assumption is inappropriate the auditor should express:

- an adverse opinion if the financial statements have been prepared on a going concern basis
- an unqualified opinion if the financial statements have been prepared on an alternative acceptable basis (e.g. break-up basis) and there is adequate disclosure of this basis. An emphasis of matter paragraph may be required.

40 Creed Computers

(1) Stock records and PCs held by directors

Weaknesses

The stock records are not a reliable record of actual stocks held because:

- customer returns have not been recorded
- some items recorded as being in stock are missing

Some 'missing' items are held at directors' own homes.

Implications

- Year end stocks may be misstated if reliance is placed on year end stock records instead of a year end count.
- Stock losses may go unnoticed until the next physical count delaying insurance claims and making theft more likely.
- Customers may not be given credit for goods returned such that trade debtors will be overstated and there may be a loss of customer goodwill.
- PCs 'borrowed' by the directors are unlikely to still be suitable for resale at their full value and may need to be written down in the financial statements.
- Orders could be accepted which cannot be fulfilled if decisions are taken based on incorrect stock records.

Recommendations

- All stock despatches should be recorded on sequentially numbered despatch notes and be subsequently matched with a sales invoice.
- All stock returns should be recorded on sequentially numbered returns notes and be subsequently matched with a credit note.
- A responsible official (e.g. warehouse manager) should authorise any movement out of stock other than for sales. These items should either be removed from the stock records and transferred to the fixed assets register (e.g. PCs used by directors) or retained within the stock records with a note as to their location.
- Physical security over stock should be improved.
- Until the accuracy of the stock records is established, monthly counts should be performed.

(2) Customer credit limits

Weaknesses

The system in operation over credit limits has been broken down as:

- credit limits are being exceeded
- credit limits are not being allocated to new customers.

Implications

- Customers may make purchases for which they are then unable to pay, resulting in bad debts.
- Customers may take advantage of the deterioration in credit control and delay payment.

Recommendations

- A credit limit must be set by a responsible official (e.g. sales director) before a new customer can be accepted.
- Before an order is accepted from a customer, a check should be made to see if that order, together with the outstanding balance on that customer's account, exceeds that customer's credit limit. If that is the case then either the order should not be accepted at that time, or an increased limit should be authorised.

Index

C

D

E

F

G

H

I

L

M

N

O

P

Q

R